# The Eternal E-Customer

How Emotionally Intelligent
Interfaces Can Create Long-Lasting
Customer Relationships

Bryan P. Bergeron

**McGraw-Hill**
New York   San Francisco   Washington, D.C.   Auckland   Bogotá
Caracas   Lisbon   London   Madrid   Mexico City   Milan
Montreal   New Delhi   San Juan   Singapore
Sydney   Tokyo   Toronto

**Library of Congress Cataloging-in-Publication Data**

Bergeron, Bryan.
   The eternal e-customer : how emotinally intelligent interfaces can create long-lasting customer relationships / Bryan Bergeron.
      p. cm.
   Includes index.
   ISBN 0-07-136479-X
   1. Customer loyalty.   2. Internet marketing.   I. Title.

HF5415.525 .B47 2000
658.8'12—dc21

                                       00-057875

# *McGraw-Hill*

*A Division of The McGraw·Hill Companies*

1 2 3 4 5 6 7 8 9 0  DOC/DOC  0 9 8 7 6 5 4 3 2 1 0

ISBN 0-07-136479-X

*This book was set in Times New Roman by Patricia Wallenburg.*

*Printed and bound by R. R. Donnelley & Sons Company.*

To Roz

# Contents

## Foreword

The advent of worldwide decentralized communication epitomized by the Internet and cell phones has been a pervasive democratizing force. It was not Yeltsin standing on a tank that overturned the 1991 coup against Gorbachev, but rather the clandestine network of fax machines and early forms of e-mail that broke decades of totalitarian control of information. The movement toward democracy and capitalism and the attendant economic growth that has characterized the 1990s have all been fueled by the accelerating force of these person-to-person communication technologies.

The impact of distributed and intelligent communications has been felt, perhaps most intensely in the world of business. Despite dramatic mood swings on Wall Street, the seemingly extraordinary values often ascribed to so-called e-companies reflects a genuine perception: the business models that have sustained businesses for decades are in the early phases of a radical transformation. New models based on direct personalized communication with the customer will transform every industry, resulting in massive disintermediation of the middle layers of distribution that have traditionally separated the customer from the ultimate source of products and services.

The underlying technologies are all accelerating. It's not just computation that is growing exponentially, but also communication, networks, biological sciences (e.g., DNA sequencing), brain scanning, miniaturization (we are currently shrinking technology at a rate of 5.6 per linear dimension per decade), the accumulation of knowledge, and even the rate of paradigm shift itself. And the underlying technologies are becoming ever more intelligent, subtle, emotionally aware, that is, more human.

Expanding access to knowledge is changing power relationships. Patients increasingly approach visits to their physician armed with a sophisticated understanding of their medical condition and their options. Consumers of virtually everything from toasters, cars, and homes to banking and insurance are now using automated software agents ("bots") to quickly identify the right choices with the optimal features and prices.

The wishes and desires of the customer, often unknown even to herself, are rapidly becoming the driving force in business relationships. The well-connected clothes shopper, for example, is not going to be satisfied for much longer with settling for whatever items happen to be left hanging on the rack of her local store. Instead, she will select just the right materials and styles by viewing how many possible combinations look on an image of her own body (based on a detailed three-dimensional body scan), and then having her choices custom manufactured.

The current disadvantages of web-based commerce (e.g., limitations in the ability to directly interact with products and the frustrations of interacting with inflexible menus and forms instead of human personnel) will gradually dissolve as the trends move robustly in favor of the electronic world. By the end of this decade, computers will disappear as distinct physical objects. Displays will be written directly onto our retinas by devices in our eyeglasses and contact lenses. In addition to virtual high resolution displays, these intimate displays will provide full immersion visual virtual reality. We will have ubiquitous very high bandwidth wireless connection to the Internet at all times. "Going to a web site" will mean entering a virtual reality environment—at least for the visual and auditory sense—where we can directly interact with products and people, both real and simulated. Although the simulated people will not be up to human standards, not by 2009, they will be quite satisfactory as sales agents, reservation clerks, and research assistants. The electronics for all of this will be so small that it will be invisibly embedded in our glasses and clothing. Haptic (i.e., tactile) interfaces will enable us to touch products and people. It is difficult to identify any lasting advantage of the old brick and mortar world that will not ultimately be overcome by the rich interactive interfaces that are soon to come.

If we go further out—to, say 2029, as a result of continuing trends in miniaturization, computation, and communication, we will have billions of nanobots—intelligent robots the same size as blood cells or smaller—traveling through the capillaries of our brain communicating directly with our biological neurons. By taking up positions next to every nerve fiber coming from all of our senses, the nanobots will provide full immersion virtual reality involving all five of the senses. So we will enter virtual reality environments (via the web, of course) of our choice, interact with a panoply of intelligent products and services, and meet people, both real and virtual, only now the difference won't be so clear.

In his brilliant and entertaining book, Bryan Bergeron has provided a comprehensive and insightful roadmap to this e-revolution now in its infancy. Dr. Bergeron describes this era not as a single transformation, but as an ongoing churning that will continually uproot and exchange one set of business models for another. What is needed, Bryan tells us, is the right set of principles that can enable businesses to flourish through times of ever-accelerating change. He discerningly bases these principles on the loyalty of the increasingly empowered customer. My advice would be to invest in any company that can successfully adopt Bryan Bergeron's principles of meeting the needs and desires of "the eternal e-customer."

*Ray Kurzweil*

T his is a book about a strategy. It is intended to be used by CEOs, CIOs, CTOs, and other eBusiness decision makers who realize that it takes more than a dotcom suffix to dominate a market niche. In short, this book is for those involved in developing, specifying, or managing the Web component of their business who need a competitive edge over the competition.

*The Eternal E-Customer* introduces this competitive advantage under the rubric of Emotionally Intelligent Interfaces (EIIs). It describes, in detail, how this technology can be strategically applied to moving eBusinesses to the next level of customer loyalty, thereby improving the bottom line. This book illustrates EII technology in a variety of forms, from textual dialogues to animated graphical figures, bots, and intelligent agents, and provides scenarios on how EIIs may carry on conversations, act as human surrogates, and achieve specific tasks.

This is a practical, solution-oriented book, with just enough technology and business theory to provide structure to the content. Although there are many wonderful books on the details of interface design and programming, this is not one of them. This book is intended to assist decision makers in formulating a global strategy for their Web presence and capitalize on eCommerce opportunities. After reading this book, the reader will:

- Understand and appreciate the significance Emotionally Intelligent Interfaces will have on the growth and survival of their eBusiness.
- Recognize that, in the competitive world of eCommerce, the key to success is customer appreciation and retention.
- Appreciate that every customer contact is an opportunity to improve upon a customer relationship and to learn more about customer needs, and how an Emotionally Intelligent Interface is the best technology for exploiting this opportunity.
- Have a roadmap detailing how to take advantage of EII technology.
- Understand the prerequisite information infrastructure required to develop and deploy EIIs.
- Appreciate that the time to act is now.

*The Eternal E-Customer* provides eBusiness executives and decision makers with a process description of how to get from where they are now to the next level of customer loyalty, from business and technical perspectives. The intent is to stress the relevance of Emotionally Intelligent Interfaces in a clear, understandable, manner, with a focus on practical, achievable results.

This book is divided into three parts: eBusiness; technology; and integrating the two. Part 1 provides an overview of the current eBusiness environment, driving home the point that the type of loyalty that can be bred by Emotionally Intelligent Interfaces can make a business more credible and more profitable. Part 1 is intended to bring IT Managers up to speed on eBusiness issues, and to provide a review for the eBusiness executive. It provides a review of business concepts that relate to customer loyalty and how the Web is a portal into customer needs and wants. It describes how a properly designed Web presence can be appreciated as a form of customer-focused decision support and as a conversation interface. It describes how EIIs, like human customer service representative, can provide customers with a sense of attachment and appreciation, and how they can act as surrogate humans that can be communicated with, and with which customers can build trust and loyalty. Most important, it illustrates how EIIs can form the nucleus of an eBusiness community based on products, services, and the free exchange of information. Part 1 also develops the concept of the Loyalty Effect, and offers a mathematical model, the Loyalty Effect Equation, to help the reader quantify the loyalty customers ascribe to their web site.

Part 2 of *The Eternal E-Customer* provides an overview of the technologies involved in creating Emotionally Intelligent Interfaces, as well as historical context for computer–human interactions work. This part serves as a review for IT Managers familiar with human–computer interfaces, expert systems, databases, and other technologies, and introduces the concepts necessary for eBusiness executives to communicate intelligently with their IT peers. It delves into the more technical aspects of human–computer interface design, but only to the extent necessary to describe the relevance of these technologies to developing customer loyalty. It describes how EIIs are based on an information infrastructure derived from customer information, driven by data from previous customer interactions, explicit customer preferences, and heuristics based on customer profiles.

Part 3 describes how the technologies discussed in Part 2 can be leveraged to convert clicks to loyal customers. It describes how, given the current business environment, the technological advances, and the promise of even greater technological advances and faster change in eBusiness, Emotionally Intelligent Interface technology can make a difference. This part outlines how successfully applying EII technology in the real business environment involves developing and maintaining customer databases and data-mining techniques, and of addressing the technical and social implications of data confidentiality and security. Part 3 illustrates how EII technology can be used to build trust and customer loyalty by offering shoppers the intimacy and individual attention they expect from corner stores. It illustrates how, in securing customer loyalty and trust, customers must be feel that the information extracted from their interactions and provided by them directly will be used in a way that doesn't violate an implicit trust, and in their best interest.

This book is meant to be read by busy, information-seeking executives who work, either directly or indirectly, with the managerial and high-level technical aspects of information technology. Therefore, each chapter ends with a condensed "Executive Summary" section that distills the chapter into three or four paragraphs. Because the half-life of many eBusinesses is measured in Internet Time, a sister Website, www.EternalEBiz.com, provides links to relevant resources and the latest examples of technologies relating to Emotionally Intelligent Interfaces.

*Bryan Bergeron*

## Introduction

Visiting the West Coast is always a joy. The relaxed pace, the pastel sweaters, the blue skies, and Pacific air are a welcome change to the hurried existence in the East. If you've visited the San Francisco area lately, however, you might find it remarkable in that the tempo of the city had increased. The tension is almost palpable as you walk down the beach over to Fisherman's Wharf while sipping a cup of Starbucks coffee. Even after the first dotcom "correction" of 2000, the air is filled with electricity generated by dotcom fever. Everyone in the shops, from secretaries to CEOs, is discussing their companies' IPO plans, the anticipated value of their stock options, and the latest twenty-something millionaire.

There is unending talk of cash-poor companies bartering stock options for legal aid, advertising, and, in some cases, even food, and of the nextdoor neighbor who has a "simple idea" that is catching on and will make him or her millions. It is difficult not getting caught up in the excitement of everyone's impending fortune. Remarkable only a few years ago, all of this prosperity—or hope of prosperity—was the result of mental capital. The prevailing attitude is that money is nice to live on, but that stock options will change your life. Not surprisingly, there is very little talk of what people are actually working on, or even thinking about. Everyone is playing their cards close to their chests.

The notion that all intellectual property is potentially worth something, and is therefore worth protecting, isn't limited to Silicon Valley. For example, there is a graduate course taught at Harvard on bringing technology to market. This year, for the first time, students have been reluctant to reveal specifics about their product or service ideas, because they have "plans to bring them public in the near future." Clearly, the current trend bucks the traditional academic model of open discussion, but when there are millions of dollars at stake, either real or imaginary, models tend to break down. You can debate whether IPO fever is greater in Silicon Valley or inside Route 128 in Massachusetts, but it's impossible to deny that the endemic exists.

While everyone in eCommerce seems to be busy chasing or making their fortunes, the traditional media are filled with pundits predicting either imminent collapse of the artificial eEconomy on one extreme, and an infinite climb to ever-increasing prosperity on the other. Optimists describe how new technologies will continually increase productivity and efficiency. Pessimists point to the unprecedented low personal savings rate, Alan Greenspan's influence, and the creeping interest rates. Most would agree that the future lies somewhere in the middle, and that, regardless of the future, *time* is of the essence. If an IPO is in your future, it's better never than late. After another round of funding and the resulting stock dilution and loss of control to the venture capitalists, you'll have to watch from the sidelines as someone else takes your company public, and reaps the lion's share of the rewards.

When we ponder the economy's future, the effect of the Web and the Internet can be likened to that of the telephone, electricity, television, the printing press, and other significant, disruptive technologies. The telephone changed how we communicated with each other. You probably don't think twice about picking up your cell phone and calling a business associate. However, you probably couldn't imagine taking an hour to use pen and ink for a routine business letter to the same associate, or meeting person-to-person to discuss every small business issue. The telephone changed everything. People were connected to each other, and to the world, as never before.

Perhaps something "personal" was lost in the move from face-to-face to telephone contact, but the loss is acceptable. Just as a typewritten letter is still seen as less personal than a hand-written letter, it's accepted as practical. No one has time to spend an hour writing a letter, even with a fine pen and high-rag stationery. Perhaps that's why hand-written letters and invitations still convey so much importance.

They're an extravagance most of us can't afford. However, even though the typewriter was accepted, it didn't do away with hand-written letters and memos. You may still send out hand-written notes on occasion, but if you are time starved like most of us, it's an occasion, and not everyday business.

Wall Street has historically been weak on predicting the eventual effect a disruptive technology has on competing technologies. For example, desktop computers and laser printers, touted as the replacements for typewriters, were initially marketed as the first step toward paperless offices. In truth, their use has resulted in more paper use, not less. The paper companies, once fearing the computer as a threat to their market, are now selling more paper than ever before. Successful paper companies changed their products to conform to the needs of laser and inkjet technologies, offering special finishes, colors, and textures.

Another disruptive technology, the telephone, didn't do away with typewriters, letters, or letter writing, nor did it obviate the need for personal contact. If anything, the telephone acted as a catalyst for personal contacts, letter writing, and other activities of normal business. We use the telephone to confirm travel reservations, to schedule meetings, and to stay in touch with our loved ones when we travel. Even though the telephone wasn't invented by a politician, it did change everything in both very subtle and obvious ways. After an initial disruptive period, when everyone was trying to determine exactly how the telephone would fit in to the scheme of things, telephone technology faded into ordinary business and personal life. Some companies were affected more than others by the telephone. For example, mail-order companies and traders in the stock market seem to have profited by the increased access and sense of immediacy provided by the telephone.

The Web and the Internet have and will have the same effect and course as the telephone, typewriter, or television. After the flurry of activity and confusion, things will settle down to a new but ordinary state of affairs. The Web will simply be another modality for conducting business and personal communications. Like the telephone, typewriter, and computer, the Web will ultimately be integrated into the brick and mortar businesses that once were threatened by it.

As we begin the twenty-first century, eBusiness *is* business. If your company isn't doing business on the Web, either it soon will be or you'll be out of business. It's that simple.

If you're a CEO of one of the many overnight dotcom startups, you're no doubt keenly aware of the challenges ahead. For a successful IPO, you have a limited time to attract and maintain traffic on your site, set up a management team, and then demonstrate revenues, or at least a potential for revenue. You'll either have to develop something of value or get out before any of the stockholders realize that your revenues won't even pay the rent. Perhaps your company will be acquired and the technologies your company brings to the table will be rolled into another company. The resulting marriage may actually provide value. Certainly, there are many exceptions to this "IPO-and-run" mentality. However, sooner or later, someone is going to be holding the bag; someone who's responsible for generating revenue and maintaining a reasonable profit margin. That means developing a loyal consumer base; and therein lies the rub.

Whether you're a traditional brick and mortar Fortune 1000 company with an evolving Web presence or a dotcom startup, the number one challenge in this era of consumerism is building consumer loyalty. Today, consumers are armed with more and more Internet-fueled information and newly acquired consumer sophistication, and these consumers are not predisposed to loyalty. They are drawn to convenience, lowest price, lowest time to delivery, and high-quality service. You can't expect customer loyalty; you have to earn it.

Building customer loyalty is the missing ingredient in eBusiness. To attract a consumer in this environment isn't too difficult; simply take a loss on an item to make a one-time sale. Retaining consumers is another matter. Consumer loyalty will become more critical as the valuation of eBusinesses shifts from revenue at any cost to a more traditional profit model. To retain consumers in this environment requires an intense and consistent focus on service strategies, with execution of these strategies enabled by technology. The escalating competitive pressure in the marketplace makes it clear that service is the primary predictor of success.

eBusinesses that focus on creating consumer loyalty excel in their markets. How do you win consumer loyalty in today's economy? Merely *satisfying* a consumer won't result in a *loyal* consumer. It's not enough to meet or even exceed a consumer's needs once and then slack off into business as usual. Loyalty is the fruit of a focused, continuous, well-executed plan of relationship building. In the traditional business world, developing a meaningful, long-term relationship with a client entails quality human–human interaction. While this remains the gold standard for company–client communications, it currently isn't practical for most eBusinesses. Given the high consumer or B2B transaction to support staff ratio, you'll have to look to technology to fulfill some of the roles you once relegated to your customer service representatives.

Even though the Web is destined to be just another innovative technology intimately woven into the fabric of daily life, today it's an exciting place, and one that's constantly evolving. New technologies are introduced through the Web at a blistering pace, and many of these will presumably increase productivity and efficiency. In a few short years, the Web has evolved from a virtual billboard to a place to find good stuff cheap to a source of information and—most recently, as a service portal. Viewing the Web as a conduit to services that can be superior to other modalities is new. The prerequisites, including information about individual users and the technologies to apply that information in ways valuable to customers, were simply not sufficiently developed in the past.

One component of the Web that was insufficiently developed, or at least insufficiently studied, is the human–computer interface, from the perspective of a service provider. Early work by luminaries such as Ben Shneiderman and Ed Tufte produced the intellectual basis for our current computer interface design and information displays. Their contributions are from a logical, ease-of-use, and ease-of-learning perspective. Building upon these qualities, you can provide service through portals that are not only intuitive and easy to use, but create some degree of emotional bond with users as well. Objects, even computer screens, have the personality we ascribe to them.

A logical interface, such as a window into an Excel spreadsheet, conveys no emotional content. It provides cold, logical answers. An Excel spreadsheet can provide a sense of mastery and of empowerment, but it doesn't give a warm and fuzzy feeling to the user. You're not going to get attached to it as you would to a good book, a favorite chair, or a video game—and sometimes that's all right. Sometimes all you want is McDonald's if you're hungry and stuck in an airport.

However, a customer-oriented Web site needs to be warm and fuzzy. Like a doctor with poor bedside manner that is otherwise competent and knowledgeable, a Web site with a purely logical interface, regardless of whether or not it gives the "correct answer," isn't something most of us can bond with. At some level we all want—and need—to feel warm and fuzzy. It's not that we subconsciously want to cuddle our PCs, but we want to feel important, respected, and cared for. We pay for service. We're hungry for attention in the increasingly cold, technological world of telecommuting, voice mail, and email.

It's time that we focus on the more human components of commuting technology. Much of the current Web behaves as though it were designed by an engineer who develops wheels and transmissions without concern for the "ride." A Volkswagen and a Mercedes both provide transportation, but most people perceive them differently. The ambiance, the music, the lighting, the feel of the wheel, the acceleration, the smell of new, fine leather, the ergonomic seats, and lighting—all define the human–machine interface. All these factors operate at a higher level than simply intuitive design, ease of use, or ease of learning.

The most important factor affecting consumer to eBusiness interactions is the user interface: what the consumer sees and interacts with to execute transactions with your eBusiness. Consider, for example, how the graphical user interface we call the Web made the Internet accessible and understandable by millions overnight. Similarly, Emotionally Intelligent Interfaces (EIIs) will enable your company to foster a feeling of trust and loyalty in your consumers. Not having an Emotionally Intelligent Interface to your service-oriented Web site—and all Web sites should provide service—would be like installing a 100-watt Blaupunkt stereo in a car with only two 3-inch speakers in the doors. Emotionally Intelligent Interfaces are the next "killer app" of eBusiness.

Emotionally Intelligent Interfaces can take on a variety of forms, from email dialogues to animated graphical figures, and may carry on conversations, act as human surrogates, and achieve specific tasks. They can be thought of as a type of consumer-focused decision support tool with a conversational dialogue—a portal into consumer needs and wants. An Emotionally Intelligent Interface can take the form of an intelligent agent with an attitude, a bot or software robot that knows you like to read Ray Bradbury and prefer cashmere sweaters to sweatshirts. Like a human customer service representative, an EII can provide consumers with a sense of attachment. Consumers appreciate being paid attention to, and Emotionally Intelligent Interfaces can provide that attention on a 24/7 basis. They are one part of the technological approach to providing service, just as technology should be only one component of an enterprise-wide strategy of customer-centered activities.

Emotionally Intelligent Interfaces can act as surrogate humans that can be communicated with, and with which consumers can build trust and loyalty. Most important, Emotionally Intelligent Interfaces can form the nucleus of an eBusiness community based on products, services, and the free exchange of information. Because Emotionally Intelligent Interfaces can provide the personal, one-on-one contact that eConsumers now demand, they are the next evolutionary phase of eBusiness.

Emotionally Intelligent Interfaces can't simply be purchased in a shrink-wrapped box from your local computer software store and set up in an afternoon. Like Customer Relations Management, Emotionally Intelligent Interfaces are really a business strategy based on an information infrastructure derived from your consumers' transactions. That is, the interface proper—what the consumer interacts with and through—is driven by data from previous consumer interactions, explicit consumer preferences, and heuristics based on consumer profiles. Creating Emotionally Intelligent Interfaces involves developing and maintaining consumer databases and data mining techniques, and must address technical and social issues such as data confidentiality and security. Consumers must feel that the information extracted from their Web transactions will be used in a way that is in their best interests and doesn't violate an implicit trust.

Consider this book a primer on how to integrate Emotionally Intelligent Interfaces into your eBusiness strategy. To increase the applicability of this book to a variety of audiences, it has been divided it into three parts. Part 1, Chapters 1 through 3, provides an overview of the current eBusiness environment. This section is intended to bring IT managers up to speed on eBusiness issues, and to provide a review for the eBusiness executive. Part 2, Chapters 4 through 6, describes the technologies involved in creating Emotionally Intelligent Interfaces, as well as a historical context for computer–human interactions work. This section is intended as a review for IT managers familiar with these technologies, and introduces the concepts necessary for eBusiness executives to communicate intelligently with their IT peers. If you're well versed in eBusiness principles, then you can save time by reviewing the condensed information at the end of each chapter in Part I. Similarly, if you're fluent with the latest IT principles that deal with interfaces, you may elect to read the Executive Summary at the end of each chapter in Part 2.

Part 3 presents the technology and eBusiness principles that address the consumer loyalty challenge. Chapters 7 through 9 provide you, the busy eBusiness executive or IT director, with a roadmap of how to get from where you are now to the next level of consumer loyalty, from business, technical, and consumer perspectives. This section details what you should be doing now to prepare the information infrastructure needed to support Emotionally Intelligent Interfaces, whether you decide to build or buy the technology.

Success in eBusiness requires attention to strategy, process, technology, and culture. Emotionally Intelligent Interfaces technology is the new face of eBusiness. With the inevitable dotCom shakeout on the horizon, the winners will be the eBusinesses with strategic advantages, such as Emotionally Intelligent Interface technology, over their competitors. What remains to be seen is how your company will take advantage of this technology in order to make your product or service the next "killer app" of the Web. Let's look ahead, shall we?

## Executive Summary

An Emotionally Intelligent Interface is a communications portal between an eBusiness and consumers that approximates the best qualities of a human customer service representative. It is personal, engaging, easily understood, polite, and gives the impression of having the consumer's best interests in mind. An Emotionally Intelligent Interface can make the difference between having merely satisfied customers and retaining long-term, loyal customers.

*The Eternal E-Customer: How Emotionally Intelligent Interfaces Can Create Long-Lasting Customer Relationships* is about developing consumer loyalty by bringing the human touch to online consumer interactions. Every customer contact is an opportunity to improve upon a customer relationship and to learn more about customer needs. Using Emotionally Intelligent Interfaces is the best strategy for exploiting this opportunity.

Part 1 examines the current eBusiness environment, where consumers demand immediate service and instant gratification. Part 2 looks at the technological underpinnings of Emotionally Intelligent Interfaces, including data warehousing, intelligent agents, and virtual personalities. Part 3 describes the steps you can take to increase the success of your eBusiness by using Emotionally Intelligent Interfaces to improve consumer loyalty and create an atmosphere of consumer advocacy.

## Acknowledgments

I would like thank my research assistant and literary guide, Nancy Mulford, for her unbridled encouragement, enthusiasm, and hard work in providing assistance on this project. Without her help, this book would not have been possible. To the staff at McGraw-Hill, especially Michelle Reed, my development editor who, with a single phone call, made this book a reality. To my readers and reviewers: Peter Leyden, John Glaser, Aaron Kleiner, Ana Maria Mezei, Lucie Salhany, Rosalind Bergeron, Ron Rouse, and, of course, Gilles, for their inspiration, insight, constructive criticism, and, most significantly, their time.

Thanks are also due to those who contributed directly and indirectly to the substance of this book, especially Rosalind Bergeron, my sister and business partner, whose thoughts and insights as an attorney specializing in human resources are contained in this work. To the editors I have worked with over the years: Paul Pagel, Terry Littlefield, Terry Monahan, Corrine Charais, Sue Frisch, Cynthia Huff, Fred Fusting, Craig Percy, Sara Gall, Sue Glover, Nancy Haiman, Conrad Swanson, George Hayhoe, Bob Mitchell, Brian Winkle, Emily Burroughs, Steven Locke, Warner Slack, Ed Hare, Clem McDonald, Frank Irving, Charlene Marietti, Reed Gardner, Bob Greenes, Geert Meester,

S. Sitharama Iyengar, Steven Lazarus, Gary Marks, Lee Klein, Rogers Piercy, Robert Perlman, JH van Bemmel, Lucinda McKnight, Nancy Collins, Pat Flynn, Robert Hogan, Nancy Megley, Richard Strauss, Ori Heller, Joel Kleinman, Dave Newkirk, and Marcel Frenkel. For those who helped formulate the emotional concepts described in this book: Ron Rouse, Nadine Nicotera, and Ellen Goodman. And finally, to my mentors, each of whom follow different philosophies and paths in life, and are separated by time, space, and context, but share supernatural (and, fortunately for me, contagious) levels of intelligence, focus, and passion: Fred Marshall, Gorst Duplessis, Bob Greenes, Mike Bailin, John Ryan, Jae H. Kim, and Ray Kurzweil. I would also like to thank the accomplished and generous Ray Kurzweil for taking the time out of his hectic schedule to write the Foreword to this book.

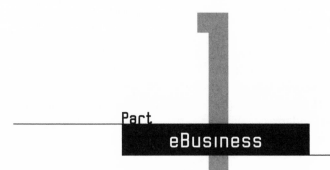

Part

**1**

eBusiness

# 1

*For tribal man space was*
*the uncontrollable mystery.*
*For technological man, it is time*
*that occupies the same role.*
                    Marshall McLuhan

As a youth at the turn of the 19th century, an oyster fisherman worked from sunrise Monday morning to sunset Friday night. Around 3 A.M. on Saturday, he would load his catch onto a large skiff and head to the fish market in town. Although he and his father had a relationship with the owner of the fish market, they always debated the quality and price of the product. With oyster knife in hand, the fish market owner would sample the oysters and state his price. On a good day, a barrel of salty oysters and 15 minutes of haggling fetched 50 cents. On a bad day, the same 15 minutes might yield only 35 cents. Regardless of the transaction details, both the oyster fisherman and the fish market owner parted with the full expectation that they'd be doing business again in one week. They had a relationship that was built on years of short, intense, personal transactions.

From the oyster fisherman's perspective, the time he spent in the actual business transaction was insignificant compared to the time he spent hauling oysters from the brackish waters in southern Louisiana and then transporting them to market. As a producer, he felt that selling was simply the final step in a long, arduous process. He didn't have time to consider his role in the value chain and what might happen if the fish market owner refused to buy his catch in favor of that of another fisherman who might accept a lower price. The oyster fisherman and the fish market owner had an unsigned deal—a relationship—that virtually guaranteed security for both of them.

From the fish market owner's perspective, the oyster fisherman was probably a normal, welcome part of his Saturday morning. After 15 minutes of haggling and another 15 minutes of the fish market owner's watching the oyster fisherman unload a dozen barrels of oysters, the oyster fisherman was gone. The time the owner invested in the relationship was the time spent transacting business. It was an efficient use of his time. Of course, it wasn't as simple as that. If the owner didn't at least satisfy the oyster fisherman's need for capital, he might have to invest time finding another reliable source of oysters.

It turns out that their relationship lasted over a decade. The demand for oysters declined and the oyster fisherman shifted to the more lucrative shrimping industry. As captain of a shrimp boat, his main concern was maximizing his weekly catch while managing a crew of six. He no longer dealt with sales; a salesman representing the shrimping cooperative negotiated with the big freezer companies for the best price. After another decade, faced with dwindling profits and fierce competition from shrimp producers in Mexico and Taiwan, the oyster fisherman graduated from hauling ice and shrimp to managing tugboats that transported drilling equipment to offshore platforms for multinational corporations.

Through the course of his work career, the oyster fisherman became involved in longer, more complex value chains. He advanced from delivering a product with a measurable quality to a service that was difficult to quantify. He moved from dealing one or two levels up from the end-consumer to dozens of levels up from domestic and international consumers. The oyster fisherman never experienced the Web, but his career illustrates a number of points relevant to the Web.

## eBusiness Clichés

According to the clichés floating around the trade magazines, we're all operating in "Internet time," "power has shifted to the consumer," "revenue is in and profit is out," and "the Internet changes everything." There may be some truth to these revelations, but in each case, it's a matter of degree. Despite the widespread adoption of the telephone, email, and the Web, business is still about creating and nurturing relationships. What has changed is the real and perceived time required to form relationships, transact business, and—most importantly—dissolve and disrupt relationships.

It's fashionable to speak of things happening in Internet time because processes on the Web simply occur faster than in the physical world. Instant communications and gratification are not only possible, they are expected. It's as though, as a species, business has been transformed from a lumbering elephant, which lives seven or eight decades, to a sprightly fruit fly, which experiences an entire life cycle in less than a month.

The Web, like the telephone and the microcomputer, is really a time machine. Just as FedEx is a modern version of the transporter from "Star Trek," capable of moving objects from one point on the planet to any other point in about a day, the Web compresses the relationship building–sales cycle. A three-second sequence of mouse clicks can replace a one-or-two hour business meeting. Because of the ease and rapidity with which symbiotic relationships can be established, there's little motivation for either side to develop loyalty toward the other. Or is there?

Several factors affect the Internet business relationship: trust, is one factor. Each side assumes that the other will abide by the agreement to exchange goods, services, or money. Trust doesn't have to go very far if the business transaction involves trading a barrel of oysters for a few coins. Both sides get what they want out of the exchange or the deal is off. But consider a business transaction for services, such as a one-month contract for house cleaning. A service, unlike a physical object, is difficult to quantify objectively. If a customer isn't satisfied by the quality or timing of the service, there may not be any recourse against the supplier other than simply not using that supplier again.

To quote a sales cliché, "The fear of loss is greater than the prospect for gain." Or, as Spencer Johnson says in *Who Moved My Cheese?*[1], "The more important your cheese is to you, the more you want to hold on to it." We—buyers, sellers, and bystanders—fear the unknown. This universally human trait provides the psychological basis for cultural development, patriotism, and loyalty. Since we are consumers in the service industry, this fear of the unknown also fuels our desire to stay with a service provider that has performed admirably for us in the past. Presumably, service providers appreciate the money paid to them for their services.

However, if they're in demand, they may not be as attached to the consumer as the consumer is to them. When the world is full of clients willing to pay for a service, one client is just as good as another.

Another factor in relationships is control. If one side can walk away from a relationship, and the other side can't or won't, the side that can walk away controls the relationship. On the Web, where so many product and service providers are only keystrokes away, control of the relationship is clearly in the hands of the consumer. According to Fisher and Ury in *Getting to Yes*[2], consumers have a better BATNA—a Best Alternative To a Negotiated Agreement. If the deal doesn't work out—if a seller doesn't meet a price point, for example—the customer can click to another eBusiness in a half-second. This scenario assumes that providers are numerous and largely undifferentiated.

The BATNA view of relationships suggests that the time invested in a relationship affects our decision to stay in a relationship. It's one thing to drop someone after one date and another to walk out after living together for a year. If a person has invested significant time in a relationship, then walking away and starting the process anew with someone else isn't very appealing. At least the time investment in an ongoing relationship is known. Starting anew, trying to develop another relationship, often has an unknown time commitment. Time is the most precious commodity on the planet, and no one wants to spend it unwisely.

As illustrated in Figure 1.1, a consumer in an existing relationship with Business A expends a known amount of energy and time managing the relationship ($e_k + t_k$). Alternatives to the current business relationship, Businesses B and C, each carry with them unknown energy and time investments. Although it may be impossible to quantify the energy and time required to establish a working relationship, the relative investment can usually be surmised. For example, Business C might be located in a different state, while Business B might be located a block away. If the consumer is looking for a supplier of physical widgets, the physical distance will probably be a major issue. From a subjective, mainly qualitative assessment, Business B appears to be the BATNA, the best alternative to Business A. That is, the customer's perception of energy and time required to establish a relationship with Business B ($e_{p1} + t_{p1}$) is greater than that required for Business C ($e_{p2} + t_{p2}$). On the Web, there may be so many competing businesses that the chances of a consumer selecting one over the other could almost be attributed to chance.

In an ideal environment where customers find an eBusiness strictly at random, market share can be calculated as the number of potential customers divided by the number of eBusinesses on the Web. In the real

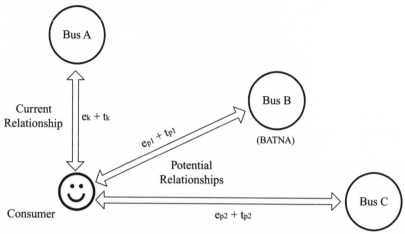

**Figure 1.1**    *A consumer in an existing relationship with Business A (Bus A) has a known energy ($e_k$) and known time ($t_k$) investment in the relationship. Moving to a new business relationship with Business B (Bus B) or C (Bus C) requires an unknown quantity of energy ($e_p$) and time ($t_p$). A relationship with Business C is perceived to be more costly in terms of time and energy than a relationship with Business B, as indicated by the longer path between the consumer and Business C.*

world, the process of creating business relationships isn't random, even on the Web. The entire focus of marketing is to make the process of a customer's locating a supplier as non-random as possible, in favor of the business behind the most aggressive marketing effort. Establishing a brand with a positive or negative image, for example, significantly upsets the randomness of the Web. A customer is likely either to search out or avoid a particular eBusiness, based on perceptions of the brand. Similarly, although geography and physicality are irrelevant concepts on the Web, the Web equivalent of prime real estate—a short, catchy URL—can have the effect that a multi-million-dollar storefront in a prime location has on sales in a brick-and-mortar business.

Brand aside, a basement eBusiness startup with a Web designer who has an eye for graphics and a programmer who knows her way around active server pages is on equal footing with a 100-year-old multi-million-dollar brick-and-mortar corporation—at least from the perspective of eConsumers. Of course, when an established business with a known brand decides to establish a presence on the Web, the physical business can give the eBusiness instant credibility.

For example, the Gap's click-and-mortar Web site (www.Gap.com) is an online extension of the Gap chain of retail outlets. The Store

Locator function allows anyone to locate the nearest Gap retail outlet. In addition, as the Web site boasts, Gap.com is about ease. A customer can order a garment from the comfort of her home. If the item doesn't fit, she can bring it to any Gap for a refund or exchange. Gap.com is also up front about collecting consumer information. A disclosure statement on the Web site states that the company maintains records of product interests, purchases, and whatever else might enable it to enhance and personalize a consumer's shopping experience.

Consider two eBusiness startups, neither one of which initially has a physical business presence. What is the differentiating factor that will successfully upset the randomness of customer hits in favor of one of the businesses? Given equal advertising and marketing budgets, it won't be brand development, unless perhaps one business has a great Web address and the other doesn't. All other factors being equal, the difference will center on customer stickiness or loyalty.

How to cultivate loyalty in the customer base is the most critical issue in a successful eBusiness. A loyal following is also important in a traditional business, but it's not as essential as in eBusiness because of practical physicality issues, such as storefront location and prospect for walk-in business. A customer is likely to continue to visit the corner grocer, even if there is a better product or service available elsewhere, simply because the store is on the way home.

# The Landscape of eBusiness

eBusinesses are spending unprecedented millions on short, catchy URLs and radio, TV, and print marketing campaigns to attract shoppers to their Web sites. Until about the beginning of 2000, hits were all that mattered. Eyeballs were where the big money was. For marketing firms, that's still the case, but for an eBusiness that delivers products or services, it's not the window shoppers, but the buyers who count. Window shoppers are good, because they represent potential customers, but buyers are best, because they add value to the eBusiness, especially if they return with more business.

As eBusinesses become smarter, the metrics of success are less about hits and more about transactions. Having visitors drop by an eBusiness is necessary but ultimately not the crucial condition for a thriving eBusiness. What's important is how many of those customers actually complete a transaction. It doesn't matter how long or often a customer visits a site if, in the end, he or she doesn't buy. On the Web, a little less than half of the adult shoppers are also buyers.

Of the four main distinguishing characteristics of a business—price, place, product, and time—the Web has yet fully to address time. For example, while customers may use the Web to look up books on Amazon.com, if they need the book immediately, they'll probably walk two blocks to their local Barnes and Noble to purchase it. Although customers may consider themselves to be loyal to Amazon.com, practical considerations often dictate that they forgo loyalty in order to save time. The point is that the eBusiness world isn't a fish tank; the brick and mortar malls are still doing very well.

Attracting customers to a Web site is still important; in fact, it's critical. One of the hottest areas of Web technology development, from an "attract the customer" perspective, is 3-D. The increasing availability of high-bandwidth DSL and cable modem Internet connections, together with affordable 3-D software, is making realistic product renderings the new "must have" of the month on the Web. The Sharper Image (www.SharperImage.com) site uses 3-D to create an online version of an actual shopping experience. Shoppers can manipulate products, such as a waterproof CD Player, which have been modeled in 3-D. Sharper Image's Web traffic is up several hundred percent since the introduction of the 3-D animation, and customers spend considerable time viewing the 3-D objects. This extra time spent shopping presumably translates to more sales, either through the Web, a Sharper Image storefront, or through the mail-order catalog.

Lands' End® (www.LandsEnd.com), the catalog clothing retailer, is using 3-D technology to help female shoppers visualize an outfit on them. Potential customers create a personal 3-D model that approximates their figure, face shape, hair style, and skin tone. With the model, shoppers can experiment, discovering which garments enhance their body type. For example, a blouse with wide horizontal stripes might look great on a sleek model, but altogether different on a voluptuous figure. Like a virtual Barbie doll, the model can be dressed in a variety of garments and then viewed from multiple angles.

In creating their 3-D surrogates, customers have a choice of filling out either a Quick or a Detailed questionnaire. The Quick questionnaire requires qualitative information, such as small, medium, or large shoulders, hips, waist, and bust. There are clearly labeled buttons for selecting hair style, hair color, skin tone, and face shape from a palette of icons. The Detailed questionnaire requires exact body measurements, including height, arm length, and rise. With this information, the Lands' End site can suggest outfits and general style advice. For example, for a woman with medium shoulders and a large bust, the system suggests avoiding double-breasted jackets.

Lands' End also offers a functional *Lands' End Live!*™ feature on the Web site that allows customers to talk directly with a customer service representative while shopping on the site. Customers with a second phone line can talk with a customer representative by phone. Those with a single phone line who are comfortable with email can have a live chat session with a customer service representative. When a customer chooses the telephone option, he can enter his phone number and a customer service representative will call him. The only information customers have to add is their first or last names. The Lands' End site also makes it easy for customers to track their orders.

At the end of the eBusiness shakeout, the winners won't be those with the coolest graphics or catchiest marketing slogans. The winners in eBusiness will win by providing outrageous service. eBusinesses that want to attract paying customers, not window shoppers, will focus on what matters most to customers: service. Customers expect prompt, courteous, personalized service. With intensified competition and uncertain brand loyalty, successful eBusinesses will focus on developing and maintaining excellent customer relationships.

## Custom Is King

Service has a personal connotation. To be treated like the masses, without the slightest hint of personalization, is not service. The American Express ads reminding Visa and MasterCard holders that "Membership has its privileges" appeal to the consumer's need to be recognized as an individual. With this pervasive attitude, it's no surprise that consumers are willing to pay handsomely for customized products and services. Consider, for example, the custom Levi's store in San Francisco. Patrons are more than willing to have their bodies scanned with lasers, submit to fingerprinting, and pay top dollar to have a pair of custom fit jeans made to their exact specifications. Not only are consumers willing to pay handsomely, but also, they are willing to forfeit their personal information for a pair of jeans.

Customization and personalization are generally easier on the Internet than in the physical world. For example, instant messaging, popularized by America Online, allows online consumers to request online customer assistance. Alternatively, a customer service representative monitoring the site for visitors may initiate the interaction, just to let the customer know that online assistance is only a mouse-click away.

Although humans are the gold standard as dispensers of quality customer service, they can be expensive, and aren't always available or in a good mood. One of the technological alternatives to human customer service is to use Intelligent Agents. Consider booking an airline reservation with the aid of one of these software programs. An agent can be programmed to find, for example, flight times and ticket prices at various airlines, saving the consumer time and money.

An intelligent shopping agent serves in the same capacity as human travel agents do with the airlines. As such, these agents are poised to become the primary interface between customers and suppliers, with the businesses that create and maintain the agents reaping most of the benefits of the transaction. The issue isn't whether agents and other software tools should or will be used, but how the technologies are implemented. As intelligent agents and other tools become commodity items on the Web, the real winners will use agents and other technologies in a customer-centric manner, with a goal of building customer loyalty.

Consider the parallel "real-world" situation with a human travel agent. Even though anyone can make reservations directly with airlines via the phone or on the Web, many customers prefer to use a human travel agent. Why use a human agent, with so many free alternatives available on the Web? One reason is that it's faster. The other is loyalty. Many customers don't feel loyalty to the airlines; the airline selected by their travel agent is usually insignificant, as long as it's one of the major carriers, and there hasn't been a major crash in the carrier's fleet within a week of the intended flight. The loyalty is to the travel agent, not the travel agency she works for, and not the airline.

## Better Never Than Late

The Christmas shopping season of 1999 was a painful wakeup call to those who took the "If we build it, they will come" approach to eBusiness. Tens of thousands of shoppers, hoping to avoid the holiday crowds in the malls, opted to make their toy purchases through one of several new eBusinesses advertising wide selections, good prices, and guaranteed delivery by Christmas.

Unfortunately, thousands of shoppers who opted for the e-solution to their shopping challenges were without the expected FedEx boxes of toys as Christmas approached. During a frantic two weeks before Christmas, their phone calls to customer service representatives produced stories ranging from "FedEx was unable to deliver to that zip code," to "I'm sorry, we're out of stock on that item." These shoppers ended up in the malls on Christmas Eve.

For their troubles, customers were offered a $10 gift certificate and a "come back again real soon" pat on the back. Clearly, the customer representatives for the online toy stores just didn't get it. The primary reason that thousands of customers chose an online toy store over the malls was to save time and avoid the hassle of shopping. Unfortunately for those eBusinesses, many customers have no intention of ever using their services again, $10 bribe or not. What the customer service representatives didn't understand was that many customers were willing—happy, even—to pay a premium for the service that the online toy store advertised. That eBusiness lost potential customers—forever. In addition, these customers may be hesitant to use an eBusiness toy store in the future, for fear that they'll be in the same predicament again.

## Killer Apps

Eons ago in Internet Time, *Unleashing the Killer App*, by Downes and Mui[3], made a stir in the eBusiness world by identifying concepts that are critical for an online business to be successful. Killer apps—the next big thing; products and services that converge in creative, new ways, such as the spreadsheet, the word processor, and the Web—are so powerful that they transform industries, redefine markets, and annihilate the competition.

The principles most relevant to our discussion of eBusiness are: outsourcing to the customer; auto-cannibalizing markets; treating each customer as a market segment of one; and, perhaps most important, from the perspective of Emotionally Intelligent Interfaces, replacing rude interfaces with learning interfaces.

As an example of outsourcing to the customer, consider the Web-based FedEx tracking system, which allows customers to obtain tracking information on their packages without involving FedEx staff. Not only are fewer FedEx employees needed to cover the customer service lines, but customers can view tracking data on a 24/7 basis. Motivations for outsourcing are numerous; there may be an economic incentive for customers to do some of the work. For example, many travel agents charge $20 to issue a domestic ticket. However, anyone can log on to the Web and reserve the same ticket directly from the airlines without the $20 charge.

Auto-cannibalizing markets refers to a company's treating its legacy operations just as its competitors do. If a company can do a better job using improved methods, Downes and Mui suggest that it toss its old operation and start on the new one before someone else does. This isn't to say that a company should raise its new multi-million-dollar facility to modestly improve production efficiency. However, if a company recognizes an advantage to offering some of its products on the Web at a discount, then it should do so, even if this cuts into brick-and-mortar profits. It's better for a company to do the cutting instead of having competitors eating away at its profits.

Treating each customer as a market segment of one is a call to customize products and services to suit individual customers. The Web can be used to capture data of sufficient granularity to predict, with good accuracy, exactly what customers want. The trick is using the data to make intelligent decisions.

Any human–human interaction has the potential to become rude. That is, if a customer representative is having a bad day, all of his or her customers will as well. One solution to this potential problem is to provide electronic interfaces for customer interactions. The advantage of this approach is that the eBusiness maintains control over the interface. The challenge, of course, is to make the interface great, not merely good enough to replace a questionable customer service representative. It's not enough automatically to capture customer information and instantly provide relevant responses based on this information. A great learning interface gives a sense of humanness, of empathy, and of customer advocacy. In other words, the interface should be emotionally intelligent.

# Reflection

Revisiting the oyster fisherman's era, it's clear that, thanks to technology, the transitions we'll experience in our lifetimes will make the changes his generation experienced seem inconsequential. Two generations ago, lifetime employment by a single employer was expected and seemingly monumental changes in work and income took decades; today's business economy appears to be moving at warp speed – with or without the Internet.

Today, the only thing constant is change, and that rate of change slows no signs of diminishing. Our grandchildren will look back on this period, when everything happens in "Internet time," just as we look back on the oyster fisherman's time—slow, imprecise, impeded by lack of communications, with both suppliers and buyers separated by layers of bureaucracy.

Technology-enabled business is in its infancy. Our Web, fax, cell phones, and PDAs will seem as antiquated to our grandchildren as an old Marconi wireless system does to us. Those old wireless systems of early radio were used with Morse code to take full advantage of the limited bandwidth of the newly tamed ether. We are still in the process of taming communications at all levels in our society and in business, and we have a long way to go. Technology will help get us there as long as we are ready and willing to accept and promote change in how we perceive and do business.

## Executive Summary

Business—not just eBusiness—is becoming more customer-centric every day. However, eBusinesses unhampered by physical inertia are evolving at a much faster rate than are comparable brick-and-mortar businesses, and customer expectations are evolving at least as rapidly. In this environment, personalization of the Web experience isn't just a nicety; it's expected.

Regardless of the short-term fate of the Web, eBusinesses with a competitive advantage will be here for the long term. While short-term goals of attracting customers are critical, what really matters in the valuation of a company is steady growth. The winners in eBusiness will be those who provide consistent, highly responsive customer relations by developing customer loyalty.

New Rules, New Game

*Learn from the mistakes of others—*
*you can never live long enough*
*to make them all yourself.*

John Luther

Players in the Internet Game are learning the hard way that many of the old rules of business don't apply. The winners, whether their business focuses on B2B, B2C, or some other point in the value chain, know which of the old rules do apply, and how best to apply them in a Web-enabled economy. These winners also know how to accommodate the new rules into their existing schema of how their businesses operate. This chapter explores the phenomena of constantly increasing customer expectations; the evolution of eBusiness models; the challenge of mass customization of products, software, and data; the new metrics of corporate success, and present and future disruptive technologies.

# Customer Expectations

Phenomenal powers of observation and statistical correlation are used by paleontologists who recreate the entire skeleton of a huge dinosaur from fossil footprints and bone fragments only a few inches long. A competent forensic pathologist can determine, with good accuracy, the height, weight, sex, age, race, and build of a victim by examining the remains of a single leg bone. An experienced clinician can make a diagnosis on the basis of only a few critical observations. In each case, someone who has experience correlating seemingly insignificant pieces of a much larger picture can often easily recreate a full entity from very limited samples. Like working with jigsaw puzzles, the ability to visualize the whole from parts may involve the scientific method to some degree, but it always requires a modicum of instinct and personal rules of thumb or heuristics.

Similarly, customers usually come away with a perception of an entire company after briefly encountering only one or two touch points. Consider "Joe's Used Auto Parts," a traditional brick-and-mortar business. Without knowing anything about the business other than its name, a customer could probably make a very good guess about the decor, the number of oil-stained rags on the desk, the type of calendar on the wall, the education level of the manager, and something about the level of service that he should expect. Now, to add to the customer's knowledge base, suppose he drives to Joe's and gets out of his car. Suppose Joe walks up, greets the customer with a toothless smile and a two-day beard, shakes his hand with his greasy paw, and tells the customer to park his car behind the building, next to the dumpster. As the customer wipes the grease from his hands so that he doesn't ruin the oyster-white leather seats of his BMW sportster, what are the odds that he'll leave his car in Joe's hands? Joe may be the best auto mechanic on the planet, but all the customer has to go on in his evaluation of Joe's business are his interpersonal skills and appearance.

When a customer walks into a restaurant, hotel, or retail outlet, the background music, the colors of the carpet and the furnishings, and the dress and demeanor of the staff prime him for an experience. These props set the mood and his expectations for everything from cost to the level and quality of service. He probably also has expectations of how things should fit together in any business that he's considering working with. The customer probably doesn't expect disco music in a fine French restaurant, nor does he expect Italian opera in a take-out Chinese restaurant. Incongruencies in what a customer expects and what he actually experiences are disturbing. It isn't that opera or disco are innately bad, or in bad taste, but it's how they're used in combination with other props that matters.

A customer walking into The Gap doesn't expect fluorescent greens and blues, but khakis and black leather. Customers want whatever a business offers to fit their ideal of what the business is about. On a first-class flight, a customer expects the steward to take her jacket before takeoff, stow it on a hanger, and return it to her, unwrinkled, just before landing. The brands Gap, Coke, and Mercedes Benz make customers think about a certain level of quality, cost, and service, based on brand identity.

Customers use a personal set of heuristics when they deal with companies. Because the heuristics aren't based on any formal statistical analysis, customers can often be misled, either intentionally or by accident. Sometimes the correlations are illogical. Perhaps a customer doesn't like a salesperson's dress, for example. Perhaps a short-tempered customer service representative reflects poorly on the quality of a product. Or a dealer who fails to return a phone call promptly gives the impression that a customer isn't welcome. A decade ago, if a businessperson's business card didn't include a fax number, people assumed that their company was either going under or was hopelessly behind the times. Two years ago, business people simply had to have an email address on their business cards.

Today, the must-have item is a Web address—preferably one with a short, catchy URL. The other must-have for a Web site is an attractive appearance. A pretty face goes a long way when it comes to computer applications, whether they're video games, business programs, or Web sites. A slick, well-thought-out interface that's clean and easy to use gives the impression that the entire program is a quality product. Conversely, if the back end of an application is elegant and powerful, but the front end dreary and clumsy to use, no one is going to consider the application of much value. After all, when so little effort has gone into the user interface—something that everyone sees—users often wonder what unseen features the designers must have skimped on below the surface. For much of the Web, it's not a case of putting lipstick on a pig; what you see is what you get.

Given this sensitivity to negative measures, or intolerance to deviation from what's expected, a company has to make a good impression at every touch point or risk never seeing the customer again. Because customers have choices in how they plan to interact with a business, the business has to be on top of all of their possible touch points. As illustrated in Figure 2.1, touch points for a typical business, from the consumer's perspective, include the physical building, personal contact,

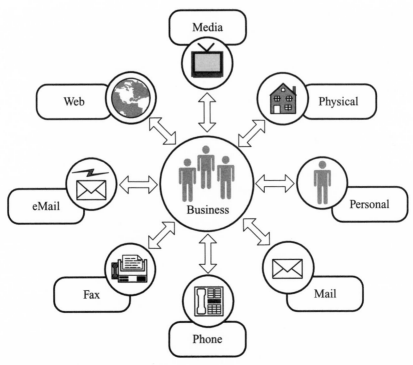

**Figure 2.1**  *Typical business touch points, from a consumer's perspective, include: Media—TV, radio, newspaper, and flyers; Physical—the physical plant, such as a showroom or retail outlet; Personal—direct people contact, including salespeople and customer representatives; Mail—correspondence, bills, and payments through the postal service; Phone—telephone communications with sales, marketing, and customer service representatives; Fax—facsimile communications, including quotes and invoices; email—communications via computer regarding orders and services; and Web—information and ordering through the Web. The arrows indicate relative significance of each touch point; this figure illustrates the state where every touch point is significant.*

mail, phone, fax, email, the Web, and traditional media advertising. Depending on the nature of the business, some of these touch points will be more prominent than others, and some may be nonexistent.

Consider the touch points for Joe's Used Auto Parts, illustrated in Figure 2.2. Joe's Used Auto Parts is predominantly a brick-and-mortar company, with most customer contact occurring with Joe at his shop. From Joe's perspective, his primary touch point may be his telephone. Perhaps he took out an ad in the local yellow pages, and his impression is that everyone who drives in saw the ad or called ahead.

From the customer's perspective, Joe's Used Auto Parts consists of Joe and his shop. There is a small amount of phone and regular mail

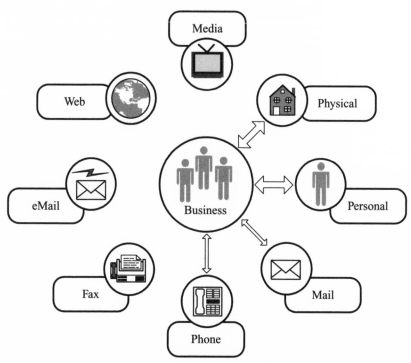

***Figure 2.2***   *Touch points for Joe's Used Auto Parts, a fictitious brick-and-mortar business. Arrow thickness indicates the significance of each touch point, from the consumer's perspective. The major touch points are Personal and Physical.*

activity as well. Joe doesn't have a fax or email, and he doesn't have a Web presence.

As shown in Figure 2.2, for anyone surfing the Web in search of auto parts, Joe's business simply doesn't exist. Whether or not this affects Joe's bottom line depends on who Joe considers to be in his list of clientele, and how interested he is in attracting new clients and maintaining contact with existing clients. Joe may not be the computer-savvy type, and probably couldn't see himself emailing former customers on specials and discounts that might bring them back to his shop.

However, Joe's daughter, Jill, has an eBusiness creating and selling computer game software. Jill is working out of the family basement, with no physical space for customers to aggregate or test her products. From the typical customer's perspective, Jill's business is a Web site supplying marketing materials for her software. As shown in Figure 2.3, from the customer's perspective, email, fax, and the telephone also have significant roles in her business.

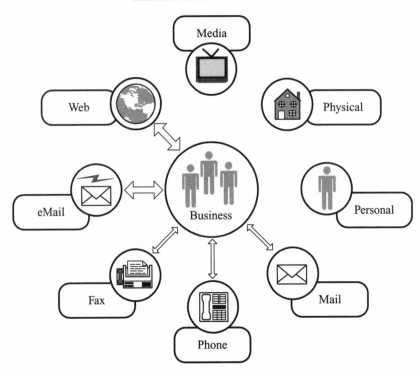

***Figure 2.3*** *Touch points for Jill's eBusiness, a fictitious software develop-ment and fulfillment house, from the consumer's perspective. Email and the Web are the main touch points.*

In the case of both Joe and his daughter, potential touch points are either accidentally or intentionally ignored. In Joe's case, he may simply be happy the way things are, and not want to complicate his life by entering the electronic world. In Jill's case, she may recognize the need to have a physical presence at some point in the growth of her company; for example, when she needs to hire a part-time programmer or perhaps administrative support. For now, however, her rent is a bargain (free room and board) and she cannot rationalize an office. Similarly, she may be at capacity, duplicating CD-ROMs on her PC, and can't see the need for a salesperson on her staff. Regardless of the rationale, an undeveloped touch point is a wasted consumer contact portal.

## Emotionally Intelligent Interfaces

Meeting customer expectations isn't rocket science. Anyone with common sense and the most superficial understanding of human nature can figure out how to deliver what some customers would consider adequate service. After all, if a customer orders a hamburger from a fast food restaurant and, without too much of a wait, receives a reasonably warm burger on a fresh bun, then the customer's expectations will probably be met.

However, if the intent of the restaurant's manager is to exceed a customer's expectations—not simply to satisfy the customer but to wow him—then business as usual won't do. If the manager of that fast food restaurant wants to develop a loyal following of customers who not only return to the restaurant whenever they want a burger, but bring their friends as well, then the customer is going to require some personal attention. Perhaps he likes a plain toasted bun instead of one topped with sesame seeds, or doesn't like onions on his burger. The manager could learn this by either asking the customer or, taking an indirect approach, by simply watching the customer remove the onions from his burger and brush the sesame seeds from the top of his bun.

Clearly, exceeding customer expectations requires specific customer data, and nowhere is exceeding customer expectations more important than on the Web. When the competition is only a mouse-click away, customer loyalty can mean the difference between a successful Internet business and disaster. In today's market, without the technology or techniques for securing customer loyalty, a Web site is hovering on the edge of catastrophe.

One of the most promising technologies for attracting and keeping customers is Emotionally Intelligent Interfaces (EIIs). Whether they are based on caring customer service representatives, computer programs, or both, EIIs build trust and customer loyalty by offering customers the intimacy and individual attention they expect from corner stores. EIIs are driven by data from previous customer interactions, explicit customer preferences, and are based on customer profiles. While Emotionally Intelligent Interfaces make sense for any customer–business interaction points, they are especially crucial on the Web, where instant gratification is expected and choices tend to be based on price, not loyalty.

# eBusiness Models

Every business has a variety of touch points, and the relative importance of these portals or channels varies from one business to the next. Regardless of the perceived relative importance of the touch points, many businesses consider themselves to be either brick-and-mortar establishments with a Web presence or eCompanies with a minimal physical presence (see Figure 2.4). However, this binary thinking is a misjudgment. Most companies exist with varying degrees of a physical and online presence. While there is the occasional commercial-quality Web site run on some thirteen-year-old's home PC, most dotcoms have a more significant physical presence. Similarly, few businesses today are content with a simple home page that says they exist. Expectations dictate a more professional approach to designing and managing a Web site.

Web technology and traditional business are on nearly parallel, intersecting trajectories. As more and more companies are fully integrating the Web into their brick-and-mortar business operations, distinctions become blurred. The synthesis of the online companies with a minimal physical presence and brick-and-mortar companies with only a Web presence is the inevitable convergence of technologies, the click-and-mortar companies. For example, Amazon.com is pouring its online revenue into a huge network of warehouses. CameraWorld of Oregon now publishes its mail order catalog under its Internet identity, CameraWorld.com. Egghead Software (www.egghead.com), once a physical storefront and then an Internet-only retailer is positioned to reopen physical doors in selected markets. The three categories of eBusinesses—the brick-and-mortar companies with an online presence, online companies, and click-and-mortar companies—are described in more detail below.

## Brick-and-mortar Companies with an Online Presence

When traditional brick-and-mortar businesses first crawled out of the primordial ooze and onto the Web, they typically did so simply to establish an online presence. It was a move to stake out territory and to one-up other businesses that they considered potential or proven competitors. The term "online presence" indicates the deadbeat "Hi, we're here" home page that provides little, if any, information that the customer couldn't find elsewhere, and probably more easily. These "flag on the mountain" Web sites are increasingly rare in business, simply because customers expect more than a banner announcing a company's name. They want to be let in, to shop, to inquire, and to roam through the virtual company.

A consumer who runs into a company's veneer Web site lacking anything of substance feels as though she's running into a locked door. The effect is often worse than having no Web site at all. After all, consumers

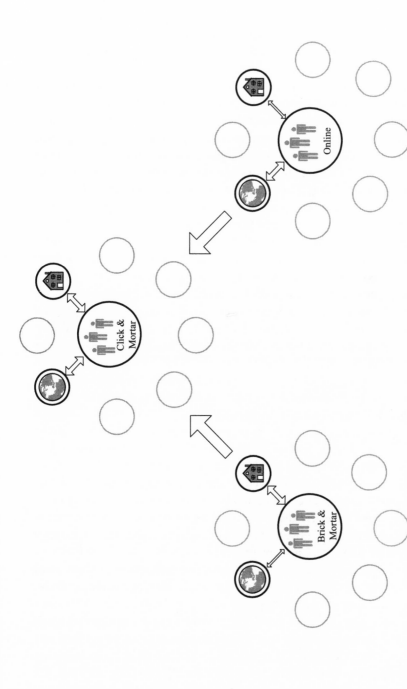

**Figure 2.4** *Evolution of eBusiness models. Companies may begin as brick-and-mortar businesses with a Web presence (left) or dotcom companies with a minimal physical presence (right). However, most companies will evolve from either of these two extremes into integrated, click-and-mortar businesses (top). The other touch points normally found in each business model are not shown.*

might blame themselves for not being able to find the site, and they fully expect that there must be a grand site, given the company's massive physical presence. Better to have potential consumers imagine a castle than to give them the reality of a barn.

Few businesses have been able to use a barren online presence to supplement and improve their image in the customer's mind. However, not all successful Web sites need to support eCommerce and comprehensive product and service information. For example, in academic medicine, there is fierce competition for quality residents to fill training slots in major U.S. hospitals. Many hospitals rely on mailings, open-house events, mailing videotapes, expensive, full-color brochures; and the telephone to entice physicians to enroll in their programs. Virtually all academic medicine programs in the United States have Web presences they use as a marketing tool. A few go beyond porting their brochures to the Web and provide a service to potential, current, and past applicants.

For example, Massachusetts General Hospital's Department of Anesthesia and Critical Care provides a job placement service to graduating residents. In addition to the usual brochure text and pictures, their Web site (www.etherdome.org) allows graduates of their program and alumni from other programs to list job openings. The goal is to build a community around graduates of the program. By providing continuity with alumni, not only are current graduates aided in their job searches, but potential applicants can see a path for themselves after graduation. The Web site is a catalyst in building a community around alumni focused on a particular specialty. Unlike a true business operation, the Web site isn't a money-making proposition—few commercial Web sites are profitable. The payback is indirect, through increasing the number and quality of the residents in the program.

Today, customers expect even a minimal Web presence to include some sort of customer-centered information. For example, many of the smaller banks advertise their interest rates, and provide location information and links to government financial information. Some larger banks offer more than a mere presence, such as full services through the Web, enabling customers to check their balances just as they can on the phone. The Web becomes another seamless touch point, allowing customers to view their financial data.

If I were to give advice to Joe about improving his business, I would tell him that he might be able to gain more customers if he put up a simple marketing page on the Web. For about $20 per month, he could have a Web presence through any of the hundreds of hosting services. For even better results, he could pay a few dollars a week to Jill to handle his email, maybe host a forum of, say, old Volvo models, and help the owners locate parts at Joe's. If Jill were really industrious, she could create a database of auto parts, provide an interface into Joe's parts via the Web, and allow potential customers to do the work of searching for what they need.

I use a custom tailor who operates out of Hong Kong and travels to the United States every few months to visit established clients and to attract new ones. Meeting him on the two days that he's passing through a major U.S. city is a major challenge. Initially, the Web site (www.noblesuit.com) was merely a presence, listing products and services offered. Today, the site lists possible appointment dates and makes it easy for potential clients to select a city, day, and time that suit them. While this feature provides value to a worldwide clientele, the next logical improvement in functionality and customer service would be to offer an online scheduling system. Such a system would allow customers to manage their own time, freeing the tailor's staff from the burden of checking his schedule and of emailing customers to verify meeting dates. As an added feature, an automatic reminder email could be sent to clients in the schedule a few weeks before the planned meeting.

As illustrated in the three examples above, it's difficult even to discuss a Web site that's merely a presence without creating a list of "should and could have" features. In the same way, potential customers who try to interact with an unresponsive, unintelligent Web site often come away dissatisfied, and asking themselves "Why didn't the company add this feature or that?" Thanks to a new generation of Web development tools, Web sites can leapfrog each other in functionality in weeks or even days, compared to months in the brick-and-mortar world. The point is that serious businesses can no longer get by with simply a presence on the Web. Consumers simply expect more from a Web site in terms of interactivity, information, and responsiveness to their needs.

The bottom line is that a simple online presence doesn't make sense except for some academic centers, small brick-and-mortar businesses like corner groceries or service stations, and small, community-limited service providers. For example, a small accounting firm, dental office, or medical practice might consider establishing an online presence.

Many modern medical practices provide a service to their current and potential patients by listing their credentials and specialty, office hours, acceptable insurance providers, and a map with directions. As in dentistry, law, and other professions, physicians have numerous options for free Web sites. Medical specialty boards, health care institutions, medical hardware vendors, and pharmaceutical companies provide no-cost options for physician home page development and hosting. Medical portals such as

WebMD (www.WebMD.com) offer home pages to paying physician members at no additional cost. In this context, a mere Web presence makes sense. Few patients expect their physician to spend time providing links from their home page to information sources, offering online scheduling, or running forums on specific health care issues—yet. The level of expectation will change with time, however, as some physicians increase services provided through their Web sites, raising the bar on what constitutes a minimal "presence."

*Online companies.*    The Web is replete with primarily online companies—businesses in which the Web is the most important touch point—and some online companies are more successful than others at attracting and retaining customers. In addition to eBay, Amazon.com, and the other dozen or so dotcoms that made headlines with astonishing IPOs, there are hundreds of online companies born and buried every day. A characteristic of primarily online companies is that they have no legacy brick-and-mortar company image or brand to fall back on. This isn't to say that they don't have significant brick-and-mortar components that aren't visible to most consumers, but they're free to experiment, to challenge old models, and to disrupt traditional businesses. Amazon.com is a good example of a primarily online company that has a significant "invisible" brick-and-mortar presence. Amazon.com has an extensive warehouse and shipping network that employs thousands of highly motivated employees.

Dotcom companies like Amazon.com are making significant changes in the text, motion picture, and music distribution and publishing industries. Not only are huge conglomerates getting into the act, but small basement studios are producing videos, eBooks, and music for distribution on the Web. The traditional print industry experienced an uproar when Stephen King published an eNovella, *Riding the Bullet*, in March 2000, a short story he made available only through the Web, with a half-million readers downloading his work the first week. Instead of his usual $10,000 that he would have received publishing through a magazine, he made about fifty times that amount. Both Amazon.com and Stephen King have been successful, not because they are changing the way their markets work, but because they are skilled at attracting and retaining customers. Stephen King does it through name recognition and the emotional bond he forms with his loyal readers. Amazon.com performs the same feat, although perhaps not so deftly, by employing a personal touch through its Web site.

A characteristic of many successful Web sites is instant gratification. For example, *Riding the Bullet* is available as an immediate download from PeanutPress.com (www.peanutpress.com) for $2.50. NetLibrary (www.netLibrary.com), PeanutPress.com's parent organization, also offers eBooks for immediate download, including King's eNovella, in a form readable on standard Windows computers, the Palm Pilot, or any number of dedicated electronic eBooks. Customers can download and begin reading an eBook in less time than it takes them to stand in line at their corner bookstore.

Another instant gratification company is Audible.com (www.audible.com), which offers "books on tape" without the tape. Customers can instantly download one of thousands of titles for $2–3 per title. The alternative, renting books on tape and paying for shipping, either directly or indirectly, and dealing with defective tapes and the delay of the mail system, is arduous by comparison.

Audible's advantage over traditional books on tape is instant gratification, especially if customers use a DSL or cable modem to download a book. The cost is also potentially lower, depending on how customers plan to listen to their books. If customers plan to use a laptop or PC, all they need is a standard sound card to enjoy a story. If they want to go portable—to the gym, for example, then they'll have to buy one of the solid-state digital audio players on the market. These MP3 players, available from Sony, and others, hold an hour or two of audio; enough for a jog in the park. Customers can also use these solid-state players with downloaded music—another instant gratification eBusiness—as well.

Many dotcom companies succeed because they focus on customer service as a product. For example, Circles (www.Circles.com), a high-end virtual concierge and convenience service, conducts most of its customer relations through the Web. Circles is looking at using bots, software robots that can work tirelessly collecting, manipulating, or analyzing Web-based data, to learn more about clients every time they visit the Web site. The goal is to become personal life assistants as opposed to a simple valet service, and give busy executive clients the ability to opt out at any time. The company envisions, for example, executives receiving personalized emails of weekend entertainment choices for their families. Circles offers everything from help paying bills to throwing a party, for a price. Part of that price is a willingness to disclose relevant personal information. However, the customer has ultimate control, because he or she can terminate the relationship at will. In addition, Circles neither bombards the customer with emails about its services, nor sells names and profiles, only aggregate data.

Because of the importance of the Web in its business model, Dell Computer offers "Premier Pages" to qualified businesses. These customized Web sites are secure, personalized Web pages that include online purchase histories, customer-specific pricing, and online ordering. Premier Pages provide small-business users with 24-hour access to their account team; online purchasing with a personal discount, based on their purchase history; product information; and a service and support section. The Premier Pages are successful because they provide immediate, personal service.

***Click-and-mortar companies.*** Fully integrated companies, those with a full complement of active touch points, as illustrated in Figure 2.1, represent the future of eBusiness. Just as the telephone was eventually integrated into everyday business, the Internet and the Web will eventually be an integral part of every brick-and-mortar company. Sooner or later, we'll all be running or working for click-and-mortar companies.

Click-and-mortar companies, which present consumers with a seamless storefront on both the Web and in the physical world, aren't born overnight. They're usually the result of a deliberate, often painstaking evolution from either a dotcom or a traditional brick-and-mortar beginning (See Figure 2.4). Look at Amazon.com, the established dotcom source of books, which is spending millions of dollars on warehouses and transportation chains. In contrast, Barnes & Noble, the 800-pound gorilla in the physical bookstore world, is frantically working to shore up its Web offerings. Eventually, Amazon.com and Barnes & Noble will meet somewhere in the middle. Consumers won't think in terms of online or offline, but online *and* offline. Expect to see Amazon.com retail outlets in the malls one day.

Successfully evolving a brick-and-mortar company into an eBusiness is more common today than adding a physical retail infrastructure to a dotcom. Even so, for a brick-and-mortar company to establish a position on the Web can be disastrous. Some attempts at becoming instant click-and-mortar companies, such as Toys 'R' Us, Inc.'s partnership with Benchmark Capital, have been economic disasters. However, some established brick-and-mortar companies, such as Kmart Corporation and Wal-Mart Stores, Inc., are transforming themselves into click-and-mortar companies through successful dotcomming deals. The concept of evolution is valid; it's simply a matter of selecting the proper mate and allowing the natural selection process of Wall Street to work its magic.

Evolution isn't cheap. It can cost millions for a brick-and-mortar store to establish a functional, customer-oriented Web site, and it can cost even more for an eBusiness without a legacy brick-and-mortar operation to establish one. It takes a tremendous marketing operation to establish online brand recognition. Hence the stories of multi-million-dollar URLs, million-dollar ad campaigns during the broadcast of the Super Bowl, and other high-viewer marketing opportunities. Many eBusinesses spend the majority of their capital on marketing, much to the delight of traditional marketing business.

The evolutionary path to click-and-mortar status isn't usually linear, and the end result of evolution may deviate from what was expected. Staples (www.Staples.com) is a successful click-and-mortar company that evolved from a brick-and-mortar company to one with a fully integrated online touch point. However, consider Egghead Software (www.egghead.com). This computer software and hardware vendor went from a brick-and-mortar company to a dotcom almost overnight. Egghead isn't doing so well, and may need to add retail shops in order to survive. Sometimes a company's physical and Web touch points can be symbiotically related without being seamlessly integrated. Gateway Country, for example, allows customers to try out various Gateway computers and then order them online (www.Gateway.com). These demonstration stores help promote the Gateway brand and steer customers to the Web site.

Although Dell and Amazon.com each have massive physical infrastructures, most consumers consider them to be primarily dotcom companies. Although Amazon.com's main touch point is the Web, most of Dell's customers use the Web and an information source, and then place their orders via telephone. Today, Dell exists in the consumer's mind as a telephone and Web company. Ultimately, online, telephone, fax, and retail outlets will exist in one seamless entity. That is, the customer's information must pass seamlessly between all touch points. It shouldn't matter if customers register their preferences online or in person, for example. Certainly, there will be exceptions.

Lands' End, L.L. Bean, and PC Connection exist as single-channel mail-order outlets for most of their customers. Both L.L. Bean (www.llbean.com) and Lands' End (www.LandsEnd.com), mail-order clothiers, rely primarily on the telephone as their major touch point. Although these companies have outlet stores, there isn't any apparent move to increase their physical presence. Their growth is directed toward the Web. PC Connection (www.PcConnection.com), a mail-order retail computer software and hardware outlet, also makes extensive use of the telephone, supplemented by the Web, for sales. In addition to selling software and hardware, PC Connection makes money by charging software houses to advertise in its mail order catalog. However, it saves money on telephone support staff by offloading to the consumer the sometimes arduous task of locating a software title. If a customer can't find something in the catalog, it's often possible to locate the product on the Web, thereby saving PC Connection the cost of having a customer service representative spend five minutes looking for an obscure five-dollar part.

Even though some companies, such as Amazon.com, may remain primarily online companies, the majority of dotcom companies will need a significant click-and-mortar presence to survive. Successful companies will appear to the consumer as seamless entities, with multiple touch points, physical and electronic. There may be one or two touch points, or several dozen, depending on the nature of the business. For example, not considered in the previous discussions in the touch point figures are B2B, buyers, booths at conventions, branded baubles, and sponsored events.

Although the economics of each transaction may be more weighty, from the perspective of what makes a successful online presence, B2B transactions are no different from B2C transactions. The interface between parties in the transaction, whether human or technological, or a combination of the two, has a direct bearing on customer retention. As long as there are people involved on the receiving side of the transaction, there will be the same issues of how to provide immediacy of satisfaction, a personal touch, and the other qualities of an Emotionally Intelligent Interface.

Creating a seamless click-and-mortar entity requires the best of the physical world and the best of online technology. This translates to establishing customer call centers, data-mining applications, and online features such as personal shopping assistants, gift registries, and other parallels of retail operation. Regardless of the technologies involved, how a Web site looks to consumers—unwelcoming, familiar, sincere, cold, logical, inviting, or friendly—sets the tone for consumer dialogues.

## Statistics and Mass Customization

The debates on privacy and right to know surrounding Census 2000 highlight our national preoccupation with statistics. Not only do the statistics from the national census affect political boundaries and funding for social programs, but they form the basis for many business decisions as well. The use of statistical tools on relatively small samples allows companies to make global business decisions on the basis of incomplete, sometimes even inaccurate data. Statistical tools make it possible for an entire population to be defined based on a relatively small sample. For example, pollsters regularly predict the outcome of a presidential election only hours into the poll results by sampling results from only a few counties in key states. The challenge is finding patterns in complex sets of data that may not be related in a straightforward way.

Although a small business owner, such as a corner bakery, can be successful without ever knowing the difference between variance and standard deviation, the more complex the value chain, the more relevant statistical analysis becomes. It's a matter of deciding what mix of goods to produce to satisfy customer demand. The corner baker knows, from day to day, and from past experience, what will sell. If he sees that a dozen poppy seed muffins didn't sell, and that he sold out of cherry muffins after only an hour, he can increase his output of cherry muffins and cut output of the poppy seed muffins the next day. (See Figure 2.5.) The matter is more complicated when the producer and final customer are separated physically and in the value chain. For example, automobile manufacturers produce models in red, silver, black, green, and so on, based on population statistics of what marketing thinks will sell. If a particular color doesn't sell well one year, colors for next year can be

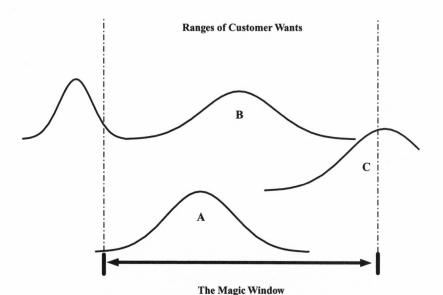

*Figure 2.5*    *The Magic Window encompasses what customers want within the range of what a business is willing and able to deliver. Customer population represented by curve A provides the best fit, while the customer population represented by curve C provides the worst fit. Consumers represented by curve B may represent a satisfactory pool, depending on the number of customers involved.*

adjusted accordingly. Because of the lag time between production and sales, and because the factory workers and management can't see what's selling on the showroom floors, they can over- or undershoot production of a particular model.

The assembly line, one of the greatest innovations of the 19th century in terms of increasing worker productivity and factory output, plays directly into the predictive production model. Standardized parts and standard processes allowed factory workers with minimal training to produce guns and cars and other widgets of standard quality. That is, until boredom, repetitive stress injuries, and other maladies of modern assembly line work set in. Worker satisfaction aside, most people know what to expect when they purchase a mass-produced appliance, car, or garment. They can decide on color and style at the time of purchase, and the manufacturer decides on the core characteristics or features of the product. Assembly line workers, whether working on automobile assembly lines in Detroit or garment factories in Hong Kong, produce runs or batches of identical product, according to their statisticians' best guesses of what customers will decide at the checkout line.

In addition to hard goods, such as appliances and tools, the assembly line process has been applied to other areas as well, such as food preparation and delivery. McDonald's, the fast-food chain built around the idea of standardization and assembly line-type operations, is popular among travelers because they know what to expect. A McDonald's in New York is going to give a customer the same burger and fries that he'd expect in San Francisco. The corner diner might give him a much more palatable meal, but there's a chance that he could end up with salmonella. In a strange city, McDonald's is simply the safer bet.

Whether it's due to the unprecedented prosperity of the 1990s or simply narcissism, custom or one-of-a-kind products are increasingly sought by those of us with thicker wallets than others'. Consider how the media has placed customization in the mind of the buyer. Ads such as "Express your individuality" for homes and clothes that proclaim "I'm different" are everywhere—and these products are all manufactured in runs of thousands.

As summarized in Figure 2.6, many factors relate to the customization of products. There are issues of cost, production capacity, and quality control, but also of communicating with the customer to understand exactly what she wants. Investigators involved in a focus group know how difficult it can be to identify what a customer wants from a universe of unlimited, open-ended options. Most customers have grown so accustomed to selecting what they want from a catalog of offerings that dealing with the decisions associated with a true custom product can be

| Mass Customization of: | Involves | Prerequisite | Marginal Cost | Example |
| --- | --- | --- | --- | --- |
| Physical Widgets | Process overhaul | Factory reworking | High | Car manufacturers |
| Clothes | Personal interaction | Trained personnel | High | Custom tailor |
| Software | Versioning | Marketing | Low | Word processors with user-specific dictionary |
| User Interface | Cookies, Data Warehousing | Consumer Information | Low | Amazon.com |
| Information | Versioning, Pricing, Modification | Access to information | Low | Online Phonebooks |
| Support | User Profiling | People or (Technology) | High (Low) | Help desks vs. Bots |

*Figure 2.6  Factors involved in mass customization.*

unnerving at first. The change can be likened to switching suddenly from an easy multiple-choice exam to difficult, essay-based exam.

Customization requires an educated consumer with a creative mindset, as well as a complete rethinking of the production process. From the customer's perspective, the issue is usually one of granularity of information. For example, suppose that during the next visit to a woman's favorite Creole restaurant, she tells the waiter to go easy on the salt and oil, and that she'd like her fish blackened. After acknowledging this reasonable request, the waiter asks the woman how much pepper she'd like on the fish, cracked or fine, black or green, and what type of wine to use in reducing the stock—and how the roux should be started. These choices, which the customer would probably enjoy entertaining if she were a cook, might serve to simply confuse her if she just wants a good meal. It's not that choices are unwelcome, it's just that the level of knowledge required to make a meaningful decision can be daunting.

At a high enough level, the decision-making process required to create or specify a custom product or experience can be fun. For example, food courts, with their dozens of restaurants, each offering a dozen or more food choices, allow customers to create a custom dining experience, based on their preferences. Customers make their choices, based first on the category of food and then one or more items within the category. The Montreal-based chain, Marché's, takes customer choice to a new level by offering ethnic islands within the same restaurant. Customers move from one island to the next, carrying their food card with them. After selecting an item, a customer simply hands the card over to a representative who stamps the card, and then prepares the meal. At the checkout line, the customer hands the card over to the cashier who tallies the total. Because the level of detail required creating a "custom meal" is minimal, Marché's makes the decision-making process fun. The same could be said for a well-stocked salad bar in any restaurant.

For most of us, even though we may not be able to describe every feature we want in our ideal custom product, we know what we want when we see it. In this regard, customization is really a matter of degree. Custom tailors, house builders, hairdressers, and other personal services aside, customization is usually a misnomer, and simply refers to an array of options available. Consider Dell Computer (www.dell.com), which offers a dozen or so basic computer models, each of which can be "customized" to suit a customer's particular needs. Of course, thousands of customers are not really getting a custom computer. They're simply selecting among options at the time of purchase; Dell defines the core unit. Customers can specify their particular requirements for the amount of RAM, hard drive capacity, monitor size, video card, processor speed, type of removable media to support, and, on some laptop models, even the color of the case. It wouldn't be cost effective—or necessary—to offer PCs designed from scratch. Even so, to the technically inept, the modest customization offerings from Dell can be daunting. Fortunately, Dell customer service representatives walk technically challenged customers through the choices available, locating the computer configuration best suited for them.

The extreme of one-on-one customization is probably a custom tailor. Anyone who has been fitted for a custom suit or shirt—not a rack suit or shirt that's simply tucked here and there for a better fit—knows how many choices are involved, and how stressful the choices can be. For example, consider a custom shirt. The customer has to decide on cuff (French or roll), and if roll cuff, then one or two buttons? How loose should each cuff be? How much larger does the customer want the cuff on his watch hand so he can pull back the cuff to check the time? How tall should the collar be in the back, and how should it taper in the front, and should the front be rounded, end in a long point, or button-down? White collar and cuffs and a color shirt, or single pattern? Full cut or trim cut? Plastic buttons or metal buttons? White or colored? Front pocket(s) or no pocket? If only one pocket, which side? And then the question of fabric—sea island cotton or French cotton, oxford or broadcloth? Then there are issues of colors and patterns. Since most of these decisions should be a function of the jackets and ties the customer intends to wear, his first custom shirt might take an hour or more to configure. Then there are the slacks and jackets to deal with. For a busy executive, all these decisions can be worse than a boardroom meeting.

Fortunately, custom tailors usually offer customers suggestions, based on a customer's personal information. In addition to taking a customer's measurements, the tailor may ask about his current wardrobe, the look he's going for, and his lifestyle, including travel habits. With this personal information, creating a custom suit or wardrobe becomes a collaborative process. For example, if the customer is a frequent traveler, then his tailor may suggest that he forgo a cashmere jacket in favor of a more sturdy wool model. If the customer is a winter person, then the tailor will probably suggest dark blues, crisp, true reds, and other bold colors for his suits and ties. In the end, the customer and his tailor work together toward a common goal—to satisfy the customer's wants and needs.

Although few of us can afford true custom homes and clothing, the appeal of custom products to the average consumer has sparked interest in mass customization, the production of goods or services at the cost of standardized, mass-produced goods. Toyota and other manufacturers of traditional products have failed at early attempts at mass customization, probably because their efforts fly in the face of conventional, assembly line-oriented processes that have taken decades to perfect.

Despite notable failures on physical widgets, mass customization is a natural with some products, such as software, information, and service. A woman caught going over the speed limit will probably receive a custom speeding ticket. The fine will be in relation to how fast she exceeded the speed limit, perhaps modified by her unique attitude toward the officer. If she tries to beat the ticket, her lawyer will probably customize a standard document in preparation for her defense, probably for a custom price. If the woman can't afford a lawyer, she might use a legal document template from Nolo Press (www.nolo.com) that can be customized for her needs. There is mass customization of tax collection service. Everyone pays a different tax, based on income, mortgage, expenses, capital gains, alimony, and other considerations. In a small startup company, an employee's salary and stock options package is probably a function of ability and performance, not simply a reflection of time with the company.

Not everyone appreciates custom service and attention in all cases. A businessman may not appreciate paying a custom price for his airline ticket when he discover that the passenger next to him paid $200 less for his ticket, simply because he went through a different Web site or travel agent. Airline tickets are mass customized by price. They'll get customers to their destination in the service level customers specify— for a price. Similarly, a customer may not want a customized sales tax based on her personal income if she's in a higher income bracket. A customer could get a custom price for his next car or for a software package he orders from the Web. He could also get custom support from the software producer. At issue is not only absolute cost but relative cost. Most of us don't mind a uniform cost, even if it's higher than expected, as much as we mind a custom cost when we're the only one paying the higher cost.

Consider mass customization from the producer's perspective. For a software product, most of the cost is in creating the first CD-ROM. After that, the cost of duplication is usually insignificant. Given this cost structure, it makes sense to address mass customization through versioning and pricing. In versioning, the customer thinks that the product is just for her. A word processor with a legal dictionary could be marketed to attorneys, and the same word processor with a medical dictionary could be marketed to physicians, for example. A company might offer the basic word processing program for $100, packaged with the legal dictionary for $200, and with the medical dictionary for $250. The marginal cost of versioning is primarily in the added support, documentation, and marketing required. The company may need more phones, more people to answer questions about each version, or training for their existing staff.

The concept of mass customization of service is illustrated by Amazon.com's interface. When a customer returns to the Amazon.com site, he's greeted by name and presented with a suggested list of book titles that reflects past purchases. Amazon.com also gives the customer the opportunity to identify preferences for gifts. He could also consider Amazon.com to be a mass customized portal to book publishers.

The mass customization challenge facing the Hong Kong tailor discussed earlier is typical of a physical, product-oriented, person-limited business. The owner, who serves as both master tailor and traveling salesman, specializes in clients who don't follow the casual Friday trend—bankers, CEOs, and other executives in brick-and-mortar businesses. His approach to mass customization is to take photos and measurements of each client, and email them to Hong Kong, where a factory of workers fashions the garments. When they're completed, the suits and shirts are airmailed directly to the customer.

There are several things going for the custom suit business: quality, for one. Highly trained labor is both plentiful and cheap in Hong Kong. However, the rate-limiting factor is the master tailor, and the need for at least one personal interview with the client for measurements and fabric selection. Adding clients—increasing the scale of his mass customization service—is the primary challenge. Eliminating the need for a personal interview would remove the master tailor from the process. In the future, it's possible that tactile feedback, like that developed for games, available through devices such as the Microsoft Force Feedback Joystick, is a potential means of allowing customers to judge the feel of a fabric. Similarly, the Gap's approach of providing a custom 3-D model capability might negate the need for a fitting, if men got into the habit of learning their exact measurements.

Since a given client can only own so many suits and shirts, expansion requires new clients. Customer loyalty often takes the form of word of mouth from existing clients. New clients value the tailor even though he's unknown to them because someone they trust recommends his services. Since the tailor limits his business to a particular demographic, he needs to find a way to reach more consumers. It turns out that his demographic—the people who buy the types of clothes he is willing to produce—doesn't typically scan the Web for custom tailors. He has to focus on other touch points, such as fax, phone, and salespeople, to grow. These are basic business issues that won't be solved by the magic of the Web. The concepts of supply and demand still hold, and conventional business methods still apply. There aren't enough customers of custom suits on the Web that fit his demographic to change his business.

***Decide what you will do and do it.***   The Hong Kong tailor's predicament illustrates an important point in approaching the mass customization model. Top-level management has to first know what it wants, and only then strive to understand what the customer wants. If management knows it is willing to deliver, it will know who its customers are. The concept of the "magic window" can help a company visualize its relationship to its customers. Viewing populations of potential clients through the company's magic window will entail telling some potential customers to take a hike, but will leave the company in a position consistently to deliver to customers who do fit their model. If the potential pool of remaining customers isn't large enough to sustain and increase a business, then management must think of a different way to achieve what it wants.

For example, let's say the tailor wants to deliver quality custom suits and shirts, regardless of the trend toward casual clothes in the workplace. He may want this because it's what he knows, or he simply enjoys working with clientele who wear suits. Regardless of the motivation, he knows what he wants. The question is how to increase the customer pool for his custom services. One option is to partner with clothing stores in each major city he visits, thereby establishing a physical presence and a point of contact that can coordinate customer fittings. The challenge he will have in this new model, which may likely bring in more orders than his plant back in Hong Kong is accustomed to producing, is to deliver quality suits consistently, and then to deliver consistently more than he promises.

## New Metrics

When technology-oriented consumers think of product reliability, many probably think of Dell Computer. When they think of reliability of delivery and ability to track the status of delivery, FedEx may come to mind. For warranty and ease of return or exchange, Sears and L.L. Bean are in the minds of most consumers. For convenience, companies such as MailBoxes, Etc., and PC Connection stand out. Customers can order computer supplies from PC Connection and pick them up the next morning at their local MailBoxes, Etc. Unlike the post office, MailBoxes, Etc. provides 24/7 access to a mailbox. The point is that most businesses can be evaluated from a variety of qualitative and quantitative perspectives, and they typically excel at one.

When management thinks of a dotcom, or the Web touch point of a click-and-mortar business, other metrics come into play: total number of hits, average session lengths, number of unique sessions in a 24-hour period, and other relatively low-level, quantifiable metrics. An increasingly popular metric for overall performance of the dotcom component of an eBusiness is the *conversion rate*. The conversion rate measures the number of visitors who initiate a transaction—buy a book or request more information—on a Web site within a particular period of time relative to the total number of visitors who visit a Web site.

Ideally, management would like every visitor to initiate a transaction, but such fanciful thoughts aren't realistic, even on the Internet. The conversion rate is a good overall metric for a Web site because it reflects the quality of the user interface, site performance, the convenience of shopping through any site that supports eCommerce, and the effectiveness of advertising, including word-of-mouth marketing. The conversion rate metric isn't perfect. It's easy temporarily to inflate the conversion rate of a site by cutting prices and other schemes of renting customers. The conversion rate also doesn't tell upper-level management what to fix if it isn't what is expected. A poor conversion rate could be due to a number of interdependent factors, such as a confusing user-interface compounded by an excruciatingly slow server, resulting in frustrated consumers who leave a company's site with a half-full shopping cart.

Conversion rate, hits, and session length aside, the most important metric for a modern eBusiness—that is, a click-and-mortar operation—is integration. If a customer does business with a mail-order firm on the phone, the customer shouldn't have to re-enter his billing and demographic information on its eCommerce site. From the consumer's perspective, the business should appear seamless from one touch point to the next. The question is how best to quantify this metric. On one level, it seems subjective. Regardless of how integrated a business really is, it's the customer's perspective of integration that counts. Billing information may flow freely from the phone, through the Web, and through personal contact directly into a corporate database, but if a customer calls to place an order and the information in the database that the customer entered via the Web isn't pulled up, then the customer is going to be frustrated. In addition, his impression will likely be that the Web site and main company are different, disparate entities.

Another metric unique to companies with a dotcom component is the relative importance of revenue over profitability. The newspapers and journals are full of stories of dotcoms worth billions that have yet to realize a profit. The metrics are revenues and multipliers. Why worry about profits when, with a multiplier of 60 to 100, a dotcom can post revenue of a million dollars, a loss of 20 million, and have a worth in excess of 60 million dollars? As brick-and-mortar companies begin to dominate Wall Street, potential investors can expect profit and other traditional business measures to reemerge as significant metrics of company health.

# Disruptive Technologies and the Need to Innovate

Disruptive technologies—the Web, the microcomputer, television, cellular telephones, the MP3 standard for music compression and distribution on the Web, bots, artificial intelligence, the graphical user interface (GUI) popularized by the Macintosh, and even the often-maligned software cookies—have a common feature in that they change our expectations. For example, we expect to be entertained by whatever happens to be on television, just as we expect that icons and folders will make our computers easier to learn and use. Rarely are our expectations met, however, given the hype that surrounds major technological innovations. Even so, disruptive technologies forever change the way we view our world.

This discussion of disruptive technologies is especially relevant to eCommerce because it highlights how seemingly inconsequential technologies, such as the Web and the user interface, can have a tremendous impact on a business. The various characteristics of the user interface and their effect on the user, once the subject of academic debate, are now the focus of corporate America. The user interface, properly executed, can turn a company's Web touch point to a pipeline of loyal customers, or shut the touch point off completely. It is therefore important to understand the significance of the user interface and other, related disruptive technologies from the perspective of their potential impact on a company's Web presence.

All technologies, including disruptive technologies, can be classified as either revolutionary or evolutionary. Most technologies are evolutionary, building upon the work of others. Sometimes the evolutionary process isn't visible or obvious to those outside a particular industry. For example, although Apple Computer popularized the mouse and GUI, and the concepts may have seemed revolutionary in the mid-

1980s, the technologies had been developed years before, and were known to specialists in the computer field. Some disruptive technologies, like the microcomputer and the Web are truly revolutionary, representing the biological equivalent of a spontaneous mutation.

Regardless of how disruptive technologies come about, they improve the efficiency or effectiveness of the generation, storage, transfer, or translation of energy. This energy may take the form of a 110V AC that feeds a customer's refrigerator or the data that flow across her phone lines. The television, for example, increases the efficiency of data transfer by providing us with a large-bandwidth information channel for image-rich media. Not surprisingly, computers touch on all areas that disruptive technologies influence; they can generate huge amounts of data, store them in RAM or a hard drive, translate the data into something more meaningful to humans, and transfer them to other parts of a network or to an output device. In comparison, the Web, like the telephone, is involved mainly as a catalyst, increasing the effectiveness and efficiency of energy (data) transfer. That is, the Web can potentially increase the ease with which you and your customers can communicate with each other.

What makes the Web potentially more disruptive that the telephone and other simple energy transfer technologies is that it can be configured to be an extension of a computer. Not only static data, but programs, cookies, applets, Active X, Java, Java Script and other executable code can be transferred and run on the Web, thereby touching the other three areas—energy generation, storage, and translation—of disruptive technology's influence as well.

We can't ignore disruptive technologies and hope that the expectations they generate will go away. Once disruptive technologies are introduced, they're unstoppable. They don't simply push the envelope, they shred it. Paradoxically, their major effect often has little to do with the original intent of their creators. For example, cellular telephones are revolutionizing communications in third-world countries, allowing them to bypass an entire generation of wired technology. Unhampered by a legacy analog telecommunications system, some third-world countries are moving directly to digital communications systems that are more useful than ours. If your major competitor introduces a new interface element on its Web site that somehow increases customer retention, then you have very little choice but to follow suit. When disruptive technologies are involved, standards become moving targets.

Artificial Intelligence (AI) was the favorite son of the U.S. military for decades, with funding fueling research and development at top universities. As is the case with most disruptive technologies, the initial push was for machine understanding of language. However, even after over a decade of research, instantaneous translation of Russian into English still failed miserably. Later, the Japanese government backed a five-year program to create a new intelligent operating system, based on Prolog, a language used in AI research. This project also flopped.

Because of hype by the press and movies such as *2001: A Space Odyssey*, most of us took it for granted that we'd be having meaningful conversations with our computers a decade ago. However, out of the ashes of the failed AI projects and research, we now have intelligent systems that use neural networks, rule-based expert systems, and natural language understanding systems that do real work and have changed the way information is handled in our economy. For example, every time a customer uses a credit card, an expert system compares the purchase against the customer's spending history and flags the retail store if the purchase doesn't fit the history. We finally have language-translation technology, available as shrink-wrapped applications for about the price of a meal at a good restaurant, but it's based on simple probability models, not the overly sophisticated AI techniques developed by academicians.

Television, once promoted as the future of education in this country, has done more to turn us into a field of mesmerized couch potatoes than any other innovation in our time. Children spend more time in front of the tube than they do reading. Television has, however, markedly changed American society, including the perception we have of ourselves, and how the rest of the world views life in America.

Like television, the Web has also had a profound effect on how much time customers spend in front of a monitor at home and at work. A system originally designed for document sharing, the Web has completely transformed the private securities investment business and traditional marketing, created an economic boom this country has never experienced before, and created hundreds of markets and job classifications where none existed only a few years ago. Document management may not have been affected much by the Web, but this disruptive technology has created a tsunami that's still moving through our economy.

By creating an intuitive, graphical user interface—a veneer of sorts—over the Internet, the Web opened up a vast communications network that was once the exclusive purview of the military and academia. The Graphical User Interface or GUI is the collection of icons, buttons, windows, and menus that makes navigating the Web less arduous. A similar phenomenon was created in the mid-1980s with the introduction of the Apple Macintosh. Apple took the high-resolution, bit-mapped screen technology pioneered by Xerox and added a few desktop metaphors to create the Macintosh GUI. Before Apple's $10,000 Lisa, the direct precursor to the Macintosh, Xerox had perfected the bit-mapped screen technology for use in applications such as missile tracking for U.S. military testing centers in the Pacific Ocean. A screen showing a clean trajectory, drawn with razor-sharp edges on a bright background, was much easier to interpret than a string of X's drawn on a black background. The Xerox Star, a $50,000 computer the size of a dorm refrigerator, had a 19-inch monochrome bitmapped screen that rivals the quality of any Windows or Macintosh display today. Many of the GUI technologies developed for the Xerox Star and other machines at Xerox eventually migrated to consumer-level computers, most notably the Apple Macintosh. The Macintosh desktop GUI was perfected and standardized by a group at Apple that had a history of optimizing fighter-pilot cockpits for the U.S. military.

User interface technology has obviously had a profound effect on computing, not only on computers running Windows and Macintosh OS, but on the multi-billion-dollar video game market as well. In about two decades, the gaming industry has gone from Pong, an interactive video game with one or two rectangular paddles and a bouncing ball, to lifelike, animated figures that look and move like humans. The Sony PlayStation 2, Microsoft's X-box, and the Sega Dreamcast are causing a stir in the gaming and home entertainment businesses because of the breathtaking realism of their interfaces. The other source of excitement stems from the fact that these and other game consoles can double as set-top devices, providing Internet connectivity and DVD player capabilities, blurring the boundaries among TV, entertainment systems, and the Internet. These systems are also enticing many consumers to reconsider their home entertainment plans.

The graphics, sound, and controller hardware capable of creating breathtaking 3-D views of a person, scene, or object are the disruptive technologies that make for a great video game. Much of the excitement generated from games can be attributed to excellent sound and graphics, but it's not enough to have simple graphics strewn about on a screen. The graphics must be properly deployed through an interface, and that's where standards come into play. Just as Windows and the Macintosh OS have standards for how they look and feel, most of the popular video games for Sony, Nintendo, and Sega have a standard feel that makes learning a new game on a particular brand of player easier. That is, the buttons on the game paddles tend to be mapped consistently so that "jump" on one game means "jump" on the next. The consistency and standardization of these game user interfaces is one reason that games are so popular with their customers.

The idea of user interface standardization, first enforced by the Apple Macintosh development team, has permeated most of our lives. Computer-enabled games aren't restricted to TV-based game boxes and personal computers. It's surprising how many incredible, disruptive technologies make their debut in this country behind the mask of a child's (or adult's) toy. Voice recognition, robotics, artificial intelligence, person-to-person networking, and other technologies have made their civilian debuts in the toy arena. For example, there have been toys that respond to a child's verbal commands, such as "stop," "go," "turn left," and "turn right" for well over a decade. Although voice recognition hasn't made significant advances in the PC until the past few years, it is now poised to revolutionize the way we interact with computers, including the Web. It may very well provide the standard interface to the new breed of wireless Web appliances that promise to be even more popular than desktop PCs.

Consider neural networks, yet another disruptive technology that will likely have a direct bearing on eCommerce. High-end 35-mm cameras, which could also qualify as adult toys, were one of the first application areas to use neural networks and fuzzy logic successfully in widely distributed consumer products. There are camera systems with predictive focusing, for example, that predict where the subject will be by the time the shutter actually opens. Photographers wanting to take a close-up photo of a sprinter without such a predictive focus system would have to focus and point the camera at some point in front of the runner, and depress the shutter release, hoping that she didn't predict too far forward or, worse still, misjudge the focus. With a fuzzy logic system, the microprocessor in the camera takes care of setting the focus for where the sprinter should be, freeing the photographer to compose the shot. Another example of applied fuzzy logic systems is the 35-mm camera that focuses the camera lens on whatever the photographer's eye is focused on, based on an infrared scan of her eye while she's looking through the viewfinder. It's easy to imagine a Web interface based on the same technology, especially when it's integrated into a head-mounted display or a handheld wireless Web panel.

MP3 is a major disruptive technology on the Web that's causing panic amongst traditional record labels, while potentially making millionaires out of a few forward-thinking Web entrepenures. MP3 is a software standard that allows music that's been digitized, such as a CD sound track, to be transferred to a computer in a compressed form. Once MP3 audio is on a computer, it can be played, mixed with other music, or saved to a portable MP3 player. Retailers and middlemen fear that MP3 will reduce their role in the value chain. Some artists fear lost royalties due to piracy. Meanwhile, cash-strapped artists are using MP3 as a way to get their music out among the masses, perhaps as a first step to a traditional recording contract. As MP3 flourishes as the de facto standard for music sharing on the Web, record companies are still fighting over what formats to use to sell music over the Web. At issue are competing technologies, such as an in-store music kiosk that sells compilation CDs, burned while the customer waits. Traditional music retailers who don't develop MP3 capabilities on their Web site may face extinction.

A disruptive technology that has its roots in AI research, interface design, communications technology, and most recently the Web is that of bots. Bots—software robots—can take on a variety of forms, most of which can live on the Web. One type is as an autonomous agent that can be sent out to perform specific tasks. WebCrawler, Yahoo, and other search engines are examples of well-known bots that have gone out under programmatic control and mapped the Web. This ongoing, seemingly infinite task that makes business on the Web possible would be virtually impossible without bots.

Another form of bot is a chatter bot, an expert system with an attitude. Some chatter bots can carry on conversations in such a realistic manner via email that real users are sometimes fooled into believing they're human. The first chatter bot, Eliza, developed in the 1960s, played the role of a psychoanalytic therapist. This program was so realistic that many people became addicted to the program, believing it to have profound insights into their psyches. While Eliza didn't have any real intelligence, it did have simple pattern recognition, an AI technique, which allowed it to play the role of a therapist with remarkable success. Eliza and subsequent bots changed the way computer scientists and the public thought about computers.

The most significant bot technology, from an eCommerce perspective, is a type of directed chatter bot that can converse with customers over the Web in response to specific questions. These context-specific bots, when supplied with customer-specific data, are being used to provide information and help to customers. Bots can assist customers in navigating through a Web site, finding specific items in an online store, or providing diagnostic assistance in some problem domain. Bots also hold the potential to provide Web sites with affordable, intelligent 24/7 customer assistance, with enough emotional cues to foster customer loyalty.

What other disruptive technologies that are just over the horizon could have a direct bearing on eCommerce? Because disruptive technologies tend to spawn not only other industries but other disruptive technologies as well, the Web is a prime incubator. As such, programs like Gnutella (http://gnutella.nerdherd.net) and FreeNet (http://freenet.sourceforge.net)

that offer true, peer-to-peer distributed networking have the potential to revolutionize computing yet again. With either of these viewers—which don't make use of the Web—other users can share computer files over the Internet. That is, instead of locating a Web server on the Internet with a unique URL to perform a search for, let's say, information on golf courses in the Palo Alto area, a golfer's search would propagate through the Internet, searching through the hard drive of every PC in the network for the information. If this technology takes off, it would turn the current Web paradigm on its head. For example, short, memorable URLs that commanded hundreds of thousands of dollars would become relatively worthless overnight. Security systems would have to be redesigned. On the other hand, DSL and cable modem providers would be inundated with business from people who wanted to become part of the network, requiring a constant connection that isn't practical with a dial-up connection to the Internet.

When pondering the next big disruptive technology, whether for its potential in eCommerce or simply to envision life in the future, it's important to recognize that we're living at a time when science fiction defines the dreams of our best innovators and entrepreneurs, and, eventually, the realities of our lives. Currently, we're grappling with how to utilize the Web and related disruptive technologies as vehicles for eCommerce, and deal with issues such as privacy, control by third-party payers, and the return on investment for this technological immersion to society. Eventually, all disruptive technologies become a normal part of our everyday existence, and we'll take no more or less notice of them than we do the telephone. Our collective future, like our current reality, depends on how we see ourselves. It's a matter of collective vision.

# Executive Summary

Customer expectations of a company and products are keyed to a variety of variables, many of which may be out of the company's control. For example, customers have shorter attention spans and a markedly diminished tolerance for deviation from what's expected. Customers expect consistency in the level of service and connectivity at each touch point, which typically includes a company's physical building, all personal contact with the company, including staff, mail, phone, fax, email, the Web, and traditional media advertising such as radio, television, and flyers.

In considering eBusiness models, Web technology and traditional business are on nearly parallel, intersecting trajectories. As more and more companies are fully integrating the Web into their brick-and-mortar business operations, distinctions are becoming blurred. The convergence of the dotcom companies with a minimal physical presence and brick-and-mortar companies with only a Web presence will ultimately evolve into the future of business—the click-and-mortar companies. Sooner or later, we'll all be running and working with click-and-mortar companies.

Mass customized products present a variety of challenges to both the consumer and the producer. Consumers must be educated regarding the options available and must be willing to make many more decisions than they usually consider necessary to acquire a stock item. Producers must determine what customization really means, from the customer's perspective. This can include detailed information from the customer.

New metrics for Web-based business, such as hits, conversion rate, and revenue have temporarily overshadowed traditional measures of business health, such as profitability. The most important metric for a modern eBusiness is integration. From the consumer's perspective, the business should appear to be seamless from one touch point to the next.

Disruptive technologies—the Web, the microcomputer, television, cellular telephones, the MP3 standard for music compression and distribution on the Web, bots, artificial intelligence, the GUI popularized by the Macintosh, and even the often-maligned software cookies—forever change the way we view our world. The computer and, by extension, the Web, are particularly disruptive technologies because they both improve the efficiency and effectiveness of the generation, storage, transfer, and translation of data (energy). Two of the most promising disruptive technologies currently incubating in the Web's womb are bots and intelligent agents. They promise to bring a level of functionality to the Web that approximates what can be expected from human assistants.

## Customer Relations

*One can do without people but*
*one has need of a friend.*

Chinese Proverb

Business is about developing a relationship with customers, whether they happen to be on an eRetail doorstep due to chance or a concentrated marketing effort. This chapter explores the business–customer relationship, first from the consumer's viewpoint, and then from the business perspective. In the consumer-centric discussion, we'll look at the standards for excellent customer service, and the factors that contribute to developing customer loyalty. From the business perspective, we'll explore the importance of defining the limits of what a business does and who its customers are—and aren't.

# A Restaurant at the Edge of the Internet

Imagine that a man awakens from a deep slumber to find himself in a small town somewhere near the end of the Internet. He doesn't know how he ended up there, but he vaguely remembers that stock options and a 401(k) plan were somehow involved in persuading him to move. After he gets up and get dressed, and starts exploring his neighborhood, he's amazed by the number of choices available for spending his modest moving allowance. For example, within an eight-block radius from his home, there are over a dozen restaurants.

In the course of a month, he visits every restaurant to learn firsthand which would be appropriate for particular social and business occasions. In each case, he starts his investigation by reading the menu posted on the restaurant door or window. He carefully examines the menus for the variety of food offered and the prices to get an idea of the quality of the establishment. After his first visit to a restaurant, he never looks at the posted menus again, but makes his dining decisions based on his experience.

Let's say that this man, a reasonable cook, eats out either as a social event or simply to save time. The restaurants in his neighborhood all offer what he considers satisfying meals. What is unique about each restaurant, and the reason that he chooses one over the other, is the experience. For example, when he's entertaining important business associates, he goes to one of the two most upscale restaurants in the area, one Japanese and one Italian, depending on his guest's preferences.

Consider what the man has come to expect for service from the upscale Japanese restaurant. When the man drives up to the front of the restaurant, the valet greets him and opens the door for him and his guest. The driver hands over the keys, and they walk a few steps to the front door of the restaurant. An attendant opens the door for them.

The maître d' greets him and his guest and escorts them to their favorite table by the window. As he's come to expect, a clean white linen tablecloth is draped over the table and the lighting is subdued. There are orchids in a small oriental vase on the table, and an instrumental oriental tune plays subtly in the background, creating a comfortable ambiance. Once they're comfortably seated, the water waiter fills the glasses with ice water and slices of fresh lemon. The room acoustics are such that they can comfortably carry on a conversation without raising their voices, or worrying about someone from another table listening in.

After a few minutes, a familiar waitress walks up, and, smiling, introduces herself. She distributes the menus and then asks if they'd like anything to drink before dinner. After they've ordered drinks, the waitress acknowledges their request and excuses herself. When she returns in a few minutes with the drinks, she asks if there are any questions about the menu. He sometimes asks about the specials, and she's good at suggesting which ones he might enjoy, because she remembers his preferences.

During the meal, the head waitress stops by to ask if everything is all right, and if they would like anything else. In her dialogue with them, she's friendly, but not overly so. There's no hint of any personal affection; her focus is on his needs, the needs of client, and her performance. In the rare event that something has to be returned to the kitchen, she handles reasonable requests promptly, courteously, and without question.

After the dishes have been cleared away, the bill is presented with a few fortune cookies. They open the cookies, and, in the usual ceremony, read their fortunes out loud to each other. He pays the bill, leaving a tip that reflects the level of service provided by the staff.

After discussing business and a bit of small talk with his guest, he heads to the front door. The valet has his car waiting; the engine is warmed. She greets him, and he thanks her, handing her a tip. They drive away, well fed and, more important, feeling well cared for. The meeting was a success.

This man's experience at the Japanese restaurant epitomizes the pinnacle of customer service available in his new town. However, sometimes he doesn't have two hours to invest in developing a relationship to simply feed his hunger. Sometimes he just wants a place to get away with one of his coworkers for lunch. Neither of them has time for a ceremonial dinner; they both need to eat and then get back to work. In these situations, he visits Maria's, a small Italian restaurant that seems more like an extended part of his home kitchen than a restaurant. He's treated there more like family, and less like a guest. It's a respite from the office, and a place where he can relax.

When he enters Maria's restaurant, the waitress, Maria's daughter, boisterously shouts hello and suggests that he find a place to sit. Since there are only a half-dozen small Formica-top tables and another half dozen booths in the restaurant to choose from, the decision isn't very difficult. He usually picks one of the booths, wiping the crumbs from the red vinyl-covered cushions before he sits down. The acoustics aren't the best, and a private discussion is out of the question.

Once he's seated, he picks up one of the menus wedged between the napkin holder and the shaker of Parmesan cheese. In a minute, the waitress, dressed in a red, short-sleeved Polo shirt, navy slacks, and an apron, appears with pen and pad, ready for his order. While she waits for his decisions, she chats about local events or suggests the special of the day. After a few friendly exchanges with the waitress, he and his associate order.

Between customers, the waitress manages to deliver two glasses of water over to the table, along with napkins and flatware. The fork tines are usually bent, but straightening them with the knife gives him and his coworker something to do while they discuss work or their latest outing. In less than five minutes, his order is brought to his table. Halfway through his meal, the waitress stops by the table en route to other patrons to verify that everything is okay, and to deposit a hand-scrawled bill on his table. She's friendly and appears genuinely appreciative of his business. He pays the bill, leaving a generous tip. As he heads for the door, Maria's daughter thanks him and invites him back soon. He usually manages to have a pleasant lunch in less than thirty minutes.

# A Carriage Ride

In the virtual world, commuting to the office and entertaining business guests aren't the only reasons people travel. Sure, many companies are located just off the Internet, and it's intriguing to hear stories of work-at-home executives and virtual corporations, but most people know that serious business is still conducted the old-fashioned way—face to face. Video conferencing and hi-fidelity, duplex speakerphones haven't obviated the need to press the flesh—yet. Frequent, often-challenging travel is a given if engaged in business—even eBusiness.

In the real world, the most arduous part of a trip is usually getting to and escaping from airports. One of the best companies that address this need in over 450 cities worldwide is Boston Coach. Why does Boston Coach enjoy such a loyal following among executives? Service. What's a typical customer interaction like? It starts with the reservation. A day before the trip, a woman's assistant reserves a sedan through the easy-to-use Boston Coach Web site (www.BostonCoach.com). After deplaning, she walks to the baggage claim area to find her driver holding a placard with her name plainly printed on it. When they meet, she exchanges the usual pleasantries, and then the driver quickly verifies her destination and the time of her meeting. He assures her that she has plenty of time to make a punctual arrival at the meeting. She then walks to the car, a current model Volvo sedan, and the driver opens the rear passenger door for her. She slides in, noticing that there is an unread copy of *The Wall Street Journal* on the seat, immediately behind the driver. The driver also slides the front passenger seat forward, and pushes the back of this seat forward as well. The seat belt isn't hidden somewhere in the crack of the seat, but is readily available. She feels as though she is flying first class.

The driver, in this case a retired CEO, is well educated and articulate. He offers information about the city and events, but isn't overly forward. When asked about Boston Coach, he is openly proud to be associated with the company as a driver. He tells her about the special two-week training period, the written and practical exams, and how good the company is to him. Even though he is only a part-time employee with Boston Coach, he and his wife are enjoying medical and dental insurance and a retirement plan. Drivers are paid whether or not their car is moving. Furthermore, drivers won't accept tips, but do receive an 18 percent bonus when they are working.

The woman's driver may also tell her that, except for a few buses and a sub-contracted limousine service, Boston Coach uses Volvos exclusively. When the odometer registers about 27,000 miles, which it generally reaches within two months, Boston Coach returns the car to Volvo. The finish on the cars is usually worn out by then, not from use or abuse, but because the drivers take them to drive-through car washes two and sometimes three times a day. Upon arriving at her client's office building, the driver stops the car, and asks her to sign a slip stating that she has been transported to her agreed-upon destination. He gets out, walks around the car, opens the door for her, and shakes her hand with a "Good luck with your meeting. Thank you for using Boston Coach."

All in all, the trip from the airport is a pleasant experience, and just what she needed to enter that meeting with a positive attitude and a bounce in her step. Five hours later, having fought for and won the contract for a high-speed connection to the Internet near her home, she's ready to head back to the airport.

On the return leg of her trip, Boston Coach is scheduled to pick the woman up in front of the client's building. However, when her assistant made the reservation, she had no idea that there simply were no parking spots directly in front of the building. So what does the driver do? He circles the block, slowing down as much as possible in front of the building until the woman spots her name on the placard posted on the rear driver's side window. On the fourth trip around the block, she jumps in. The driver is the most exciting person she's seen all day. "How are you, ma'am? Isn't it a GREAT day!" are the first words out of his mouth. His enthusiasm is contagious, and just what she needs after an intense five hours of meetings.

When he's asked about his job, he says that he "adores" it. Then he tells the woman that the Volvo is like a second home. He actually enjoys sitting and driving in traffic, enveloped in a climate-controlled leather cocoon, even though he has to get up at 4:30 A.M. to arrive at work on time. He is friendly and yet very professional. For example, he remembers the airline, but asks her to verify it just the same. She arrives at the airport terminal within five minutes of her predicted time. And, as the previous driver had done, he comes around and opens the door for her and offers a warm handshake. Smiling, he says, "Have a great day, and thanks for using Boston Coach."

How many employees display such infectious enthusiasm around their clients? Obviously, Boston Coach knows how to treat their people. Their drivers display contagious enthusiasm, love their jobs, feel good about themselves, and care about *their* customers. That is, they own the business–client relationship. Boston Coach manages to get their customers where they are going on time, and makes them feel like VIPs in the process. Cost is never an issue.

Behind the driver's seat of every Volvo, there is a postage-free service evaluation card addressed to Russell Cooke, President and COO of Boston Coach. The card asks for feedback on its executive sedan service. Customers are encouraged to comment on whether the reservationist was courteous and knowledgeable, the driver was prepared, friendly and professional, whether or not they were picked up on time, and the cleanliness of the vehicle. Clearly, Boston Coach understands the importance of creating a positive customer experience at every touch point.

Back home, customers can print out a receipt of their trip's expenses from the Boston Coach Web site. Their customer profile page requires only their name, email, and home phone number. The only personal information, apparently to verify the identity of a customer, is the customer's home town of birth. Optional information on the customer profile is information on how they may be contacted at work with phone, fax, and pager numbers. There's also an area for credit card numbers that will be used to pay for their rides.

The information requested by Boston Coach is probably less than what a travel agent has on file for each customer in her computer system. The agent knows more than just seating preferences, special food requirements, and favorite airline, hotel, and rental car agencies. She knows where her customers travel for work, when and where they vacation, and which charge cards they use for work vs. vacation. In exchange for this information, customers can count on their travel agents to find the best fares at the times they like to travel. Customers trust their travel agents with this information, in part because they have an ongoing, longstanding business relationship, and in part because the travel agents have always done what's in their best interest.

# Service Standards

The better to anticipate what will meet—and exceed—customer expectations for service in the evolving click-and-mortar world, consider the level and nature of the service provided by the restaurants and the carriage service. These illustrate the ideal service standards that all customer-centric businesses should strive to provide. Excellent service includes:

- Providing the appropriate level of service. For example, customers don't expect to pay for ambiance, fresh-cut flowers, and an expensive sound system at Maria's restaurant. They do expect a good meal and efficient, courteous, economical service.
- Connecting to customers through clear, non-ambiguous language. Boston Coach drivers don't discuss religion or politics, but are happy to discuss their company, the city they're visiting, and other non-controversial issues.
- Using shared metaphors, contextual clues, experiences, and mental models to aid in communications. Service is about communicating and relating to the customer. The best service business, like the best sales organizations, gets into the customer's head by using words and scenarios that he understands.
- Not only listening for what the customer explicitly wants and needs, but also anticipating his expectations. The restaurant staff was ready to provide whatever was ordered from the menu, but the water waiter didn't have to be told to fill the glasses.
- Suggesting relevant solutions to the customer's problems in a non-obtrusive manner. The waitress at the Japanese restaurant didn't simply deliver her monologue describing the specials, but asked first whether her customers would like to hear them.
- Displaying demonstrable knowledge and credibility, and, above all, professionalism. Regardless of an employee's level within her organization, she is expected to act professionally and to be knowledgeable within her domain. For example, we expect the wine waitress in a restaurant to know the particular qualities of the various wines she sells.
- Empathizing with the customer when appropriate. Everyone is a customer at some level, and everyone has had trouble with service. No one appreciates—or forgets—feeling neglected and taken for granted by a business.
- Seeing problems from the customer's perspective—and the businesses'. This isn't to say that management should always side with the customer. There are always non-negotiables in any relationship,

and management has to know what they are. It may not be possible or appropriate always to see things from the customer's perspective. Excellent service doesn't mean always saying yes to the customer. It is bad for business and ultimately for the other, reasonable customers who will have to bear the economic burden of the problem customers. It's the service provider's responsibility to understand—and enforce—the boundaries of his Magic Window, as described in Chapter 2. That is, management has to decide, for example, if the company is competing with other businesses on quality, price, or quantity.

Excellent service goes beyond remembering a customer's name—it's knowing how and when to enter into a joint problem-solving exercise.

When the man and his guest dined at the Japanese restaurant, their basic needs were met. They were seated and fed, and enjoyed a quiet place to discuss business. If the goal was to be seated and fed, and to talk business, then the dinner was a complete success. From that perspective, dinner at McDonald's might have been equally successful in satiating their appetites, but his guest may not have been so eager to transact business—unless it was for a contract to mow his lawn. Serious clients don't take time away from their families for a night on the town simply to be fed. They eat out for the experience, and expect to be shown a level of respect in line with the relative importance of the relationship between the customer and the business. In other words, the subjective experience reflects not only the host's taste, but also the host's view of the guest.

Now consider the man's experience at the Japanese restaurant. Service begins before he even enters the restaurant, with the courteous valet service. Then there is the greeting at the front door. Once inside, the ambiance adjusts his senses and expectations. Everything speaks of quality, from the table linens to the staff's dress to the background music. It is also clear from the attentiveness of the staff that the establishment is interested in cultivating a regular customer, not simply in serving him and his guest a meal.

The staff at the Japanese restaurant is friendly, but not familiar. The waitress does a good job at balancing her attention between them and her other responsibilities. She is collaborative, cooperative, friendly, and quick to offer a suggestion after verifying that one is desired. In other words, she is able to identify and develop opportunities for collaboration. She asks about their preferences to create a problem-solving relationship with their best interests in mind. The unspoken barter is their personal information in exchange for choices.

A man's experience with the restaurant service staff sets his expectations for the quality of meal to be served. His focus on the dining experience only peripherally includes his subjective reaction to the food served. If the ambiance and service is top notch, the actual composition of the meal is almost irrelevant. Consider that most consumers never actually meet the chef of their favorite restaurant, and that they never see the meals being prepared. The dining experience tells a customer that the food is good. However, the process of procuring, preparing, and serving the food doesn't typically interest most customers. What matters most is the interface between the food preparation team and the customer. The staff, not the food, makes the customer feel welcome, special, and deserving of the service.

What makes the experience work? There's a sense of familiarity, but it's not too overt. The maître d' remembers where particular customers like to sit. The waiter remembers the customer's preferences, and is better able to recommend something that they would probably enjoy. The restaurant's staff is working under certain assumptions while presenting options and choices. For example, the waitress asks whether her customers would like to hear the specials before any information on the special is given, providing the option of avoiding a potentially distracting description. The information she gathers she uses to make the customer's experience more enjoyable. She doesn't intrude, asking, for example, how their family or business is doing. She doesn't assume a false familiarity or a relationship that is reserved for close friends.

Great service providers know when to stop asking questions. They sense when the quantity of information they're asking for is too much, even if it is otherwise appropriate. In addition, they realize that the questions must be in line with the service they offer to the customer.

To be comfortable with sharing personal information, the customer must be certain that the information is being requested in his best interest, and not simply out of curiosity or for the sole benefit of the business. For example, a doctor may ask a woman about her sex life, private feelings, and intimate habits. If she's like most patients, she'll feel comfortable discussing these and other personal issues because she trusts the doctor and because she feels that it's in her best interest to be open and honest.

Note that in both the restaurant scenarios, the men were treated with respect and courtesy even after they had paid for the meal and tipped the waitress. At the Japanese restaurant, when they left their table for the car, the valet had it ready for them. She anticipated their needs. Similarly, at Maria's, there was a sincere good-bye and an invitation to return. In both cases, there was an underlying assumption that they enjoyed the experience so much that they'll be back for more, and will recommend the restaurant to their friends.

The cases above illustrate that great service is based on bilateral trust and something in common, either a belief or an activity. Great service is also constant and predictable, and familiarity is comforting. Consider what customers have come to expect at Maria's. As in the Japanese restaurant, the waitress anticipates the needs of its customers. For example, if a woman orders a burger, she'll ask if she wants fries with it. If she's not too distracted with other customers, she might remember the customer's name, along with what she likes to drink or eat. She may ask if she wants "the usual," for example.

Great service is immediate. A voice mail system that takes five minutes to circumnavigate isn't great service. Another characteristic of a business that delivers great service is that it doesn't ask customers to reenter information simply because they're using a different touch point. It may, however, ask if their demographic information has changed, and offer them the opportunity to update it. A mail-order company providing great service doesn't ask its customers to repeat its internal tracking number in the yellow box at the back of the catalog. Customers know that it's for the company's tracking information, and not for their benefit. A mail-order business providing great service doesn't break a trust by telling a client what another client ordered. A business that provides great service knows when to break the rules and, from the businesses perspective, can differentiate between a troublemaker who should be dropped and a client truly in need of assistance.

## The Satisfaction—Loyalty Connection

Customer expectations are increasing, partly due to the popularity of the Web. For example, even though tea and fortune cookies are rarely listed on the menu of an Asian restaurant, customers usually expect them at their table, and at no charge. In fact, customers might feel outraged at restaurant management if their meal, no matter how wonderful, wasn't accompanied by a small pot of tea and followed by a five-cent fortune cookie. For a business to develop loyal customers, it isn't enough to simply satisfy them. Satisfying a need is a necessary but by no means sufficient requirement along the path of cultivating a loyal customer.

In any type of business it is important to provide a service at some level. That means selling something that customers can't see or hear; what the business is really offering is an experience. Services, unlike products, are delivered, experienced, and personal. In contrast, products are produced, purchased, and often used in impersonal ways. From the consumer's perspective, buying a service is more risky than buying a product, simply because services don't really exist until they're delivered. A hair cut, for example, is a contract for something unseen that can't be returned once it's delivered. A man may be able to recoup his monetary outlay, but the results of bad service (such as a bad haircut) may be with him long after he's forgotten about the money.

Services are more difficult to sell than products. Even the innovators and early adopters tend to shy away from new services. It isn't generally difficult to locate customers who want the first copy of a widget, but very few customers want to be the first to try a new service. It's safer, for example, to let someone else try the new dry cleaner in the neighborhood before dropping off a favorite cashmere sweater for cleaning, or try one of the personal shopping services, such as HomeRuns or Peapod. Regardless of the hurdles associated with selling a service, businesses want their customers to be so surprised and delighted with it that they volunteer positive references.

In Louisiana, the concept of a little something extra thrown in for free is called lagniappe. On the East Coast, it's called a baker's dozen— the extra bagel thrown in for buying a dozen. The problem is that once a customer has received a baker's dozen, he begins to feel entitled to it. The "gift" is no longer a free token of friendship or good business. It's like the free second-day delivery from some mail-order companies. Once it's instituted, taking the service back or charging for it is often viewed as a punishment, or going back on the company's word. Consider the airlines, which went from not-so-great meals to peanuts or pretzels on many flights. Just when everyone thought the food couldn't get much worse, it did—it disappeared.

How is it possible to surprise and delight customers with service when the better the service is, the better it has to be next time? There are three ways to improve service. From the business perspective, customer satisfaction results from reducing unnecessary or inappropriate variations in service, enhancing the overall level of service, and eliminating unacceptable performance of the customer service staff. However, from customers' perspectives, the primary issue is not merely satisfaction—they want to be delighted.

In experimental psychology, it's understood that if a long-lasting behavior change is the goal, it's much better to reward someone randomly for excellent performance than to reward someone after every performance. If someone is consistently rewarded after every great performance, as soon as the rewards stop, the behavior reverts to the previous state very quickly. If, however, the rewards are randomly distributed, and then removed, people assume that they will come, eventually. They keep working hard for a much longer period of time before their behavior reverts to their previous pattern. Of course, it takes longer for the behavior modification to occur using a random reward system, compared to a constant reward scenario. However, if the goal is to create a long-lasting behavior change, not a one-time action, then it makes sense to focus on the long-term behavior of consumers.

This type of behavior modification assumes multiple, frequent encounters. It also assumes that there's no competition or distractors. For example, if a rat is being trained using randomly distributed rewards (food pellets) for desirable behavior in a maze test, the training won't be effective if there are multiple food pellet dispensers, each running in parallel, dispensing rewards at random. Even a dumb rat will simply wait for one of the food pellet dispensers to dole out a pellet. Why run around a maze for possible rewards from one dispenser when there are so many dispensers offering food?

A business has to deliver satisfaction at some baseline level of service that customers can come to expect. Next, the business can create a random reward system that doesn't elicit an entitlement response from its customers. McDonald's does it by providing frequent contests, where the prizes are free meals and cash. The added value to the business relationship is random and, more important, customers know the prizes are given at random. They don't feel entitled to win a free meal every time they walk under the golden arches. However, customers do expect consistent, quality meals for their money. The occasional free drink or sandwich doesn't excuse McDonald's for any slip-ups in the basic business, nor does it fail to delight customers who win. Most fliers remember the first time they were given a "surprise" free upgrade to first class from coach.

Providing seemingly random rewards for customer attention isn't new. In the retail business it's called a *sale*. One reason for the popularity of malls in the 1990s is that, in addition to their being places to socialize, customers were able to quickly move from store to store, taking advantage of sales. If a woman is in the market for a particular appliance, going to a mall versus a single store increases her odds of finding what she's looking for on sale. Web shoppers share the same mentality; only the mall is virtual and virtually endless. Someone will have what a customer wants, and at a great price. The "Web" becomes the store, and the particular Web site takes on the significance of the cashier at a store in a large shopping center. With this mindset, customers have no loyalty to a particular store or Web site. In other words, if a business tries to compete on price alone, it will never survive on the Web. The business has to offer something else of value.

Whether a business is serving hamburgers through a drive-through window or auctioning cars through the Web, the challenge is to develop a loyal following of customers. Loyal customers, like loyal friends and loyal employees, can't be bought. Management can apply behavior modification theory to get customers to buy from the business until something better comes along. But, for a healthy business in the long term, it's important to consider the business relationship from the customer's perspective. As described below, the customer's perspective in the business relationship can be understood in terms of the Loyalty Effect, which illustrates the importance of providing value and personal attention to the customer.

# The Loyalty Effect

To improve something, assume that it first must be measurable. Therefore, businesses need a tool for measuring customer loyalty. A common measure of consumer loyalty, stickiness, or customer return rate, leaves a lot to be desired. From a bottom-line perspective, if customers return for business, that's success, and they can be considered loyal. However, consumers often patronize a business located on their way home from work simply because it's convenient. Perhaps they buy gas from a service station because a multinational corporation that's damaging the rain forest owns the competing station just across the street. If someone on the Web is looking for a book, she might stay with Amazon.com simply because she doesn't know of any other Web sites that sell books. Maybe a business has prices that are lower than the competition's, and as soon as the competition lowers its price, customers will flock to the competition.

Management can theorize forever and never know for sure what motivates customers to do business with their company; all management can be certain of is customer actions. Loyalty implies the presence of an inner feeling or emotional bond, but all that can be observed and measured is external behavior. Therefore, it's more useful to quantify the behavior commonly associated with loyalty, and the factors that apparently affect this behavior.

The Loyalty Effect describes the quantifiable behavior normally associated with loyalty. Why should management concern itself with the Loyalty Effect? Because quantifying what appears to be loyal behavior may help management to get at what factors contribute to gross stickiness measures. The Web tends to decrease the Loyalty Effect because it decreases the energy required for a customer to move from one supplier to the next. With this knowledge, management should be better prepared to fine-tune a business and to ensure that it is doing everything possible to encourage loyal behavior in their customers.

The Loyalty Effect, from the customer's perspective, can be divided into internal and external factors that act upon his relationship with a business. As illustrated in Figure 3.1, internal factors include the customer's perceived value of a product or service, the amount of time and energy a given customer has invested in doing business with the company, and the emotional bond a consumer has with the business. External factors include the number of affordable alternatives customers have to the product or service, and the difficulty they have in locating alternatives for the products or services. The level of frustration a customer experiences while doing business with the company is an additional internal factor.

When expressed as a mathematical expression, the Loyalty Effect a consumer displays toward a business appears as:

$$\text{Loyalty Effect} = (\text{Value}_{(0-10)} + \text{Investment}_{(0-10)}) \times \text{EB}_{(1-5)} - \\ (\text{Affordable Alternatives}_{(0-10)} \times \text{FL}_{(1-5)}) + \\ \text{Difficulty Locating Alternatives}_{(0-10)}$$

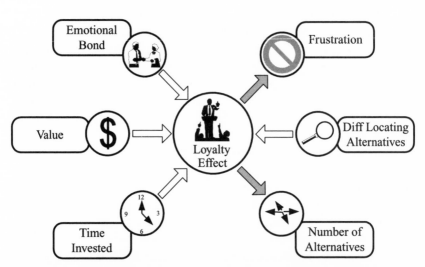

***Figure 3.1*** *Factors affecting the Loyalty Effect include the customer's emotional bond with the business, the customer's time investment in the relationship, the customer's perceived value of the product of service that the business offers, the number of affordable alternatives available, ease of locating these alternatives, and level of frustration with the relationship. Factors with white arrows add to the Loyalty Effect; dark arrows lead to factors that diminish the Loyalty Effect.*

*Loyalty Effect* is a relative value, expressed as a number between 0 and 110, used for comparative analysis. For example, a relationship with a Loyalty Effect of 38 would be better than a relationship with a Loyalty Effect of only 13. Although not intended as an absolute measurement, for calibration purposes, the following ranges can be applied:

0 to 30 – Poor
31 to 60 – Moderate
61 to 90 – Good
91 to 110 – Superior

The absolute ranges can be useful in providing a guide for defining the initial value of the variables in the Loyalty Effect equation. For example, if the analysis of every successful business in a given field has a Loyalty Effect in the Poor range, then it's likely that the value assigned to the variables in the equation may be lower than it should be. Conversely, if even mediocre businesses rank in the Superior range, then the value of the variables may be higher than it should be. The absolute ranges may be helpful when more than one person is involved in the analysis, since the value ascribed to the variables has a subjective component.

In the Loyalty Effect Equation, *Value* is the perceived value that a consumer places on the product and services that a business offers. *Value*, expressed in the equation as an integer between 0 and 10, can be related to price, aesthetics, performance, reputation, brand, peer pressure, trendiness, association of a product or service with a particular group or self-image, and service. At the most basic level, the business must offer something the customer wants or needs. That desire or demand can be daily or seasonal, depending on the business. For example, if a business offers landscaping services in the Northeast, business will be slow in the winter months. If a business supplies RAM to consumer-targeted computer manufacturers, then it will likely see a rise in need as the manufacturers increase computer inventories in preparation for holiday sales. Obviously, marketing and advertising have a large impact on customers' perceived value of a product or service, either by making them want the product or by making them realize that they need it. A man doesn't wear a gold Presidential Rolex because he's interested in keeping accurate time. For that, a plastic Timex Triathlon watch is the superior instrument. People wear Rolexes for prestige.

*Value* can also be a result of brand development, where one brand is valued more highly than another. For example, cars with the brand Mercedes are generally perceived to be of greater intrinsic value than, say, those branded Chevrolet. In the context of the Loyalty Effect, a brand is a "trust mark." Perceived value can also be a function of cost. A more costly service is often perceived as better than a less expensive service, and potentially more valuable. Similarly, a black box manufactured in Japan or Germany is generally valued more by American consumers than one manufactured in the United States.

The perceived value of a relationship with a business can be a function of scarcity, whether the product is art from a dead master or a company is one of the last suppliers on the planet of a particular widget. Scarcity can be real or imagined. For this reason, car dealers typically keep extra stock behind their showrooms and out of sight to give the impression that the cars on display are relatively scarce. The hope is that customers perceive the lone cars as more valuable alone, compared to when they are sitting among a hundred other identical models in the parking lot.

Products with relative scarcity, especially when a time element is involved, appeal to certain types of consumers, especially *early adopters*. Early adopters will go to great lengths to acquire a product before it is widely available to the general public. Although they expend a great deal of energy to be first among their peers with a new widget, early adopters may not return to a company for more of its products unless the company offers more "must-have" technologies. Otherwise, they'll be off chasing new products from other vendors. Consider the uproar among early adopters over the highly publicized Apple Newton personal digital assistant. Even though the Newton flopped in the consumer market, it was hotly sought after by early adopters who were willing to stand in line for hours and pay top dollar when it was first released. Many of those same early adopters were first in line to buy the Palm Pilot when it debuted.

A customer's perception of the value of a company's products and services is highly influenced by referrals. In some markets, word of mouth accounts for the majority of sales. In the health care industry, for example, clinicians are notorious for ignoring traditional advertising, preferring to rely, instead, on the referrals of their fellow clinicians. This behavior is in part due to years of medical equipment manufacturers and software vendors making false promises to get a quick sale, leaving unwary clinicians holding worthless technology.

Customers will often place a higher value on products with which they have a personal, sentimental connection. If a business sells a product that reminds customers of their youth, for example, they may place a much higher value on the product than would customers with different histories. In short, nostalgia and sentimental value sell. Finally, and most important, the value a customer ascribes to a business is a function of the quality of the products and service that the company provides. In other words, of all of the factors described thus far, a customer's direct experience with a company's products and services has the greatest impact on *Value*.

The value one customer perceives for a business may be transferred to a potential customer. For example, in an online dating service, customers who marry due to the company's efforts probably place little value on an ongoing relationship with the business. However, they may strongly recommend the company's services to a friend. This illustrates how the perceived value of a relationship with a business can be greatly influenced by word of mouth. A negative endorsement from a trusted friend or associate is unquestionably one of the best ways to lose a current or potential customer permanently. For example, even a long-time customer may walk away from a relationship with a business if it fails to honor a warranty or sells a defective product to one of her associates.

One assumption about *Value* in the Loyalty Effect Equation is that a consumer's perceived value is non-negative. Even if *Value* is zero, customers may be interested in maintaining a relationship with a business due to their investment in time and energy in the business, as well as any emotional bonds they have formed with the business, and its staff.

In the Loyalty Effect Equation, *Investment* is a customer's total investment, in time and energy, in the B2C relationship, expressed in the equation as an integer between 0 and 10. This investment includes, for example, the customer's taking time to obtain information on the product or service offered, and negotiating with the company's marketing and sales division. Because energy is involved in starting and maintaining any relationship, a five-year relationship with a company has a greater Loyalty Effect than a single, five-second transaction. Over time, friendships develop, as do trust and a bond derived from working out the kinks of a business process together.

*Investment* is also a function of the frequency of B2C encounters. For example, if customers stop by a coffee house every morning on their way to work, the Loyalty Effect is greater than if they stopped by only once a month. Another investment that businesses want their customers to make is *criticism*. Loyal customers have a willingness and desire to give meaningful criticism to improve a business. Of course, businesses need a process in place so that their loyal customers can express their desires for improvement. Lack of an outlet can frustrate customers who would otherwise be a company's best advocates. An additional aspect of *Investment* is lost opportunity costs. By virtue of consumers' doing business with a company, they are forgoing opportunities to establish relationships with the company's competitors.

A key internal factor contributing to the Loyalty Effect is the Emotional Bond, *EB*, between a business and its customers. *EB*, expressed in the equation as an integer between 1 and 5, reflects trust, and, to a lesser extent, accountability, respect, and other emotional issues. The emotional bond has a multiplicative effect on *Value* and *Investment*.

Without an emotional bond (i.e., $EB = 1$), the Loyalty Effect is limited to the contributions of the customer's perceived value and investment in time and energy in a business. To have a Loyalty Effect, the emotional bond must be positive. A negative experience with a company, either directly or through word of mouth, for example, is reflected in the Frustration Level, *FL*, described below. A positive emotional bond between customers and a company could be the result of personal interactions with the customer, through telephone conversations with the company's support staff, through shared activities or sponsored events, and all other touch points. Because the emotional bond has a multiplicative effect, it should be developed and closely monitored.

*Affordable Alternatives*, expressed as an integer between 0 and 10, refers to the number of alternative businesses that offer comparable services or products in the same price range. As illustrated in Figure 3.2, the Loyalty Effect decreases when customers have an increasing number of affordable alternatives. Commodities such as personal computers and cellular phones have a large number of affordable alternatives, and a correspondingly lower Loyalty Effect. For example, when cell phones are one cent plus the cost of a service contract, the difference between Nokia, Motorola, Radio Shack, AT&T, and other brands of cell phones can seem insignificant (i.e., *Affordable Alternatives* approaches 10).

The Frustration Level, *FL*, expressed as an integer between 1 and 5, represents the customers' level of frustration with their relationship with a business. At a certain level of frustration, even a company's most loyal customers will move to the nearest alternative, regardless of their history with the company. For example, if customers are hungry enough, or don't have time to wait an hour to be served, they'll forgo waiting in line at their usual restaurant and walk into the nearest restaurant that can seat them immediately. It doesn't matter if the alternate restaurant is Chinese and the customers had planned on Italian for dinner. At some level of frustration, customers will use anything in a product or service category to satisfy a want or need.

Frustration can come from a variety of other sources, but the most egregious frustration is generated within a business. For example, suppose a woman is running a mail-order clothing store that is offering, for

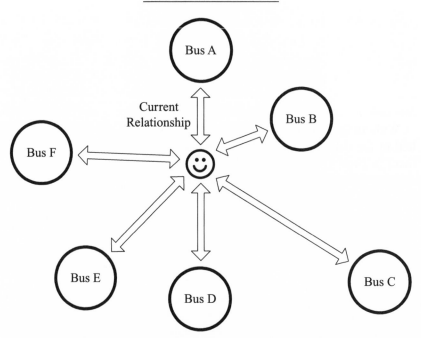

**Figure 3.2**    *The Loyalty Effect is diminished by increased numbers of affordable alternative business relationships. The current relationship between Business A (Bus A) and the consumer (center) is threatened by potential relationships between the consumer and Businesses B through F (Bus B)−(Bus F).*

two weeks only, a discount to customers who place orders over the Web. However, her regular phone-in customers may learn about the discount only after they've called in an order. Since they have already given their names and credit card numbers, it may seem ludicrous for them not to be given the same discount without visiting the Web site. If she makes customers hang up and reenter their information online to receive the discount, they won't likely be very appreciative. They won't think of the savings on the Web as a discount at that point, but will infer that the customer-support person is lazy and inept, and that her company doesn't appreciate their patronage. Like the emotional bond, EB, the frustration level has a multiplicative effect. Therefore, maintaining a low FL is critical to maximizing the Loyalty Effect.

Figure 3.3 illustrates how the factor *Difficulty Locating Alternatives* in the Loyalty Effect Equation relates to practical difficulties customers have locating alternatives to a business. This difficulty may be imposed by geographical and transportation constraints. Perhaps a business is the only one in the United States that can supply particular widgets

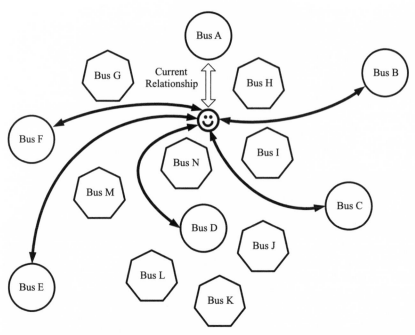

***Figure 3.3*** *Difficulty locating alternative business relationships (circles), due to geographical constraints or superfluous hits on the Web (hexagons), increases the Loyalty Effect.*

overnight, for example. On the Web, alternatives, even if they aren't plentiful, can be mere mouse-clicks away. *Difficulty Locating Alternatives* is expressed in the equation as an integer between 0 and 10, with 10 representing the greatest difficulty. The easier it is for customers to locate alternatives to a business, the lower the Loyalty Effect. For example, a "loyal" customer has stopped by the same bakery every morning for the past two years on his way to work. If a Starbucks Coffee house (Business B in Figure 3.3) opens up two doors up from the bakery, it is likely that the customer may try it. If he does visit the Starbucks, the bakery manager runs the risk of the customer's placing greater value on Starbucks' coffee or service.

Figure 3.4 illustrates how the Web can act as a catalyst for customers moving from one business to the next. The Web increases customer access to affordable alternatives, assuming there are affordable alternatives to be had. For brick-and-mortar products, a customer may have to travel two hours to another town to find a business offering widgets at a better price. In contrast, on the Web, a business (Business B in Figure 3.4) with a better price may be two mouse-clicks and a search away. The

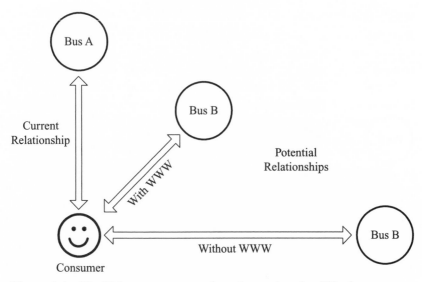

*Figure 3.4*    *The Web serves as a catalyst, decreasing the difficulty associated with locating affordable alternatives (Bus B) to a current business relationship (Bus A).*

Web is a catalyst for business transactions because it decreases the energy required for a customer to move from one supplier to the next. In other words, the Web tends to decrease the Loyalty Effect, even though it encourages new, seemingly random, transactions.

## Applying the Loyalty Effect Equation

The Loyalty Effect Equation, just one way of modeling the complex issue of customer loyalty, highlights the importance of the emotional bond (EB) in cementing the relationship between a business and its customers. In qualitative measures, a business would have to quadruple the value a customer places on its goods and services to have the effect of doubling the emotional bond the customer has with the business. How does management go about enhancing the customer's emotional bond? As described earlier in the restaurant and carriage service, the best of the traditional service industries illustrate how personalized, experiential, customer-centric service enhances the emotional bond, thereby increasing customer loyalty.

Let's look at some examples of applying the Loyalty Effect Equation. Consider the extreme case where the business is a lemonade stand well past the end of the Internet and the customer, a lone Java programmer, is lost, thirsty, and on foot. Furthermore, there isn't another vendor of any type for as far as the eye can see. The customer has been frequenting the lemonade stand for about a week, not long enough for him to get to know the business.

In this scenario, the customer places great value on the product (*Value* = 10). His investment in time and energy is minimal (*Investment* = 0), the emotional bond is non-existent (*EB* = 1), there are no affordable alternatives (*Affordable Alternatives* = 0), there is no frustration working with the business (*FL* = 1), and it's almost impossible to locate alternatives (*Difficulty Locating Alternatives* = 10). The Loyalty Effect is calculated as:

$$\text{Loyalty Effect} = (\text{Value} + \text{Investment}) \times \text{EB} -$$
$$(\text{Affordable Alternatives} \times \text{FL}) + \text{Difficulty Locating Alternatives}$$

$$\text{Loyalty Effect} = (10 + 0) \times 1 - (0 \times 1) + 10 = 10$$

On the absolute scale, the Loyalty Effect is Poor. What we have is a dependency—a customer without any options. The customer has no reasonable alternatives to doing business with the lemonade stand. However, as soon as an alternative appears, the consumer may switch to the alternative, if for no reason other than to break out from the dependency. Dependency isn't loyalty. True dependency, perhaps the Holy Grail of many Application Service Provider (ASP) eBusinesses, occurs when a business supplies mission-critical functionality to its customers.

For example, suppose a company provides small business owners with a Web-based budgeting and tax preparation application, and it maintains all client information in a proprietary format on its servers. If the system fails or the company folds, the customers may have to wait months or years before they can access their data. Even when the business is operating normally, customers can't easily migrate to competing systems, simply because the company archives all their data on site, and in a proprietary format. That is, customers are held captive.

Similarly, several businesses are promoting the use of Web-based patient scheduling and electronic medical record systems for medical practices with fewer than ten clinicians. With these systems, patients can arrange their own visits, and physicians can create medical records that automatically conform to government-standard guidelines for content. Clinicians can be up and running with only a PC and a service contract that costs less than $100 per month—a significant cost savings, compared to a $30–$40K small-practice system. However, what happens to the practice if the remote servers crash, or the data are lost due to a natural or manmade disaster? Insurance money is nice, but it won't recreate patient records if they're lost.

Revisiting the utility of the Loyalty Effect Equation, suppose a man oversees a parking garage business. Since it's expensive, the garage is rarely filled to capacity. Now, imagine that on a Saturday night one of his regular weekday customers has been driving around for twenty minutes in a frustrating search for on-street parking. There's added pressure on the customer, in that the concert she's scheduled to attend starts in ten minutes. The customer no doubt places a high value on a parking spot, in part because of actual scarcity. There's no substantial investment in time or energy in the parking garage business, and no emotional bond. Alternatives are non-existent, and there isn't any frustration with the business.

In this case, the customer places great value on service (*Value* = 10). The investment in time and energy in a relationship with the business is slight, due to the existing workday contact with the business (*Investment* = 1). Similarly, there is probably a small emotional bond between the customer and the staff because the customer uses the garage on weekdays (*EB* = 1). There are no affordable alternatives (*Affordable Alternatives* = 0), and, as yet, the customer hasn't had any frustration working with the business (*FL* = 1). It appears that the garage is the only one available, and it's almost impossible for the customer to locate alternatives (*Difficulty Locating Alternatives* = 10).

From this data, the Loyalty Effect is calculated as:

$$\text{Loyalty Effect} = (\text{Value} + \text{Investment}) \times \text{EB} - (\text{Affordable Alternatives} \times \text{FL}) + \text{Difficulty Locating Alternatives}$$

$$\text{Loyalty Effect} = (10 + 1) \times 1 - (0 \times 1) + 10 = 20$$

Assuming that the garage is the only unfilled parking lot in the area, the customer will undoubtedly use the service. This situation isn't quite a dependency, but the customer really doesn't have an opportunity to exercise his choice. In absolute terms, the Loyalty Effect is Poor, but much improved over the lemonade-stand business.

In further exploration of the utility of the Loyalty Effect Equation, let's add two other parking garages to the mix, located just across the street, both offering competitive parking rates. Let's also say that not only does the customer have a weekday contract with the business, but over the years she has come to know the parking attendant on a personal level. Perhaps the attendant helped her fix a flat one day, or loaned her a set of jumper cables when her car wouldn't start.

The perceived value of a space in the parking garage is less than it was in the previous scenario because there are now two alternatives. The customer has invested a modicum of time and energy in dealing with the company, and there may be a significant emotional bond with the company, especially if the customer hopes to meet her friend, the parking attendant. There are nearby, affordable alternatives, and the frustration factor is irrelevant.

In this scenario, the customer places a high, but not great value on service (*Value* = 7), the investment in time and energy in a relationship with the business is slight (*Investment* = 1), there is a significant emotional bond with the business because of a personal relationship with the parking attendant (*EB* = 4), there are at least two affordable alternatives (*Affordable Alternatives* = 10), there is no frustration working with the business (*FL* = 1), and it's easy to locate alternatives (*Difficulty Locating Alternatives* = 0).

The Loyalty Effect is calculated as:

$$\text{Loyalty Effect} = (\text{Value} + \text{Investment}) \times \text{EB} - (\text{Affordable Alternatives} \times \text{FL}) + \text{Difficulty Locating Alternatives}$$

$$\text{Loyalty Effect} = (7 + 1) \times 4 - (10 \times 1) + 0 = 18$$

Because of the competing businesses across the street, there is a lower Loyalty Effect than in the previous example. However, because of the emotional bond that developed between the parking attendant and the customer, the customer will likely park in the garage.

Now, consider the parking garage business one month later. In the intervening time, the parking attendant has been fired because he was late for work one time too often. He now works at one of the nearby competing parking garages. The former attendant feels as though he was fired unfairly, and it happens that the customer sides with the attendant. Even so, the customer still has a weekly contract with the garage because it is through her employer. It's the weekend again, and the customer is in search of a parking space. In this scenario, even though the customer's perceived value of a parking spot in the garage is high, the emotional bond with the company is gone. If anything, the customer is frustrated with the business because she believes the attendant was fired unjustly.

In this scenario, the customer places a high value on service (*Value* = 7), the investment in time and energy in a relationship with the business is slight (*Investment* = 1), she has no emotional bond with the business (*EB* = 1), there are at least two affordable alternatives (*Affordable*

*Alternatives* = 10), there is a great deal of frustration working with the business (*FL* = 5), and it's easy to locate alternatives (*Difficulty Locating Alternatives* = 0). The Loyalty Effect is calculated as:

Loyalty Effect = (Value + Investment) × EB −
(Affordable Alternatives × FL) + Difficulty Locating Alternatives

Loyalty Effect = (7 + 1) × 1 − (10 × 5) + 0 = 0

There is no Loyalty Effect. Given this scenario, the customer will likely park in the garage that hired the parking attendant, her friend and the company's ex-employee. From the competing garage's perspective, the Loyalty Effect is positive because of the emotional bond the customer has with its attendant. The same activity can be observed when salespeople or hairdressers move from one company to the next; their loyal customers tend to follow them.

As a final example, consider a client's relationship with one of the most popular corporate gift businesses in the United States, Harry & David (www.HarryAndDavid.com), a mail-order catalog and now Web-based company that sells fruit baskets and other food items for all occasions. Suppose one of their customers, someone who has been doing business with them for over five years, decides to surf the Web in search of alternative sources of gift baskets. Let's also suppose that the customer has developed a good working relationship with Harry & David. She appreciates, for example, the pre-filled–in order form every Christmas with the names, addresses, and suggested items for everyone she gave Harry & David gifts to the previous year. The customer has invested a substantial amount of time, familiarizing herself with Harry & David's offerings, and has never had any bad dealings with this company. In fact, she appreciates the no-questions-asked return policy for all its products. In surfing the Web, the customer locates hundreds of companies offering fruit baskets, many substantially cheaper than those at the Harry & David Web site, and advertising the same guarantee.

Using the Loyalty Effect Equation as a means of predicting the customer's behavior, we see that the customer places a moderately high value on Harry & David's service (*Value* = 8), the investment in time and energy in the five-year relationship is moderate (*Investment* = 7), there is some emotional bond with the business (*EB* = 3), there are hundreds of affordable alternatives only a click away (*Affordable Alternatives* = 10), there is no frustration regarding working with this business (*FL* = 1), and it's easy to locate alternatives (*Difficulty Locating Alternatives* = 0). The Loyalty Effect is calculated as:

Loyalty Effect = (Value + Investment) $\times$ EB $-$
(Affordable Alternatives $\times$ FL) + Difficulty Locating Alternatives

Loyalty Effect = $(8 + 7) \times 3 - 10 \times 1 + 0 = 35$

When using the Loyalty Effect Equation, remember that it has predictive value only as a relative measure. It should be used only to compare similar types of businesses. The loyalty effect for Harry & David can't meaningfully be compared with that calculated for a parking garage. The equation is designed to compare Loyalty Effects in relative terms. In absolute terms, as a calibration point only, the Loyalty Effect is considered Moderate in this case. As an exercise, locate a competitor to Harry & David and run the Loyalty Effect Equation.

The above series of examples illustrates the importance of the emotive component of a relationship in developing and maintaining customers. A business can produce the best products and services, and yet the emotional factors, both positive and negative, have an overriding effect on customer behavior. As most salespeople realize, customers make a buy decision on what they want based on emotion. Customers use logic when buying what they need for survival—and most of what customers buy isn't related to survival needs.

It's important to remember the Loyalty Effect Equation is a model—a simplified view of reality. It should provide enough predictive value to be useful in a business. However, it's also important to remember that human behavior is very difficult to predict, especially when the prediction is based on only a few variables. For example, if a competing bagel shop opens across the street from a bagel shop, and a customer of ten years suddenly, and without a word, takes his business to the competition, what did the first business do wrong? It may have developed a great emotional bond, provided the highest-quality products and services, and yet the customer turned out to be disloyal to the business. Management at the first bagel shop may never know what the reasons were, and they might not have been able to change the customer's behavior even if they did. For example, perhaps the customer simply wants to try something new. Maybe he changed jobs and now wants to avoid running into his ex-boss. Perhaps a friend of his owns the competing bagel shop. The point is to let those situations go, and focus on what can be controlled.

# Privacy

The most sensitive aspect of customer relations is privacy. Americans are privacy conscious, and most of us feel invaded if someone records our buying habits without our permission. All of us have boundaries, and don't trust people who become too familiar too soon.

From the business perspective, ubiquitous data and information that flow seamlessly from one touch point to another represents nirvana, regardless of the business model. The goal of every service-conscious business is to understand not only all customers, but their circumstances as well—and this requires information. In addition to the obvious business opportunities, there are numerous consumer benefits to the ready access to personal information, no matter where the location. For example, any authorized clinician in any emergency room could pull up a patient's medical records. The information in the record could save the patient's life if, for example, it contained information on drug interaction problems that the patient experienced in the past. If a woman loses her credit card, driver's license, and other identification, she'd still be able to make do on a vacation. Think of the implications of having all of a patient's personal data available at someone's fingertips in a usable form. Many in the government, private sector, and business have thought long and hard about the implications of ubiquitous data access. Full-scale, transparent integration of everyone's personal data is years away in the sprawling United States. However, looking at our neighbors in Europe suggests what we can reasonably expect, assuming that we can come to a consensus as to how personal information should be handled in this country.

One possible future of information privacy is represented by Finland, a country of five million. In terms of the integration of communication and data technology, the relatively homogeneous citizenry is far ahead of every other country. Over sixty percent of the population owns a mobile phone, and most use it as their only phone. A Finn's identity is closely attached to his phone, in part because he uses it like a virtual smart card. For example, if someone wants to purchase a soft drink from a vending machine, he simply dials the number listed on the machine and a soft drink appears. The charge appears on the customer's phone bill. It's the same for banking and trading some stock. All that's needed is a cell phone.

However, consider what happens when a Finn is stopped for a speeding violation. A police officer simply keys in the speeder's phone number through a link to the tax bureau, and the officer knows the alleged speeder's annual income within seconds. A person's annual income is important, because, by law, the fine imposed on speeding is a function of income. The more someone makes, the more she pays for a given speeding violation. The idea is that the "sting" should be equivalent but not equal, and a function of income. Before everyone's tax information was available through the phone system, those caught for speeding would sometimes lie about their income. Now, there's no hiding it.

The census 2000 in the United States has provoked protests, especially from groups that are furious about the need to disclose their income, race, and other personal information. In this political milieu, it isn't likely that voters will submit to having everything about them made available online to "authorized" individuals, whether the sentiment is due to mistrust of government, or big business, or doubts of security on the Web.

Most online customers recognize that they have to pay a price for convenience and service. The issue, in online privacy matters, is control, in the form of freedom to choose. It's one thing to ask a customer for her preference in reading materials, for example, and quite another for an eBusiness to take it without asking. For example, when a woman hands over her discount card at her local grocer, she understands that someone is tracking her purchases. In exchange, she is given the privilege of enjoying the "special" discounts. She can register a false name, and her privacy will be maintained to a degree. The first time she's short on cash and uses her charge card, however, her name and address and Visa card will be linked, and her true identity will be known to the system. Most people don't worry about it, or at least don't care much about who knows that they pick Charmin bathroom tissue over a competing brand.

Whenever a man use his cell phone in the United States, his location is instantly knowable—to someone. The FCC approved rules that require cell phones to be trackable by law enforcement. There is also a record of every phone call he's ever made from his home or office, and his charge card companies have information on where he spends his money, vacation time, and life. To the dismay of many privacy advocates, the government often works in concert with businesses, freely exchanging private information in exchange for money.

Paradoxically, the Internet initially gave the illusion of privacy and of anonymity. People could voice their opinions on any subject, view pornography, and read about any topic they wanted, without disclosing their identity. However, it was a very short, temporary illusion. In the workplace, emails are often monitored, as well as employee activity on the Web. Medical records are also sometimes used in unfair (and illegal) hiring decisions. As more medical records are posted online, the potential for abuse increases. Not only will it be easier for clinicians to follow patients from one clinic to another, but it will also be possible for an intruder to learn everything there is to know about the personal health of a potential employee or insured family member.

There is currently a hot debate over the rights of companies to create dossiers on consumers without their knowledge and then sell the information to third parties. While companies like DoubleClick (www.DoubleClick.com) received a lot of media attention for the intentional use of consumer data, other companies, such as America Online, which have much more consumer information at their fingertips, have maintained a low profile. America Online, for example, maintains information on 21 million subscribers, including demographics, credit card numbers, and where they spend their time within its service. Although America Online is not currently in the business of selling consumer data, it sells names and addresses to bulk mailers, and buys information about subscribers for targeted advertising. Some service providers intentionally track subscriber movements, with subscribers' knowledge, and sell the information to third parties. In return for the extensive personal profiles that result, subscribers are given free Internet access.

Because federal law on online privacy is currently limited, it's uncertain what right consumers have to privacy over the Internet. The legal system simply hasn't kept up with the exponential growth of issues surrounding the Internet. For example, it may be that content acquired through cable modem connections to the Internet is treated differently from that acquired from dial-up modem and DSL connections, since there are federal laws concerning privacy and cable companies. California has state laws that protect consumers against privacy abuses. Regardless of the law, it's clear that there's a social contract between information requesters and consumers. One way to turn away a potential eConsumer forever is to violate his sense of trust by selling or otherwise disseminating information gained from him, either directly or indirectly. Friends don't dig into each other's file cabinets without permission.

Tracking consumer-purchasing patterns isn't always used with the consumer's best interest in mind. For example, personal tracking data are often used in yield management, a technique designed to maximize revenue and profitability. The idea is that some customers are more profitable than others, especially those placing orders with short lead times. Since suppliers can charge higher prices for orders with short lead times, they reserve capacity for such orders and turn down less-profitable, long-range orders. As customers are ranked in terms of profitability and system compatibility, not long-term profitability, less-profitable customers are taken off the list and their orders are declined.

For example, a company may not be able to purchase hotel rooms in bulk for conferences unless its conferences are a certain minimum size. This mechanism is great for businesses, but may not be appreciated by customers, especially those who are bumped from the supply chain.

When the above discussion is distilled to its essence, it's clear that customer relations are based on a timeless, technology-independent triad—service, trust, and loyalty. Customers have to trust that a business is working with their best interests in mind. Without trust, the major contributor to the emotional bond between a business and its customers, there can be no relationship. Furthermore, even the best intentions are worthless without action. A business must repeatedly provide a valuable, consistent service to prove to its customers that the company stands behind its marketing rhetoric. As illustrated by the Loyalty Equation, if a business provides its customers with a valuable service and develops a trusting relationship, the business has done all it can to galvanize a loyal customer following.

In the next section, I'll explore the technologies that make information gathering and analysis possible. I'll also review how technology can help answer customer demand for immediate service and instant gratification, while enhancing loyalty by offering highly personalized service.

## Executive Summary

Business is fundamentally about customer relations and due to the Web, customer expectations are increasing. As a catalyst for communications, the Web provides customers with unprecedented power to compare prices instantly and squeeze profit margins from even the largest suppliers. However, customer information gleaned from on-Web activities can be used to offer highly personalized products and services.

The best of the traditional service industries provides excellent examples of personalized, experiential, customer-centric service. Customers expect the service provider to be reliable, helpful, trustworthy, knowledgeable, credible, empathetic, competent, friendly but not familiar, unobtrusive, and clear in communications. It's clear that a prerequisite for excellent service is knowing how and when to enter into a joint problem-solving exercise with customers.

One of the greatest challenges in business is to develop a loyal following of customers that, like loyal friends, can't be bought. The customer's perspective in the business relationship can be understood in terms of the Loyalty Effect Equation, which depends on: the customer's perceived value of a product or service; the amount of time and energy invested in doing business with a company; the emotional bond a consumer has with the business; the number of affordable alternatives to the business products and services; the difficulty in locating alternatives products and services; and the level of frustration with the business. The Loyalty Effect Equation suggests that the business must provide both value and the personal touch to develop loyal customers.

Part **2**

# Technological Underpinnings

## The Human-Computer Interface

*When the eyes say one thing,
and the tongue another,
A practiced man relies on the
language of the first.*
Ralph Waldo Emerson

At this dawn of the new millennium, many brick-and-mortar businesses may be dipping their toes into the alluring pond of Web technology and either deciding to add a Web touch point or delay committing until clear winners in the battle for standards and market share appear. In contrast, for many customers, the Web is enough to fill their lives with pleasure, education, entertainment, and, for many investors, handsome profits. They view the Web and the seemingly endless parade of faster, more-compact computers and higher-speed networks as tools that allow them to function with increased effectiveness.

With our increasing dependence on information technology, the economy is continuing to evolve into a system based on the transfer of every variety and form of information. For example, the traditional process of purchasing, playing, and storing prerecorded music on CDs is being threatened by Web sites that allow music fans to download music from the Internet and store it on their hard drives, memory stick, or other media. It's clear that in the future virtual reality will have a central role. Within the first two decades of this millennium, acquiring a stylish new wardrobe, a slimmer waist, a different partner every night, or the latest in home furnishings will entail no more than running a program that will alter everyone's perception of people, places, and objects in the real world. While everyone may not look with favor on a future, information-dependent world in which perception is everything, the issue today is how best to cloak not the planet, but the computer systems that will one day make a synthetic world a reality.

This chapter examines the human–computer interface, the veneer that hides the intricacies of the microprocessor and its operations of zeros and ones, and presents customers with images, sounds, and graphics with which they can interact on a human level. Why is the human–computer interface, usually referred to as the *user interface*, relevant to eBusiness? Because one of the main purposes of the user interface is to focus the computer user's attention on what's being presented. In other words, it should reduce the cognitive distance between customers and the images on a Web site or the sounds emanating from their speakers. If customers are shopping on a Web site for a widget, they should be thinking about the widget, and not how to get to the checkout page.

Interface designers know that focused attention results in expectations of success, confidence, and goal achievement, and an overall positive experience that many users return for. Conversely, poorly focused attention results in boredom, slow progress, fatigue, and confusion, which users rarely want to re-experience. Think of the interface as part of the supply chain of information flowing from the computer to the user. That is, data coming from the information source are transmitted through a medium, and are received by customers. The interface is the medium through which the data flow.

# JoesUsedAutoParts.Com

Revisiting Joe's Used Auto Parts from Chapter 2, suppose that Joe's daughter set up a Web site for the business. The first version of the Web site was a simple listing of parts and prices, with a "have a nice day" slogan at the bottom of the page following Joe's telephone number, address, and other contact information. Joe was content with the Web site, but his daughter realized that she wasn't taking advantage of the full potential of the medium. Within a month of the initial Web site unveiling, she created a sophisticated back-end, complete with a database to store customers' activity on the site, previous orders, and preferences. With this information, she was able to develop a new user interface. She was confident that a personalized, well-planned, informative, and easy-to-use interface would boost Joe's image and help develop a loyal customer following.

Consider what a returning customer might see when he logs on to Joe's new Web site. Assume for this example that this customer's previous order was for parts to a 1974 VW Beetle, and his age is known from an online form he filled out when he placed the order. When the customer returns to the site, there's a message greeting him by name, a listing of all specials that pertain to VW Beetles, and an image of a vintage VW beetle in the background. An online bulletin board panel lists want ads, public safety notices, and any other timely information that pertains to 1974 VW Beetles.

In addition to an image of a VW Beetle in the background, other graphics complement the layout, but not to the degree that they would be confusing to the customer if he didn't actually own a VW. For example, the VW parts he ordered may have been for a friend. If the customer is in his fifties, the graphic treatments might include nostalgic images, such as images of a flower power banner, a peace symbol, and a pair of torn jeans. If the customer is in his twenties, then images of a Porsche-designed radio and a view of fresh flowers in the front dash holder of a new Beetle could be used. If the customer is a 34-year-old woman who ordered parts for her 1999 Porsche 944, her presumed tastes would be reflected in the background image and supplemental graphics.

The motivation for moving from the old interface, a generic table of parts and prices, to the new, personalized interface with customer-specific images and information, is to increase the chance that customers will return for more business. Creating a personalized interface involves more than simply selecting graphics for the home page. Not only is an initial investment required to create an infrastructure capable of tracking, capturing, and utilizing customer data, but there's the continuing overhead of maintenance and the inevitable modifications inherent in any complex system. Regardless of the complexity and technical marvel of the database and related back-end processing, the customer sees and interacts with the user interface. Ultimately, this interaction with the user interface defines a customer's opinion of a Web site, and, by extension, the business as a whole. As described below, defining and creating a great user interface for a Web site—or any computer application, for that matter—involves much more than deciding between images of flowers and a peace symbol.

# The User Interface

When a typical computer user talks about a user interface, she's usually referring to the quality, quantity, and arrangement of the graphics, buttons, and menus on her computer screen. For example, most computer users probably recognize the Macintosh OS and Microsoft Windows 95/98/NT user interfaces. However, programs running under these operating systems, such as Internet Explorer and Netscape Navigator, also contribute to the user interface. The diminutive and highly efficient Palm Pilot, with its stylus pointing device, displays yet another user interface. While these interfaces share the trait of communicating with the user, they vary significantly in form and function. The user interface is much more than what someone sees on a computer screen.

Even the simplest user interface is a complex, multi-tiered structure that supports a dialogue or communications channel between the user and the computer and between the user and the concepts presented by the software executing on the computer. As illustrated in Figures 4.1 and 4.2, the user interface can be segmented into hierarchical, interdependent levels. The model in Figure 4.1, which portrays the elements of a user interface, illustrates that the user interface minimally consists of a physical interface between the user and the computer. The user interface may also include Graphical, Logical, Emotional, Intelligent, or even Emotionally Intelligent Interface components.

This hierarchical model is especially relevant when discussing multimedia interfaces, which use graphics, video, sound, and tactile feedback. It also reflects our heavy reliance on visual information for communications—hence, the separate level for the Graphical Interface. Except for the recent rise in popularity of voice recognition as a user interface, most of the interface work with computers has been graphical in nature, at least from the computer-to-user leg of the communication channel. The hierarchical interface model also emphasizes the visual, tactical, and, to some degree, the auditory aspects of human–computer interfaces. Taste and smell, while used in some experimental user interfaces, aren't included in this model. Multimedia interfaces are a subset of *multimodal interfaces*. The latter involve visual, auditory, tactile, olfactory, and taste information. Multimedia interfaces typically focus on visual and auditory information, sometimes augmented with simple tactile information as well.

The user interface of a Web site can be compared to a human customer service representative. For example, Physical Levels I and II in Figure 4.1 correspond to the basic physical structure of the representa-

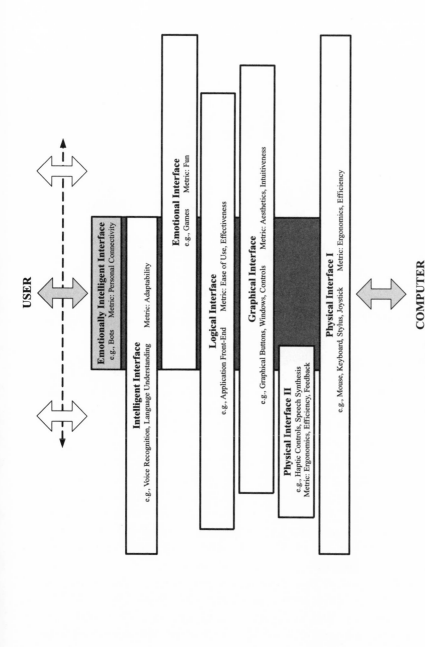

**USER**

**Emotionally Intelligent Interface**  e.g., Bots   Metric: Personal Connectivity

**Intelligent Interface**  
e.g., Voice Recognition, Language Understanding      Metric: Adaptability

**Emotional Interface**   Metric: Fun  
e.g., Games

**Logical Interface**  
e.g., Application Front-End   Metric: Ease of Use, Effectiveness

**Graphical Interface**   Metric: Aesthetics, Intuitiveness  
e.g., Graphical Buttons, Windows, Controls

**Physical Interface II**  
e.g., Haptic Controls, Speech Synthesis  
Metric: Ergonomics, Efficiency, Feedback

**Physical Interface I**   Metric: Ergonomics, Efficiency  
e.g., Mouse, Keyboard, Stylus, Joystick

**COMPUTER**

*Figure 4.1   Human–Computer Interface Hierarchy. Emotionally Intelligent Interfaces, which represent the highest evolutionary stage of interface development, are dependent upon the proper implementation of lower interface forms for functionality.*

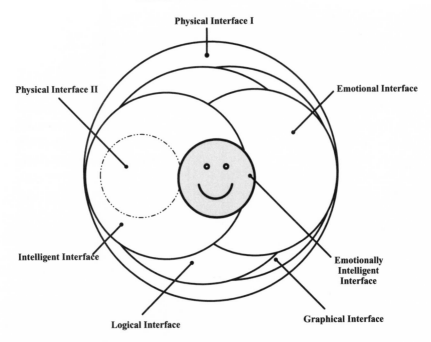

**Figure 4.2**    *Human–Computer Interface Hierarchy, top view. This view, together with Figure 4.1, highlights the various possible interface combinations and dependencies.*

tive, in terms of height, weight, sex, age, build, posture, eye color, and hair color. The Graphical Interface corresponds to the representative's suit, in terms of color, fit, material, and tailoring; accessories such as shoes; and hair cut. The goal of a customer service representative—and the user interface—at this level is to match the client in taste. The Logical Interface is equivalent to the representative's education and training. The Emotional Interface corresponds to the representative's disposition, either positive or negative. The Intelligent Interface level is equivalent to a representative who has street and book smarts, and can adapt on the fly to customers' needs. At the highest level, that of Emotionally Intelligent Interfaces, the ideal customer service representative fully engages the customer, and develops a strong working relationship based on caring, personality, and integrity.

Figure 4.2 illustrates the classifications of user interfaces as partially overlapping coins stacked on each other, with the Physical Interface at the bottom, and the Emotionally Intelligent Interface at the top. A Graphical Interface—one that relies on windows, buttons, and controls for the primary mode of communications—is dependent upon Physical

Interface I and possibly Physical Interface II. Similarly, a Logical Interface may depend on a Graphical Interface but definitely depends on one or both types of Physical Interfaces.

The traveling arrow on the top of Figure 4.1 signifies this variability in dependency. For example, moving the arrow to the far left at the level of Intelligent Interfaces shows a dependency on only Physical Interface I. That is, it is possible to create an Intelligent Interface without a Graphical Interface, for example. Conversely, centering the arrow squarely above the center of the stack reveals that Intelligent Interfaces can be dependent on Emotional Interfaces, Logical Interfaces, Graphical Interfaces, and Physical Interfaces. These and other user interface types and their interdependencies are described in more detail below.

## Physical Interface I

The first physical interface layer, Physical Interface I, communicates a user's physical actions *to* the computer. This is the base transducer level, responsible for translating mechanical movements—a key press or mouse-click, for example—into electronic signals that are interpreted by the underlying computer hardware. Depending on the computer system, this could entail the use of a keyboard, mouse, trackball, stylus, microphone, joystick, touch screen, digitizer pad, video or still camera, data glove, or a data suit. There are also dozens of specialized devices, such as those that track eye movements, fluctuations in skin resistance, heart rate, neural activity within muscles, and infrared movement, but these devices have yet to be widely adopted by the computing public. Some devices, such as retinal imagers and fingerprint recognition devices, are employed in high-security biometric systems. Other devices, such as data rings that track contact with other people and objects, and data suits that monitor the user's physiological status, are still under development.

Unless users are employing a data glove or data suit to manipulate synthetic 3-D objects in virtual reality simulations, they're probably using Physical Interface I level technology that hasn't changed much since the inception of the microcomputer. For example, the mouse, first developed by Douglas Engelbart in 1963, is basically identical to the design popularized by the Apple Macintosh in the mid 1980s. Similarly, a computer keyboard is probably modeled after the inefficient, finger-twisting QWERTY design developed to limit the speed at which typists could press the keys on early mechanical typewriters.

The metrics normally applied to Physical Interface I relate to the efficiency and effectiveness of this organic–mechanical–electronic interface, and include factors such as ergonomics, tactile feedback, efficiency, "feel," accuracy, precision, noise, and stability. If a businessman uses a laptop or PDA, form factor, keyboard layout, and weight may be critical metrics. For example, a featherweight sub-notebook may have excellent technical specifications, but if the keyboard is tiny and he has big hands, he'll never be able to use the keyboard efficiently. As the foundation of the user interface hierarchy, Physical Interface I is a crucial element in the overall interface because it establishes the limit of quality and fidelity of all communications between the user and the computer. For example, a cramped or sticky keyboard or an erratic mouse will limit and negatively color the user's experience of whatever Web site he's viewing.

Users have some degree of control over this level of the interface. In order to address deficiencies in the basic system, users can buy either add-ons or new computer systems that suit their needs. For example, a woman can buy ergonomic keyboards and mice to alleviate any pain she may have associated with extended keyboard use. She can buy a full-size keyboard extension to make more efficient use of her laptop when she uses it at her desk. If the woman works with graphics, she can purchase a high-precision mouse or trackball. Similarly, digitizer pads are available with different levels of resolution. If she's a wizard at the keyboard, the woman might want to buy an intentionally noisier model so that she can hear the positive feedback of key-clicks while she is typing. If she's a lefty, she can buy a left-handed mouse to replace the default right-handed version that ships with many desktop systems.

## Physical Interface II

The second layer, Physical Interface II, includes specialized hardware components that build upon elements of Physical Interface I. The common element in Physical Interface II is feedback from the computer to the user. Monitors; Liquid Crystal Display (LCD) panels; force feedback controls; audio, including music and synthetic speech; and complex mechanisms such as robots all fit within this layer of the user interface. As in Physical Interface I, the metrics applied to this level include ergonomics and efficiency, but also include a component that reflects the quality and nature of the feedback.

***Displays.***    Monitors and LCD panels, analogous to the speakers in a good stereo system, limit the quality of graphics and text that can be displayed. The most recent marketing activity in screen technology is centered on flat-screen monitors because they have an ergonomic advantage over traditional Cathode Ray Tube (CRT)-based monitors. Not only is glare less of a problem with a flat screen, but the refresh rate is high enough to eliminate flicker, an annoying problem with CRT-based systems that are still standard equipment on most desktop computers. LCD panels, available as an expensive add-on to desktop computer systems, are standard equipment on laptops because of size, weight, and power limitations. Traditional monitors and LCD panels are evaluated in terms of refresh rate, resolution, color depth, aspect ratio, brightness, and contrast.

Although wearable monitors, such as heads-up LCD displays and laser displays, are several years away from general consumption, they will eventually replace desktop monitors. The most exciting displays use a low-powered laser to paint an image directly on the wearer's retina. The result is a virtual, wide-screen display that appears to float in space directly in front of the wearer. In addition to computing uses, such as surfing the Web, there are obvious entertainment applications as well.

***Sound.***   Sound is an important component of the user interface because it can provide a medium-bandwidth communications link between the user and the computer. Imagine someone's disappointment at logging onto America Online and not hearing the "Welcome! You've got mail" message. The relative emphasis on sound as an interface component is evident from the changes in computer hardware during the last ten years. Only two or three years ago, a cheap set of plastic speakers was standard equipment on desktop computer systems. Today, even inexpensive consumer units ship with powered speaker systems, often with subwoofers, capable of reproducing game sound effects and music downloaded from the Internet with remarkable fidelity. A quality sound system adds to the overall impression of the applications that are running.

***Speech synthesis.***   Related to sound is speech synthesis, which generates understandable speech, usually from a text document. This Text-to-Speech (TTS) capability runs on standard computer hardware, such as a standard Creative Solutions SoundBlaster card and a set of speakers. TTS programs are commodity items. Top contenders in the speech synthesis market include Elan TTS speech engine (www.elantts.com/speech/shared/ess2nav.htm), L&H RealSpeak (www.lhsl.com/realspeak), Lucent Text-to-Speech Engine (www.lucent.com/sspeech/productss.html/), and Willow Pond WillowTALK (www.willowpond.com/nav/products/ willowtalk/). The challenge not yet fully addressed by these or any other commercial speech synthesis products is that of creating speech that doesn't sound computer-generated. It's much easier to generate quality graphics than it is to synthesize realistic sounding speech that has the appropriate rhythms and inflections. Anyone interested in using synthesized speech to enhance computer-enabled communication with their customers, through customer support, for example, will want the speech to sound pleasant, welcoming, and confident. The challenge isn't creating intelligible text, but expressive speech.

The problem with mechanical-sounding synthetic speech is that its use often diminishes the perceived quality of the underlying application or Web site. (See Figure 4.3.) For example, AnaNova (www.AnaNova.com), billed as the world's first virtual newscaster, uses synthesized speech

**Figure 4.3**    *AnaNova. The world's first virtual newscaster conveys a limited range of human emotions through her facial expressions. Courtesy of AnaNova Ltd, UK.*

from Lernout and Hauspie technology. Although the graphics are phenomenal, and the cyber-anchor portrays a limited range of human emotions through her facial expressions, the synthetic speech takes away from the illusion of reality. For example, on her debut on April 19, 2000, AnaNova reported a story involving a bomb at a restaurant. However, because of the imperfections in the speech synthesis system, the report sounded as though it was about an "A-bomb"—an atomic bomb, because of the stress on the "A" and the abnormally short pause between "A" and "bomb."

Stated another way, the increased accuracy of the video increases expectations in speech synthesis capabilities. The effect is like talking to a child who appears to be five or six years old because of his physical stature, and then discovering, through verbal communications, that he is only three or four. An adult talking to a child not only has to recalibrate the level of speech complexity to make certain that the child understands them, but the adult's expectations of the child are diminished as well. Despite AnaNova's speech imperfections, her debut was impressive, and portends a future where she will be indistinguishable from a live newscaster.

***Haptics.***    One of the more intriguing physical interface possibilities is haptic controllers: specially constructed electromechanical mice, joysticks, steering wheels, and flight yokes that can provide the computer user with computer-mediated tactile sensations. Haptic devices translate digital information into physical sensations. The electro-mechanical devices in haptic controllers translate digital information into physical movement or resistance, allowing users to experience the elasticity of springs, the viscosity of liquids, the texture of surfaces, and vibrations. For example, when someone works with a haptic mouse, what the hands feel corresponds in some programmatic way to what is being displayed on the computer screen.

Haptic controls, also known as force-feedback devices, are popular in the game community. Haptic joysticks and game controllers pull, jerk, or vibrate, depending on what's happening in the game environment. A force-feedback joystick jerks in response to the simulated recoil of a gun, the tug of a fish on a simulated rod and reel, or the pull of a racecar as it makes a turn. Some dedicated game hardware, such as Sony's PlayStation II, comes with haptic game controllers as standard equipment. For example, Microsoft markets a force-feedback joystick and Logitech offers a force-feedback mouse.

Most vendors of haptic devices rely on technology licensed from Immersion, Inc. (www.Immersion.com), which offers a free Windows application, Immersion Desktop. When a game enthusiast uses this desktop with a compatible force-feedback device, such as a force-feedback mouse, she can feel the desktop and Web pages when she navigates. That is, she can feel the cursor slip into the groove of a slider bar or menu bar, experience a window stretch like a rubber band when she resizes it, and sense the weight of a folder's contents when she tries to drag it across the desktop. The main limitation of haptic interfaces is that the hardware has yet to become standard equipment on desktop computer systems.

The multi-billion-dollar game industry aside, haptic controllers have serious uses as well. They give impressions of texture—such as skin and various types of cloth. Online clothing stores will someday offer haptic-compatible interfaces to their cloth samples. A woman will be able to "feel" the coarseness of denim, and smoothness of silk products from the comfort of her home or office. Force-feedback devices also have a future in medicine. Haptic interfaces can be used to simulate surgical techniques, where tissues, displayed on a computer screen, are "cut" with a virtual knife that pulls and responds the way a real scalpel would in the same situation. In the field of telemedicine, physicians can remotely examine patients in a separate location using robotics at the patient site and a force-feedback glove in the physician's clinic.

Despite the attraction of all the politically correct applications of haptic devices, the first commercially successful applications will likely be related to sex. Following the trajectory of the popularity of the VCR and the Web as vehicles for erotic images, there will undoubtedly be a large number of clients who are willing to pay to use their force-feedback mice or joysticks fully to explore the contour, texture, and elasticity of the skin and hair of a scantily clad male or female model displayed on their computer monitors. Full-body haptic interfaces, anatomically correct suits with sensors and mechanical force feedback mechanisms, are rumored to have been developed to explore the limits of virtual sexuality in more detail.

***Graphical interface.***    Moving up the user interface hierarchy, above Physical Interface I and II is the Graphical Interface layer, commonly referred to as the Graphical User Interface or GUI. In the context of the interface model presented in Figure 4.1, this layer represents everything displayed on the computer monitor, including the older textual command line interfaces supported by Microsoft DOS. Some of the early computer systems in the 1950s used graphical displays and pointing devices but weren't popularized until Apple's marketing effort with the Macintosh computer. Today, the Graphical Interface—the collection of windows, icons, menus, buttons, and other controls drawn on a computer screen that map the user's actions to the physical layer(s) below— is synonymous with Microsoft Windows, Macintosh OS, and the Web browsers they support.

In addition to making the Web possible, the Graphical Interface level is important because it is the first level at which companies can make a major difference in connecting with their customers. Unlike the underlying physical layers, which are defined mainly by a customer's choice in computer hardware, businesses can commission the design of a graphical interface to suit their particular needs. Businesses have a tremendous amount of flexibility in deciding what their customers see and how they communicate with them, within the constraints imposed by their operating systems, Web browsers, and the bandwidth of their connections to the Internet. This flexibility carries with it a responsibility that not everyone takes seriously—witness the vast number of poorly thought-out Web sites on the Internet.

Designing the graphical layer of the user interface isn't simply about determining which image to paste into the background of a Web site. Good graphical interface design is an art, one that's difficult to master, and one reason great Web designers are in demand. Even subtle differences, such as the color, size, and style of the font used on a Web site, can have a profound impact on how visitors perceive the site and the company it represents.

In developing a graphical interface, accomplished Web designers take into account dozens of subjective and objective factors. They need to know, for example, what sort of image the business wants to project to its customers—carefree, serious, or responsible? What is the typical customer's experience with the Web and computing in general—novice or pro? What do typical customers do for a living? What is their cognitive style—mainly visual or auditory? Everyone has built-in perceptual filters, based on prior knowledge and beliefs about a given topic. Perhaps the customers are visual thinkers, thinking in terms of images. Perhaps they're more aural, learning and absorbing more from the spoken word. Or they may be primarily kinesthetic, and learn best by touch and movement.

This and other information is necessary for a Web designer to determine, for example, the modes of interaction a Web site should support, the role of mental models in the interface, the appropriate level of graphic complexity to use, the optimal mix of power versus ease of learning that should be provided, and how to provide situational awareness.

*Modes of interaction* include the components of Physical Levels I and II that should be supported by the Graphical Interface. Some components, such as a mouse or other pointing device, are assumed. Others, such as simple sounds, music, and synthesized speech, depend on the purpose of the Web site.

*Mental models* are the metaphors that give a Graphical Interface meaning. Examples of successful metaphors include the desktop metaphor popularized by the Xerox Star and Apple Macintosh computers, and Microsoft Windows, the spreadsheet metaphor supported by Microsoft Excel software, the book metaphor in Click2Learn's Toolbook software, and the card metaphor used by Apple's HyperCard. The desktop metaphor exemplifies how a metaphor can be used to provide a large number of users who have diverse backgrounds with a conceptual model of how and where information in a computer operating system fits together. The desktop metaphor makes use of objects common to an office setting—the desktop, trashcan, documents, and file folders. Users with even a passing familiarity with an office setting have a reference point that tells them where they are, how to move on to another point, and where they have been.

Thanks to an established mental model of a paper-based spreadsheet, accountants and others experienced with paper spreadsheets seldom have trouble making the transition from paper to Microsoft Excel or some other electronic spreadsheet. Of course, the electronic spreadsheet is so popular today that most MBA students never see a paper spreadsheet. The point is that Graphical Interface designers have to make assumptions about the previous experiences of the typical user for an interface to work.

Following Piaget's theories of assimilation and accommodation, metaphors can provide customers with a familiar form into which new information can be placed. For example, an obvious metaphor for JoesUsedAutoParts.Com might be a garage, with separate rooms for tires and engine parts, a paint room, and so on. A virtual cash register might be used for checkout.

The *level of graphic complexity* most appropriate for a Graphical Interface is a balance among the need to focus a customer's attention on some aspect of the site, hardware limitations, and the resources necessary to create a Graphical Interface. For example, a Graphical Interface with less-complex graphics may be easier for customers to understand, and also easier to test and modify. The market pressure to increase graphic complexity is to make an application come to life. The most popular video games, for example, have incredible detail and complexity in their displays. Detail promotes fantasy, and fantasy can make the activity emotionally appealing.

*Easy-to-learn interfaces* benefit from the judicious use of graphics, online help, support for point devices, menu bars, dialog boxes, intuitive icons, informative error messages, and robust error handling. However, despite all the hype from Apple early on, and more recently from Microsoft, a graphically rich user interface doesn't guarantee that the resulting environment will be easy to learn or provide enough power. For example, a Graphical Interface that relies on descriptions of spatial relationships may be useless for examining logical relationships. Similarly, the Microsoft Windows environment doesn't handle temporal issues very well. For example, it takes effort to determine which files were most recently used, for example.

*Situational awareness* is one of the most important features of a Graphical Interface. When customers navigate through a Web site, they need to know where they are, where they can go, and where they've been. Providing ample situational awareness cues, in the form of graphics, text, or sound, and an appropriate level of graphic complexity can help users maintain situational awareness. A confused or lost customer always knows how to move to another Web site—leaving his shopping cart behind.

Getting everything right is challenging enough when the customer base is located in a closed geographical area. However, localization— making a Web site equally appealing to customers in other countries and with other languages—can be a major undertaking. Not only is accurate textual translation an issue, but even subtleties such as the colors used in graphics and buttons can have a profound effect on the perception of the site. In certain Middle Eastern cultures, for example, the image of an unveiled female in a business suit is considered inappropriate.

*Logical interface.*    Terrific graphics and sounds might entice customers to linger a moment at a Web site, but if they can't quickly and easily accomplish the task at hand—purchase a widget from the site, for example—they won't bother doing business through the site and won't return. The Logical Interface level is about rules, guidelines, and standards of interface behavior, such as how an interface should display the results of a calculation. For example, customers won't respond well to the need to click once on a hypertext link on one page of a Web site and three times on another page to follow a link. Logical inconsistencies in a user interface confuse customers.

A well-designed Logical Interface layer, like a properly executed Graphical Interface layer, allows customers to focus on the problem at hand, such as ordering a widget from a Web site, rather than on the mechanics of operating the interface. Logical Interface design relies heavily on the concept of information design, which deals with the organization, presentation, clarity, and complexity of information. Information design focuses on communications and on developing a framework for expressing information, not aesthetics. The primary metric for assessing the degree to which an interface supports a logical model is *cognitive ergonomics*. In other words, trying to figure out a user interface shouldn't give customers headaches.

***Emotional interfaces.*** Most office applications, utilities, and Web sites never extend beyond the Logical Interface level of the user interface hierarchy. Games are a different matter, however, in part because game designers have relatively few external limitations. Since developers can go wherever they need to in order to create a specific emotional effect, some of the best user interfaces have been developed for games. Because these interfaces are so compelling, many game players form emotional bonds—love and hatred—with synthetic beings or obstacles that keep them coming back for more.

An Emotional Interface can be fun. Consider EverQuest (www.EverQuest.com), one of the most popular games on the Internet. This massively multi-player game, which can accommodate over 50,000 simultaneous players on a single evening, is about bonding with other players. The game is configured so that players must first buy a CD-ROM containing the game, and then sign up for a small monthly service charge. Each player has the power to define a virtual alter ego. Unlike the ever-popular QUAKE and other shoot-to-kill games, EverQuest encourages and rewards players banding together. The bonding pressure is so compelling that many players spend hours every night conversing with their virtual group companions as they explore the landscape. Similarly, Microsoft's futuristic Allegiance game (www.Microsoft.com/games/allegiance) is a multi-player Internet game that rewards team efforts, not individuals. Not only does Allegiance support synthetic speech, force-feedback, and instant voice-chat between squad-mates, but the 3-D graphics are stunning as well.

The most exciting interfaces in existence today are those developed for dedicated game hardware from Sega, Nintendo, and Sony. Not surprisingly, Sony refers to the microprocessor in its PlayStation II as the "Emotion Engine." Unbridled by the need to support a Windows or Macintosh desktop interface, game designers are free to use custom interface designs to instill a sense of mastery or, alternatively, of fear and uncertainty, in the player. All computer users may not agree with the premise of the QUAKE series, for example, but they'll have to admit that they don't get as worked up about their word processor or spreadsheet program. Games address some of the player's basic needs, whether to release aggression in a socially acceptable manner, express competitiveness, or overcome obstacles to master an environment.

Games highlight the basic components of an Emotional Interface. There must be some element of risk, the prospect of a reward, either physical (e.g., a good deal) or mental (e.g., a verbal pat on the back), a degree of uncertainty, and the process of interaction, and/or the end-point of the game must elicit some form of emotion in the player. The emotions resulting from user interactions with an emotional interface could range from simple pleasure and fun to horror and fear. For example, PriceLine.com (www.PriceLine.com) is really a game of chance. The game may appeal to players who enjoy a modicum of risk taking, with some likelihood of getting a bargain. One could argue that, by providing rapid responses and unhampered transaction support, many of the online stock trading houses have become casinos of sorts for a new breed of amateur investors and professional day-traders. Many Emotional Interfaces appeal to the competitive nature of many customers. Erotic Web sites certainly cater to their customers' emotional needs at some level.

*Intelligent interfaces.*    Intelligent interfaces, often referred to as knowledge-based interfaces, build upon many or all of the user interface layers discussed so far. The primary feature or processes supported at this level of user interface sophistication is adaptability, provided by a range of pattern recognition techniques. In addition, speech recognition, machine translation, natural language processing, and intelligent agents operate at this level. Experimental areas, such as machine vision, where a camera is used to capture facial expressions and then deduce the user's emotions, may be found in this level as well. The goal at this level of the interface hierarchy, from the perspective of the Web, is to improve the range and richness of meanings that businesses and their customers can share. Customers who develop a deeper understanding of a company tend to be more loyal than customers who do not.

*Adaptability.*    Adaptability, typically the result of a process called *machine learning*, is the ability of a Web site to change what it presents to a customer. By monitoring a customer's activity on a Web site, an Intelligent Interface may learn, for example, how a customer likes her desktop arranged, that she buys more fiction than non-fiction books, and that her preference for wine is white. The primary limitation of intelligent interfaces is in how they can acquire customer data. It's far less obtrusive simply to watch what a customer does online—as long as the customer understands that she's being monitored in order to make her experience on the Web site more enjoyable and productive.

Ideally, an intelligent interface learns customer preferences by monitoring responses to certain situations, tailors the experience to current customer interests, and never demands that customers explicitly state their preferences. For example, the first time a man shops for groceries on PriceLine.com, the default categories of items reflect what most customers order. However, when he returns to PriceLine.com, the default categories change to reflect his past orders. When he plays QUAKE III, the game learns his defenses and adapts its tactics accordingly. The result is that as he plays, his opponents become much more difficult to defeat.

Even though customers may only be aware of subtle changes in the way data are displayed on an adaptive Web site, the inner workings of an intelligent interface may be very complex. For example, the back-end may contain an elaborate knowledge base coupled to an expert system or statistical analysis program. The aim of all this processing is to come up with a best guess of what a customer wants to see or interact with on a Web site.

***Speech recognition.***    Speech recognition has become almost mainstream with the advent of three milestones. First, the vocabulary is basically unlimited.   Modern speech recognition systems offer active vocabularies of over 100,000 words with recognition accuracy better than 96 percent (four errors per hundred words). The second milestone is the ability to recognize and translate continuous, natural sounding speech, instead of the single-word droning required by older, discrete recognition systems. The third milestone is price. Affordable voice recognition systems are now available from several vendors, including IBM, Lernout & Hauspie, and Philips. These systems interface directly with Web browsers, allowing users to perform searches and other routine tasks with speech control.

Recent advances in speech recognition technology have moved the price/performance ratio of speech recognition systems to the point where powerful, affordable systems are becoming attractive alternatives to the conventional mouse and keyboard. The greatest challenge to overcome is that Web browsers are optimized for point and click operations, not speech recognition. Using speech recognition with Internet Explorer or Netscape Navigator is akin to directing someone blindfolded to "go right three steps, stop, go forward six steps, stop, go back one step, stop." To realize the full potential of the Web as a delivery medium, future versions of Web browsers will need to be optimized to work with speech recognition as well as current browsers work with the mouse.

***Machine translation.***   Machine translation, the automated conversion of text from one language to another, has the potential to open Western Web commerce to non–English-speaking countries. Although about 80 percent of Web content is in English, almost the same percentage of computer users are non–English-speaking. At this stage of development, fully automated translation is limited to *gisting*—translations with occasional errors but with enough meaningful content to get the general idea across. Most of the work in the area of machine translation has been done in English, French, German, Italian, Norwegian, Spanish, and Portuguese.

Babel Fish (www.babelfish.altavista.com), e-lingo (ww.e-lingo.com), FreeTranslation.com (www.FreeTranslation.com), InterTran (www.tran-exp.com:2000/InterTran), Systran (www.systranet.com), and TransBot (www.transbot.com) are well-known examples of machine translation Web sites. For example, Babel Fish converts English into most European languages. Using Babel Fish, a potential overseas customer can convert an English-language Web page into German or French, for example. InterTran is unique in that it provides a phrase-by-phrase translation service between dozens of language pairs, such as English–Romanian or Greek–Welsh. Machine translation has obvious potential in interconti-nental and inter-cultural B2B communications.

***Natural language processing.***   Like machine translation, natural lan-guage processing (NLP) deals with the written word. However, instead of translating from one language to another, NLP is concerned with interpreting text within a given language. NLP is most often used to provide a natural language front-end to Web searches. For example, Ask Jeves (www.askjeves.com) uses an NLP front end to its Web query engine, allowing customers to ask questions such as "What is the tem-perature like in Orlando?" The Ask Jeves NLP engine converts ques-tions into a database query (e.g., SELECT "Temperature" FROM WeatherTable WHERE Location = "Orlando"), selects the appropriate database, and performs the search. NLP front ends can make a Web site more approachable and more useful, especially for customers who are unfamiliar with complex Web-searching procedures.  NLP front ends are available as off-the-shelf products from a variety of vendors, such as Microsoft.

***Intelligent agents.***   Intelligent agents are a broad range of intelligent programs that perform specified tasks on behalf of customers. For example, Ask Jeves is one example of an intelligent agent that performs complex Web searches. Intelligent agents are independent programs capable of completing complex assignments without intervention, as opposed to tools that must be manipulated by a user. These programs are discussed in depth in the next chapter.

## Emotionally Intelligent Interfaces

At the highest level of the user interface hierarchy, and building upon concepts and features found in the Physical, Logical, Intelligent, and Emotional Interface levels, is the Emotionally Intelligent Interface or EII level. An EII may make use of Logical Interface components, but the overall goal isn't simply to get numbers into and out of a program. A spreadsheet program may be logically correct, but emotionally void. And, for a spreadsheet, that's probably all right. If an accountant is using a spreadsheet to calculate the return on investment on a potential deal, she wants the bottom line, and doesn't expect to feel good about the process. Two Web sites, each using a logical interface of equal complexity and ease of use, can support different levels of emotional intelligence. The difference is in how that information is imparted to customers.

***Characteristics of an EII.***    An EII, properly executed, brings all the components of the user interface hierarchy together in a cohesive, resonant structure. For example, an interface may be logical and intelligent in that it changes characteristics and presents data to reflect information about the consumer, but that doesn't mean that it is emotionally intelligent. In practical terms, user interfaces can only approximate emotional intelligence. A fully emotionally intelligent interface would not only express emotions, but it would know how to manage those expressions and how to use its emotions to modify the behavior of the customer.

Creating an EII involves more than simply anthropomorphizing a GUI. An expressive talking head can aid in communicating information from a Web site to customers. However, an anthropomorphic interface doesn't improve customer-to-Web communications, or how the information that the talking head delivers to the customer is determined. That is, there must be some sort of intelligence behind the interface, whether elementary pattern matching or sophisticated user modeling.

Consider what it takes to be a great customer service representative—self-control, conscientiousness, empathy, and service orientation, all characteristics of anticipating, recognizing, and meeting customers' needs. Similarly, an EII is:

*Respectful.* It doesn't waste the customer's time. In addition, when information is needed, the interface asks, but doesn't demand it of the customer. When a particular course of action is required, such as proceeding to the checkout area, it suggests, and doesn't demand action from the customer.

*Helpful.* It has the ability to facilitate the task at hand.

*Empathetic.* It can develop a rapport with a broad diversity of customers, typically by matching components of the interface to suit the customers' tastes and personality.

*Socially adept.* It can adapt to specific contexts, including an ability to match the customer's vocabulary and style. It also limits the information exchange to what the conversation demands. For example, a business could offer to mail a brochure to customers in exchange for their mailing address. However, the business wouldn't ask for the customer's email address, because that has no bearing on the brochure, from the customer's perspective.

*Truthful.* An EII provides correct data, and doesn't attempt to obfuscate data in order to influence customer behavior.

*Unambiguous.* An EII supports clear, unambiguous dialogue between a business and its customers. Customers should feel that each message from a Web site has but one meaning.

*Anticipatory.* It can anticipate a customer's needs.

*Persuasive.* An EII can use social skills to persuade the customer along a course of behavior.

*Responsive.* An EII responds to the customer's feedback.

*Emotive.* An EII emotes in context-appropriate ways. For the purposes of our discussion, EIIs regulate emotions through responding to customers in a way that positively influences their emotions—for example, acting suitably helpful so that the customer feels respected. An EII is most valuable if it can create feelings of joy, hope, satisfaction, relief, pride, and gratitude; and suppress feelings of distress, jealousy, fear, disappointment, shame, reproach, dislike, or anger.

The interface needn't actually feel emotions as a human would to affect the emotional state of the user. After all, a few words or a single image can have a profound effect on the viewer's emotions. In the same way that people never know what other people actually feel but are only aware of what they appear to feel, if a designer wants to endow an interface with the ability to feel emotions, it only has to give the impression that it does. An EII can appear to emote, and that's good enough. Actors emote, and we make the leap of faith, often confusing the role of the actor with the actor. That is, we typecast actors and actresses. For example, despite his other roles in the film industry, Leonard Nimoy will always be Mr. Spock to most viewers. We often confuse what's real and what isn't. Computers, or people for that matter, are deemed intelligent because they appear to be. We expect doctors to wear a white coat and stethoscope around their necks, not a three-piece banker's suit. Perception is what counts, not reality. We often accept what only seems real.

Some attributes of human customer service representatives, such as variability, including "bad days," irritability, and negative transference, and some normal attributes shouldn't be replicated in an EII. For example, consider small talk. Suppose a customer is on the phone ordering a CD-ROM from a company, interacting with a live sales representative. While waiting for the customer's card to process, she might ask about the local weather. Such small talk adds a certain flavor, if done appropriately. However, customers don't want to waste their time telling a computer screen about the local weather.

***Rationale.***    Why devote energy into developing an EII? The primary motivation is to increase the emotional bond between a company and its customers. As illustrated by the Loyalty Equation in Chapter 3, a greater emotional bond betters the odds for creating increased customer loyalty. Properly implemented, an EII can improve the perception of a company. It also adds a differentiating factor—independent of price or time to delivery. Think of the role of newscasters and syndicated talk show hosts. They're simply delivering data that can be had at a variety of portals, and yet many listeners tune in to a particular television network because they feel a bond between themselves and the newscaster. Perhaps it's simply a matter of familiarity, but in many cases the newscaster's personality comes through, flavoring the news.

Another reason for developing an EII user interface to a Web site is that, when properly implemented, it provides a level of consistency not usually possible with human customer service representatives. An EII can be utterly consistent on a 24/7 basis, whereas humans vary their moods from day to day, and there's always the issue of turnover and training new employees. In developing an emotional bond, consistency is critical. In fact, unlike the typical approach of constantly changing the face of a Web site to provide the customer with a "fresh" experience, fresh isn't necessarily good when it comes to EIIs. A new GUI may be fresh, but an old EII is comforting. Using the newscaster parallel, it's okay to change the anchorman or -woman's suit, but not the person. In addition, even when it comes to newscasters, most users come to expect a certain level of consistency, even in their dress. Viewers form an impression of the newscasters' personality by what they wear. Walter Cronkite didn't become a trusted American icon by wearing conservative suits one week, and leisure suits with tie-dyed shirts the next. In developing an image for a Web site, it's imperative to develop one that complements the business' objectives and to stick with it.

Thanks to the Web, the Internet has heavy traffic by consumers who also happen to be computer users. That is, they are consumers first, and the computer and their Web connection are simply a portal or touch point. They don't necessarily care about the human–computer connection; they want service. As such, human customer service representatives set their expectations. For most online customers, what makes a great customer service representative also makes a great user interface. Human customer service representatives are ideally self aware, good facilitators, motivated toward self-improvement, and empathic, developing a rapport with the customer. They also have social skills that aid in persuasion. In reality, few customer representatives display all these traits on a consistently high level.

Even greater variability in customer service exists among Web sites. Consider, for example, the differences between BarnesAndNoble.com and Amazon.com, both excellent online outlets for music, books, software, and more. BarnesAndNoble.com's interface is aesthetically appealing, and easy to use, and provides a logical interface. Amazon.com, in comparison, goes one step further. Not only is the interface easy to use and logically laid out, but it's personalized. As a returning customer, a woman is offered specials and advice on books she might like to read, based on her prior selections of books and music. Because of this difference, the BarnesAndNobel.com site has the look and feel of a generic, albeit well-run eStore. When she visits Amazon.com, she's much more likely to feel as though she's a welcomed, returning guest. She might also feel an emotional bond to the huge company, even though, rationally, she knows better. After all, she's just a data point in a huge information system. Even so, Amazon.com has developed what appears to be a loyal customer following.

Amazon.com is orders of magnitude ahead of BarnesAndNoble.com as an EII. Note that there aren't any talking heads, dancing dogs, synthetic voices, or anything out of the ordinary, from the user interface perspective. Given sufficient bandwidth and more widespread acceptance of technologies such as speech synthesis and voice recognition, it's conceivable that the Amazon.com of the future will become even more of an EII. Consider logging in to Amazon.com and being asked, "Good morning, what are you looking for today? Something in fiction perhaps?" Amazon.com is primarily an eBusiness, whereas BarnesAndNoble.com is one of several touch points of the large Barnes and Noble bookstore chain. That is, Barnes and Noble employs many more, presumably more expensive, human customer service representatives than does Amazon.com.

Although profound differences exist in the sophistication of user interfaces among Web sites, they're most disconcerting when they occur within a company. This disconnect, called *touch point dissonance*, occurs when a company's touch points appear to be uncoordinated and provide customers with a different or inconsistent level of service. For example, consider the popular mail-order firm for running shoes and apparel, Road Runner Sports, Inc. (www.RoadRunnerSports.com). When a runner calls to place an order, the customer service representative has access to his complete order history, as well as notes about how many miles he runs per week and on what sort of terrain. If he's ordered shoes in the past, they'll ask how his shoes are doing, and whether he needs another pair. They'll ask if he needs to replace socks and other accessories he's ordered in the past as well. The customer service representative gives the runner the impression that he's talking with one of his running buddies, who happens to be working as a Road Runner representative. This approach seems to work; most customers bond with someone with whom they share an interest or common goal.

RoadRunner's Web site, in comparison, doesn't convey the same level of enthusiasm for customer service. The same runner can look up items and specials, but it isn't customized for running style or distance. It would be great, for example, if runners could review the same information available to their human customer representatives, such as shoe and accessory preferences, and these items could be offered at a discount. Even though the Web site performs remarkably well as a surrogate to RoadRunner's mail order catalog, it isn't configured to understand or at least recognize customers' needs and match them with their products. Like the majority of otherwise excellent retail sites on the Web, RoadRunnerSports.com doesn't reach the level of an emotionally intelligent interface—yet. Unlike its excellent telephone touch point, RoadRunner's Web site is passive; it doesn't seek out active ways to increase a customer's satisfaction and loyalty, such as by offering customized assistance, taking the customer's perspective, or acting as a trusted advisor.

Emotions play an essential role in rational decision-making, perception, learning, and other cognitive functions. Affective computing relates to, arises from, or deliberately influences emotions. One day, computers will be able to recognize and express emotions. Such *affective computers* are probably better suited to evoke emotions in a customer. Emotionally Intelligent Interfaces don't require the speech and facial expression recognition technologies of affective computing.

# Interface Dialogues

Another way of looking at a user interface is as an ambassador of sorts, mediating the dialogue between the customer and a Web site. As illustrated in Figure 4.4, the user interface defines the nature of the dialogue that can occur between customers and a Web site. This dialogue not only affects the customers' impression of a site, but ultimately influences how well the site provides customers with an effective environment for locating supplies of widgets and services and completing transactions.

As listed in Figure 4.4, if the user interface to a Web site is only configured to the level of a Logical Interface, and simply accepts data and provides answers, there is no emotive bond. Like a spreadsheet application, it's a cut-and-dried process. For a Logical Interface, the rules are obvious. For example, the spreadsheet answers will always be related to the input data by some clear mathematical formula. Unless customers have a thing for pure logic, there isn't any emotional bond associated with this kind of user interface.

At the level of the Emotional Interface, such as a customer might find when interacting with a Web-based game, or even an online stock trading site, the dialogue is described in terms of a stimulus and a response. The customer might place an order for stock, for example, and may or may not receive the stock at the desired price. Or, in a game situation, she might decide on a particular course of action. The result or response is often uncertain, and the rules may not be known or even knowable. For example, we can only speculate about the rules behind the stock market, except at the grossest level. An important quality of the dialogue in an Emotional Interface is that it is usually highly emotive. In a game, the dialogue can be centered on life and death situations. In the online stock trading market, the dialogue can be even more serious.

Finally, at the level of an Emotionally Intelligent Interface, the dialogue typically involves inquiries and orders from the customer and information and products from the Web site. If properly executed, the dialogue between the customer and the Web site, which serves as a virtual customer representative, creates a highly emotive bond. Depending on how the site is constructed, the virtual customer representative and the site may be one and the same, or the virtual customer representative could be an anthropomorphic figure within the site. In either case, the rules of the dialogue are clear and obvious.

Emotionally Intelligent Interfaces are concerned with influencing emotions in the customer. (See Figure 4.5.) For this reason, some form of pattern recognition, in the form of a *predictive engine*, is needed to

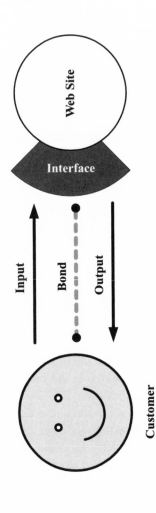

**Customer**

Input

Bond

Output

**Interface**

**Web Site**

| | Input | Output | Bond | Application | Note |
|---|---|---|---|---|---|
| | **Interface Dialogues** | | | | |
| Logical | Data | Answer | None | Spreadsheet | Obvious Rules |
| Intelligent | Query | Diagnosis | None | Expert System | Hidden Rules |
| Emotional | Stimulus | Response | Emotive | Game | Hidden Rules<br>Highly Emotive |
| Emotionally<br>Intelligent | Inquiries & Orders | Information &<br>Products | Emotive | Customer Service<br>Representative | Obvious Rules |

***Figure 4.4*** *Computer Interface Dialogues. The customer (top, left) communicates through an interface to an application (top, right). The application may be a standalone program, a Web browser, or a Web-enabled application.*

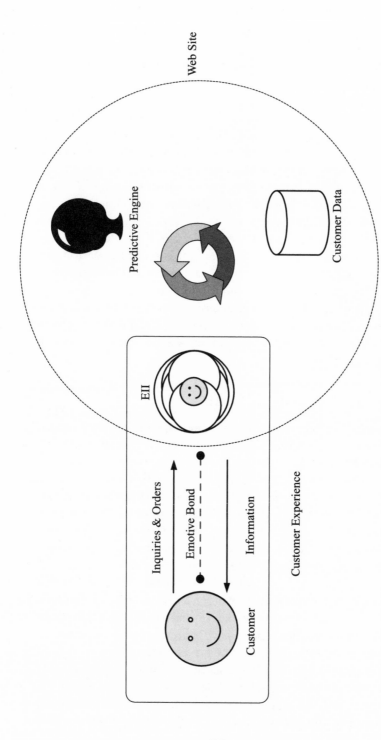

**Figure 4.5** *B2C Interaction through an Emotionally Intelligent Interface where the customer (left) interacts with a Web site (right). In this example, the Web site incorporates a mechanism for storing customer data, and a predictive engine to make use of the information.*

recognize what emotions are likely to be generated in a given situation. As illustrated, customers interact with a Web site through an EII user interface. Based on data from previous customer encounters or a profile of the customer, a predictive engine determines how to best manage the dialogue. The end result, if all goes as planned, is a positive customer experience and a strong emotive bond with the customer.

For example, providing customers with choices of action through an EII dialogue can give them a sense of mastery and control. The EII system doesn't have to understand what's important to the customer, but it must be able to recognize what's likely to be important in certain situations. Recognition, not empathy, is the immediate goal of EII interfaces. A human customer service representative learns to recognize when a customer is getting upset from the tone of the customer's voice, for example. An EII might monitor the length of an interaction, assuming that anything over a certain time limit is related to customer frustration. For example, if the average customer transaction takes two minutes, a customer still trying to move a transaction through the system after five minutes probably needs assistance. As illustrated in Figure 4.5, these heuristics or rules of thumb are handled by a predictive engine that uses both real-time and previously stored customer data.

# Interface Personalities

Anyone who has ever referred to a "stubborn nail," "finicky toaster," or "temperamental thermostat," knows how easy it is to ascribe human traits to inanimate objects. Even though at one level everyone knows the objects they're working with don't have feelings or emotion, certain characteristics of inanimate objects tend to fit neatly into human behavior descriptions. Virtually everyone is guilty of anthropomorphism at some level. All interfaces, whether on a computer program, Web site, or vending machine, have personalities. Even a copier has a personality. For example, a copier's error messages define a major component of its personality. "Paper Jam" talks down to the user, whereas "Paper Jam – Please Check Area three" is collaborative. Most people don't respond well to the "blinking time" on their VCR after a power outage, and would prefer a message like "Power interruption. Please press TIME to reset clock."

The major personality axes, whether applied to humans or objects, are dominance, submissiveness, conscientiousness, emotional stability, and openness. (See Figure 4.6.) While everyone expresses each trait to some degree, it is the expression of each trait that defines one's personality. Similarly, the expression of each characteristic defines objects,

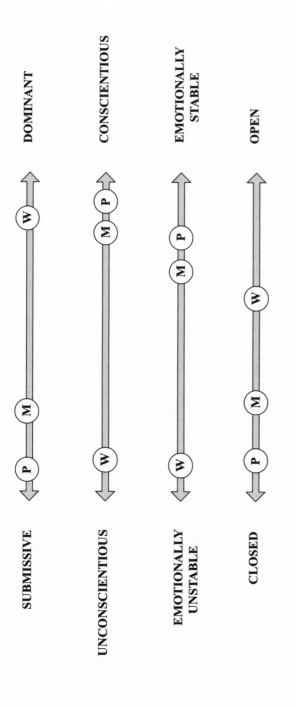

SUBMISSIVE                                    DOMINANT

UNCONSCIENTIOUS                               CONSCIENTIOUS

EMOTIONALLY
UNSTABLE                                      EMOTIONALLY
                                              STABLE

CLOSED                                        OPEN

Ⓜ = Macintosh OS      Ⓟ = Palm Pilot      Ⓦ = Windows OS

**Figure 4.6**  *Interface Personality Profile. Comparison of Macintosh OS (M), Windows 95/98/NT (W), and Palm Pilot (P) Interface Personalities.*

such as user interfaces, as well. The previous chart illustrates the personality profiles for the Macintosh OS, the Palm Pilot, and Microsoft Windows. For example, Windows is more dominant than the Macintosh OS. That is, the Macintosh OS has more collaborative error messages, is more flexible, and has a more submissive "feeling" than a Windows environment.

The Palm Pilot is even more submissive than the Macintosh OS in that it obediently responds to whatever commands users enter. Both the Macintosh OS and Palm Pilot are more conscientious than the Windows environment. It's much easier accidentally to delete files and make other non-recoverable errors in the Windows environment. Similarly, both the Palm Pilot and Macintosh OS are more emotionally stable than the Windows environment. That is, every application on the Pilot acts like every other. There aren't many variations possible. Windows, in contrast, supports everything from command-line input to unique utilities that don't abide by general standards. Finally, the Palm Pilot is a much more closed environment than Windows. For example, users can't easily modify the look and feel of the Pilot, or examine files from a variety of perspectives or views as users can in Windows.

The ability to classify the personality of a user interface is important because it may be possible to modify it to better suit the customer. For example, dominant customers may prefer dominant interfaces. Dominance may be realized through naming, the language used, the gender attributed to the interface, and real or synthetic voices used. For example, gender has a stereotypic effect. It's important that the personality of an interface be identifiable. If it's ambiguous, no one will like it or be able to relate to it.

Artificial intelligence, special graphics, and natural language processing (NLP) aren't necessary to endow a computer with personality. Personality is easy to create with a few words—witness a good book. Flattery works. People think more of the computer when it praises them; less if it provides negative feedback. Virtually all game players respond positively to the applause or "good job" message at the end of a good performance.

# Evaluating User Interfaces

The goal in evaluation, the final stage of user interface development, is minimally to verify that the interface is learnable, useable, and transparent. Evaluation can entail subjecting a Web site to attack by dozens of testers, hunting for bugs that can cause the Web site to crash, slow down, or otherwise fail. Programmers and programming management typically attend these meetings, observing and documenting errors.

User interface evaluation is also concerned with higher-level issues. For example, can a customer complete a task without getting lost in the site? Are buttons clearly labeled, and is their use intuitive? How long does a customer have to wait for a response? If it's too long, how can frustration be reduced? These interactions, which are frequently taped for analysis later, typically use expert subjects; for example, doctors for medical sites and accountants for business sites. Graphic designers, documentation support writers, and marketing staff are equally involved in these evaluations.

A typical Web review focuses on value, documentation, support, how well it performs stated functions, ease of use, and browser compatibility. There is usually no mention of anything remotely emotional. Logic rules in the software evaluation process. However, customers don't buy based on logic; they buy based on emotions.

Games go through the same verification, validation, and usability testing as well. However, questions game testers ask are: Is the game fun? Is it challenging? Does the user want to play again? Does the plot appeal to the targeted audience? If it's character-based, which characters do the users relate to? Are the levels appropriate? Web designers often think about emotive issues in user interface evaluation, even though they may not be explicitly tested. If the evaluation is defined in emotive terms, the interface is more likely to meet those criteria.

In evaluating a company's success at providing its customers with an EII interface, management can't simply look at the Web site in static isolation. Customers have to interact with it. After all, it's how the customers feel during and after using the Web site that counts. They have to feel good about the experience, just as they feel after an encounter with a great customer representative at a retail store.

Interface evaluation is an art, and different standards apply to each level in the interface hierarchy. It's obvious that EIIs aren't readily amenable to cut-and-dried mathematical analysis. Furthermore, an interface appropriate for one purpose may be ill suited for another. That is, the appropriateness of a particular user interface is task dependent.

# The Future

We are just beginning to explore the potential and power of user interface technology. The Web is a prominent portal into human-computer communications. Because the Web touches so many lives, it opens up countless opportunities for technologies that can be applied to creating a better dialog between a business and customers. For example, customers today communicate their emotions to a Web site through text generated from their keyboards. However, we communicate our emotions through facial expressions, voice amplitude and intonation, gestures, posture, and pupillary dilation. Less obvious indicators are respiration, heart rate, temperature, muscle action potentials, blood pressure, and electrodermal response. All of these physiological responses and more could be monitored and transmitted as indicators of our current emotional status. In the future, the user interface will broker emotional communications directly between humans—perhaps between customers and human customer service representatives surfing the Web.

Eventually, everyday objects, such as shoes, toilets, bathroom scales, and refrigerators, will become data interfaces. Within a few years, for example, a "smart toilet" will detect changes in a man's physiology, as indicated by an automatic urinalysis exam. The results will be sent to his physician's computer, where an intelligent agent will sound an alarm if the results are abnormal. If necessary, the alerted physician will prescribe the appropriate medication. These everyday or invisible interfaces, while covering up extremely sophisticated technology, are simple. Fortunately, most customers like simplicity; witness the Palm Pilot.

In the move to intelligent objects and invisible interfaces, it's important to note that the current desktop metaphor may actually hinder a shift to the next level of user interface development. Like DOS users resisting the move to a Windows user interface because they already climbed the learning curve, many customers may resist having their personal information distributed.

Although research in affective computing may one day address the ability to provide computers with characteristics of intelligence and sensitivity toward humans, Emotionally Intelligent Interfaces can be created now, with human intelligence. It's important to note that the move to create synthetic, cost-effective customer service representatives—through EIIs, for example—can go too far. The next chapter will explore the world of bots, intelligent agents, and the technological underpinnings that make them possible.

## Executive Summary

The evolution of the human–computer interface is the evolution of modern computing. The Graphical User Interface that was refined at Xerox, popularized by Apple's Macintosh, and later incorporated into

Microsoft Windows, and the simplicity of the Palm Pilot, are examples of how significant the user interface is in integrating technology into our lives.

The user interface can be described in terms of a seven-layer hierarchical model, ranging through the Physical Layers I and II, Graphical, Logical, Emotional, Intelligent, and Emotionally Intelligent layers. Each of the higher levels is heavily dependent on the people below them. The user interface can also be described in terms of the dialogue each type of interface layer supports.

Evaluation of user interface design, especially of Emotionally Intelligent Interfaces, is an art. In the evaluation of an EII, the issue is how the customer feels after interacting with a Web site, not a cut-and-dried mathematical equation.

## Bots, Intelligent Agents, and Virtual Personalities

*Real knowledge is to know the
extent of one's ignorance.*

Confucius

To succeed in the digitally aware economy, a business has to do more than just erect a pretty Web site. When customers visit a site, all the fancy graphics and advertising on traditional media won't lessen—and in fact may increase—the need to deliver on fulfillment and service. It may help to think of a Web touch point as a living, breathing entity. In this scenario, management is a talent scout trying to fill a high-visibility touch point vacancy with the best hire it can find. The task is like that of hiring a VP of eCommerce who personifies the qualities of an ideal Web site. Most businesses want to attract someone with a clearly defined, amiable personality—one that their customers can relate to, and one that complements the company's image. Management would also want someone with integrity, and a good head on her shoulders, who delivers on her promises and is able to communicate clearly and honestly. The ideal VP should also be attractive, charismatic, and exude confidence. It's quite a bit to ask for from a candidate, but a business creating a Web site from the ground up, can have whatever it wants, within the limits of its resources.

This chapter builds upon the premise of Part One: that every customer contact is an opportunity to build a relationship and to learn more about customer needs. It also follows the last chapter in supporting the premise that an EII is the best technology for exploiting this opportunity. This chapter introduces the back-end architecture and processing required to create an emotionally intelligent user interface, as well as intelligent agents, bots, and other technologies that live on the boundary between the user interface and back-end processes. The goal of this chapter is to provide readers with an understanding of the technologies involved in supporting the personalized, emotive interfaces that will increase the odds of customers' returning to their Web sites for repeat business.

# The Back End: Memory

There's nothing wrong with a pretty face. After all, it can get someone noticed—and maybe even promoted. But even someone with a beautiful face will need at least a semblance of personality and intelligence to earn people's trust and confidence. It's the same with a Web site, and all a company's touch points. Good looks, in terms of the user interface, are necessary to increase the odds of an initial encounter. However, the dialogue between customers and a Web site has to be meaningful and worthwhile if the relationship is going to evolve into anything more than a passing fling.

Even the simplest life forms have memory, whether learned or instinctual. Similarly, a Web site requires some form of memory, whether to maintain a record of customers' activity on the site, including their order history, create an accurate customer profile, or provide statistical data for simple pattern matching and other behind-the-scenes embedded logic or back-end processing. This memory usually takes the form of a virtual storage cabinet where customer information, including information gleaned from other touch points of a business, is saved in one easily searched filing system.

## Data Warehouses

Every business transaction, whether on the Web, in person, or through some other touch point, generates data. For example, consider the simplified data generation and flow related to a transaction through a Web site that supports an Emotionally Intelligent Interface, shown in Figure 5.1. Customers engage in a dialogue through an EII, exchanging inquiries and orders for information. Customer data flow to a virtual representative, which may be a bot. Data then flow from the virtual representative, through the EII, and to the customer. If a business transaction takes place, a fulfillment process is initiated, resulting in products and services' being delivered to the customer. Data from all these processes are stored in a data warehouse, where they serve as the basis for business decisions and customer support. For example, data in the data warehouse can be processed by cluster analysis or one of the techniques discussed earlier, and the resulting relationships discovered in the data can be used by a predictive engine to determine how the virtual representative can best respond to the customer's requests or anticipate the customer's needs.

Customer data may also be acquired from the government, banks, credit card companies, online retailers, and other third parties. These data can range from a customer's demographics, product choices, and charge card numbers, to his desired method of shipping. Another source of data is cookies, small data files created on a customer's hard drive upon a visit to a cookie-enabled Web site. The files, which usually contain a unique tracking number, can be read by the Web site and stored whenever a customer returns. A cookie, which can be as simple as a random number, can be used to track a customer's activity on a Web site from one visit to the next.

Of course, the direct approach is online customer satisfaction surveys, and online registration is another major source of customer information. Data may also be generated and archived in the business' marketing department, and some may be relegated to the accounting, fulfillment, or technical departments. However, regardless of which department initially owns the data, they must be readily and seamlessly accessible to anyone in the organization involved in business decisions. Enter the data access and management system known as the data warehouse.

A data warehouse is simply a central repository of the most important information generated by all aspects of a business—a standard database with a slight twist. The ideal data warehouse captures the various aspects of a business process, not simply the data elements, in a way that can aid management in decision-making and serve customers' needs (See Figure 5.2). For example, it may be important to know which widget a customer orders, but it may be even more valuable for management to know which touch point was used, and the exact time

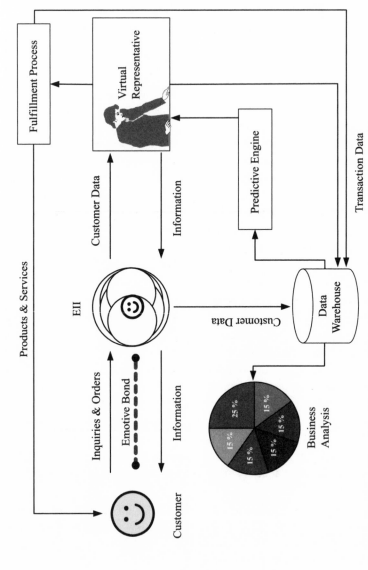

*Figure 5.1* Data generation and flow related to transactions through an EII-equipped Web site.

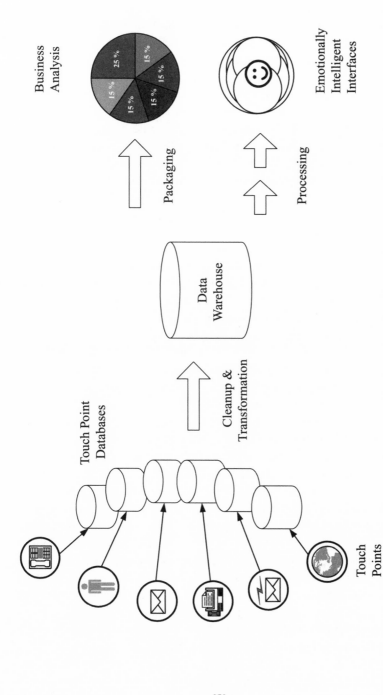

**Figure 5.2** *A data warehouse serves as a repository of customer interactions through every touch point. As data are moved into the data warehouse, they are cleaned, translated, and made available for decision support and to drive Emotionally Intelligent Interfaces.*

and date of the transaction. For example, did the customer visit the business' Web site and then call in an order? If he called in first, with whom did he talk? The data warehouse should be the only place management or customer support staff have to look to discover everything they need to know about their business. The alternative, poking around each departmental application, combining data in an ad hoc fashion, takes too much time and is prone to error.

What really separates a data warehouse from a database of favorite restaurants in someone's Palm Pilot is that a data warehouse contains current data from multiple, disparate applications. Because of the way most businesses operate and grow, each department tends to start with its own computer system, selected by the department to support its unique needs. There typically isn't much thought of integrating systems on a company-wide basis until the company expands beyond a few dozen employees. For example, if a woman runs a small startup with only a handful of employees, then her company's phone-in orders are probably tracked on one computer system, and her company's Web-based orders are tracked on another, different system. Perhaps the business is even mixing computer hardware platforms, using Macs in the production areas and PCs in the accounting area. This scenario is fine, as long as information held captive in one system isn't required, in real time, by someone using another system.

However, what of the customer who places an order on a Web site and then calls the company's phone support line to inquire about a delay? If the phone support staff can't query the database supporting their Web site, then that touch point is effectively cut off from the business. Similarly, suppose a company's marketing group needs to identify customers who visit their retail outlets and frequent their Web site, but don't necessarily make purchases through the Web. How is management going to solve the marketing department's dilemma if the company's storefront system is based on one computer system, and their Web site support group uses another?

For a one-time problem, such as identifying customers who visit a business' Web site and their retail outlets, it would be possible to query both databases for customer names, generate the appropriate reports, combine the results, and then write a program that identifies duplicates. This manual approach, however, will not solve a company's customer support challenges. For the long term, a company could replace all of its legacy systems with an integrated set of applications from a single vendor. If management is lucky enough to find one system that suits such a need, it is likely to be very expensive. A company could also build a system from scratch, but the time involved might translate to centuries in Internet time. Unless the company has plans to enter the application development business, this isn't a valid option. In either case, there will be the added costs of down time during system installation, inevitable time spent working out the bugs in the system, and the cost of training everyone on the new system.

Unless management has lots of time and money on its hands, or doesn't have a legacy system to contend with, the best way to provide information for customer support and business decisions is to create a data warehouse. Building a data warehouse needn't disrupt a business' normal operations, and everyone can keep their existing applications. Development of a data warehouse can occur in the background, without disruption of normal daily activities.

Data warehousing can be time-consuming and expensive, without proper planning. The most important task in the planning stage is to identify the subset of data residing in each departmental application that has to be warehoused. For example, to support customers from any touch point, management may decide to warehouse their order history, mailing addresses, and product preferences. The planning stage is also the time to specify database design; provide for maintenance, security, backup, authorization, and periodic modification; and estimate storage requirements and other factors that may affect computer hardware requirements.

Once data to be included in a data warehouse have been identified, the next step is to create a process in which the data are checked for errors, transformed if necessary, merged, and then stored in the warehouse. Misspelled names, duplicates, and other errors should be carefully cleaned, and some data will have to be transformed into a data warehouse–friendly form. For example, if the customer database in a storefront system maintains customer names in the sequence "First Name, Last Name," and both the databases behind a Web site and the data warehouse use separate fields for first and last names, then customer name data will have to be parsed from the storefront system to fit the data warehouse format.

At the core of every data warehouse is a database management system (DBMS), such as Oracle or Sybase, that provides tools for accessing, manipulating, and sharing data. In addition to file management, the DBMS provides for security, integrity, synchronization, failure analysis, failure recovery, and data management. Data management has undergone an evolution from early file and record management techniques to hierarchical, network, relational, and, more recently, to object-oriented systems. The relational model, the most popular technology used in data warehouse implementation, is based on the concept of a *data table* in which every row is unique. The attraction of the ubiquitous relational model is that it is mature, stable, reliable, well understood, and well suited for a number of different application environments. The basic concepts involved with the relational model are that data are populated into rows and columns in a table, and separate tables are associated with one another by joining fields that match in the two tables. Because the software industry has a great deal of experience with relational models, database engines built on this model tend to be stable, maintainable, and very fast.

As noted earlier, one aspect of a data warehouse is that it minimally disrupts existing processes. Additional screens will need to be provided to staff on the front line that interact with customers so that they can access information in the warehouse, but they won't have to learn another system. The ideal data warehouse system automatically downloads a subset of individual application databases, performs any necessary conversions and other translations, and combines them into a central database. A properly constructed warehouse takes care of timing issues, automatically performs any conversion in data representation, and populates a central database in a way that supports business decisions and customer support functions. It's up to the business to use this information so that what customers see as they walk the virtual aisles of an eBusiness is tailored to their needs and preferences.

# It's Only Logical

Given a data warehouse, creating an optimum Web site still requires an element of logic; that is, an ability to reduce the complexity of data enough to recognize patterns in customer behavior and predict future behavior. For someone running a tape rental business, for example, it may be important to know that customers with a fondness for *Blade Runner* are likely to enjoy *The Matrix*. This intelligence can range from elementary pattern matching and cluster analysis to sophisticated artificial intelligence techniques, such as various forms of machine learning.

***Cluster analysis.***    Cluster analysis is one of several computationally efficient techniques that can be used to identify patterns and relationships in large amounts of customer data. Cluster analysis can work with seemingly unrelated customer data, such as age, sex, whether or not the customer purchased a given product in the past, number of visits to a site, the time of year of the purchases, and perhaps the model of computer used. The data are then normalized or scaled so that yes-no and numerical values of different units can be compared. A typical result of cluster analysis might be that males between 35 and 40 who live in New England account for 20 percent of a company's widget sales in the winter, whereas females in this area account for only 2 percent of sales in the same period. With this information, a company can target their marketing efforts for more cost-effective outcomes.

The challenge in working with cluster analysis, and where the art of working with large volumes of data comes in, is in selecting how many and which criteria to include in the analysis. If enough criteria aren't selected, then relationships in the data may remain hidden. For example, if management failed to include the customer's sex in the example above, then it would have missed the significance of male customers on widget sales. If too many criteria are chosen, then there will be too many redundancies and the computational burden will be unnecessarily increased. For example, if the computer operating system (e.g., MacOS versus Windows 95/98/NT) were included as criteria, it wouldn't be expected to provide any additional information over using the computer processor manufacturer (e.g., Apple vs. Intel) as a criterion. In addition, even though cluster analysis is a relatively efficient process, adding only one or two unnecessary criteria may significantly extend processing time.

***Expert systems.***    Machine learning systems, software tools that rely on some degree of self programming, simulate certain aspects of human intelligence, especially decision making. These systems may be based on rule-based expert systems, neural networks, or genetic algorithms. Expert systems use rules or heuristics stored in a knowledge base to draw conclusions about a particular case. Sometimes called fuzzy logic or rule-based systems, these are programs that attempt to duplicate the expertise of a human in a particular subject area. Rule-based expert systems use a rule-base—a set of IF–THEN rules—to make decisions. Examples of simple IF–THEN rules, expressed in simple English, include:

*If the weather forecast is for rain then you should wear a raincoat.*
*If the weather forecast is clear and sunny then you should wear a hat.*

Someone could then ask the expert system what accessories to wear, and the system would suggest a raincoat or a hat, depending on the forecast.

Some expert systems can process data directly from example cases and formulate their own rules. For example, the system could be presented with a list of observed associations, such as:

*Rain – Raincoat*
*Sunny – Hat*

The system would then translate the association into a set of internal IF–THEN rules, just as a human programmer would. Because the list of observations can come directly from transaction records and doesn't require the use of a special syntax or programming language to set up, case-based expert systems are easy to set up. However, the results of a case-based expert system are generally not as predictable as those of rule-based systems because the logic of a list of hundreds of example cases may not be obvious to a human observer. Regardless of how the underlying rules are established, the purpose for creating expert systems is to make the working knowledge of an expert in a given field available to others at any time and place.

Rule-based expert systems are often called *fuzzy logic systems* because they are designed to handle concepts that are neither absolutely true nor absolutely false. That is, the rule base is not a binary yes/no or true/false system, but within the rule base, each IF–THEN clause is associated with a certainty factor. If a clause is true, the certainty factor provides a level of confidence for the associated decision. For example, the clauses:

*If the customer's first name is "Robert,"*
*then the sex of the customer is male.*

might reasonably have a certainty factor of ninety-nine percent. The one percent covers females who happen to be named Robert, as well as genotypically female customers who identify with the male sex and have assumed a masculine name. Obviously, it helps if the rules and the certainty factors are generally defined by someone with considerable expertise in the area covered by the expert system.

Following are rules for a hypothetical expert system that can predict video rental preferences, based on a customer's demographics and past purchases.

*If the customer rented* Blade Runner *within the last two years,*
*then the sex of the customer is male (70%).*

*If the sex of the customer is male,*
*then the customer is a fan of science fiction (65%).*

*If the customer is a fan of science fiction,*
*then the customer will like* The Matrix *(95%).*

Now, if a manager could interact with the hypothetical expert system, a typical exchange might be:

Computer: *Is the sex of the customer male?*
Manager: *Unknown*

Computer: *Did the customer rent* Blade Runner *within the last two years?*
Manager: *Yes*

Computer: *The customer will like* The Matrix *(43%).*

Ordinarily, an expert system designed for prioritizing content and personalizing customer interaction wouldn't engage management in dialogue, but would monitor customer transactions on a Web site.

Expert systems generate rules by *induction*, synthesizing general rules from specific examples. One virtue of an induction system is that it analyzes IF–THEN clauses to eliminate redundant information. In addition, this induction approach can identify contradictions in the IF–THEN clauses. In the example above, based on the manager's responses, the expert system concluded that there is a 43% chance that the customer will like *The Matrix*. The 43% certainty factor reflects the probability that the customer is male (70%) and that he also is a fan of science fiction (65%). Since probabilities add through multiplication, the final certainty factor represents 70% $\times$ 65% $\times$ 95%, or 43%. The rule base for a real expert system might have hundreds of IF–THEN clauses, each associated with a certainty factor.

Rule-based expert systems are relatively easy to construct, in part because the IF–THEN clauses are nearly natural language statements, as opposed to some obtuse programming language. That is, the reasoning behind predictions can be examined and modified if necessary. However, because the rules can combine in combinatorially different ways, testing and tweaking can become very resource intensive. For this reason, rule-based expert systems with less than a few hundred rules work best. Because rule-based expert systems execute efficiently, they can be used for real-time customer support and business decisions.

*Neural networks.*   Another type of machine learning approach uses neural networks, which are simulations of how neurons in the human brain work. In simplest terms, neural networks are "black box" pattern matchers that learn by associating an input pattern with an output pattern. Unlike a rule-based system, there are no IF–THEN clauses to write. A neural network is simply fed with huge amounts of input–output data and it will learn to associate patterns without human intervention. For example, if information about video rental purchases were to be fed into a neural network, then it would presumably discover the relationship between the sex of the customer and his potential preference for renting *The Matrix*.

The pattern matching ability of a neural network can be used to learn and classify consumer behavior automatically on a Web site. Audit trails of user activity on a site can be compiled and encoded in a form suitable for processing by a neural network. After each interaction, a neural network can be used to categorize a user's responses and combine this response pattern with its current model for a given classification of user; for example, a browser versus someone who is likely to purchase an item.

The problems with neural networks are that they have to be trained, they're computationally inefficient, and they really are "black boxes." Training, teaching a neural network to associate certain output conditions such as customer purchases, with input conditions, can take days or weeks, depending on the computer hardware available and the size of the database used. In addition, because neural networks are simulations of huge parallel networks, they don't execute very efficiently on standard computer hardware. One approach to reducing execution time is to use hardware neural networks instead of software simulations. The other, often a more economical approach, is to convert the input–output relationships discovered by a neural network into IF–THEN clauses in a rule-based expert system. The final, often disconcerting, attribute of neural networks is that someone can't look inside to see what's going on. For example, a programmer can't manually tweak a relationship as he could in a rule-based expert system. Modifying the behavior of a neural network means retraining it by feeding it carefully selected data.

Because of their computational inefficiency, neural networks may not be applicable for a business' real-time customer-support functions. However, they are nonetheless attractive for decision-support applications because of their ability to generate rules that are refined with experience or training. Another advantage of neural networks is their relatively high resistance to inevitable errors in customer data. A neural network can usually identify patterns in customer data even if there are occasional mismatches in input and output data. In addition, unlike rule-based systems, which are limited to a specific domain, the same neural network design can be used in a variety of areas.

***Genetic algorithms.*** Genetic algorithm programming is another approach to reducing the complexity in customer data because it can identify patterns in what otherwise may appear to be unrelated information. Genetic algorithms are so named because they are modeled after the processes of evolution, mutation, and crossover that occur in genetics. They can be used to identify patterns or solutions through a mechanism that allows only the fittest solutions to survive and have offspring. This "survival of the fittest" approach uses a random selection of solutions and determines, within each generation, which solutions should survive into the next generation. The subjective or problem-specific component of a genetic algorithm is defining the fitness function, which measures a pattern's fitness to survive as a parent in the next generation.

Although genetic algorithm programming is a powerful approach, there is a tradeoff between the computational time required to find a pattern and the certainty in the resulting pattern match. It might take 100 generations of mutating, breeding, and spawning new solutions to discover that the customer's sex is related to product purchases, and another 10,000 generations to discover patterns in males of various ages. In other words, genetic algorithms, like neural networks, are better suited for making off-line business decisions and determining how to personalize a customer's Web experience than for real-time customer support.

# Bots and Intelligent Agents

An emotionally intelligent interface can be thought of as a life-form with memory and logic—perhaps even a semblance of intellect—that isn't complete without a corpus or some other way of effecting change in its environment. Bots, software versions of mechanical robots, are one approach to creating emotionally intelligent interfaces for Web sites. The term bot, short for robot, is derived from the Czech word robota, meaning work. Bots, which predate the Web, are autonomous programs that project intelligence and a personality, and usually perform a service. Bots don't have any innate intelligence, but, as the definition suggests, the viewer should form the impression that the bot nonetheless is operating under some form of intelligent control. Since one definition of intelligence is simply the ability to adapt, customers may deem a program that adapts to a customer's actions on a Web site as intelligent. Similarly, a bot may not have a personality, but what is important is that the viewer perceives some sort of human behavior in the bot. This can be derived from complex back-end processing, or simply by anthropomorphizing the bot in some way. Bots are autonomous in that they can do their work without direct supervision. It may help to think of a bot as an expert system with an attitude.

Intelligent agents, in contrast to bots, are servile automatons. Agents take directions, such as "Find the best price for golf clubs on the Web" and return with answers. In other words, agents are gofers; they do what they're told. An intelligent agent is closely related to a bot in that it gives the impression that it is operating under intelligent control. For example, some agents can improve their performance with experience. Agents, intelligent or not, don't project a personality, and always perform a service. Despite these differences between bots and Intelligent Agents, there is considerable overlap in the technologies. As such, the terms bot and intelligent agent are often used synonymously. To avoid further confusion, the term bot will be used for both bots and intelligent agents in the following discussions.

Bots are usually categorized on the basis of their functionality. For example, a very important form of bot on the Web is a spider, an agent that travels from one hyperlink to the next, retrieving HTML documents along the way, and indexing the information it finds in them. The Lycos spider was one of the first bots used to compile a list of URLs that form the heart of the Lycos search engine. Similarly, shopping bots crawl from one site to another, compiling databases of products available through online stores. Bots also have utility in data mining operations. Like the process of cluster analysis and the use of neural networks described earlier, bots tirelessly comb through the Web in search of patterns in data. Furthermore, bots can perfect searches of the Web on their own, saving customers countless hours of frustration.

Other types of bots that can be developed to interact with customers include game bots, mail bots, news bots, search bots, stock bots, fun bots, and, most importantly, chatter bots. Game bots can play—and win—against human players, or assist them in winning a game. Some would argue that playing the stock market is a game, and one that customers are keen to win. Mail bots automatically filter email and perform other routine email functions. News bots can be used to create a custom newspaper from newspapers around the world. Search bots comb the Web for information. For example, LawCrawler (http://lawcrawler.findlaw.com) combines a search bot with the AltaVista search engine to create legal Web searches. Stock bots monitor stocks and can email customers with any change in prices or trends, or press releases. Fun bots play games, using virtual environments, predictions, and virtual reality characters.

The first bot, Eliza (http://botspot.internet.com/bot/description.html), developed in the mid-1960s, is an example of a chatter bot. A typical dialogue between Eliza and a woman would look like this:

Woman: *Did you know that you talk like my mother?*
Eliza: *Who else is in your family?*
Woman: *Rosalind.*

Eliza: *Please go on.*
Woman: *Can you help me?*
Eliza: *Why do you ask?*

Eliza uses the woman's answers and simple pattern recognition algorithms to formulate yet another question, and the process continues until the woman terminates the conversation. Although subsequent chatter bots can engage in much more realistic conversations, Eliza can give the impression of a controlling intelligence, even though there is none.

In addition to simply carrying on a conversation, chatter bots can also be much more goal directed, as when they're used in customer support. As a virtual customer support representative, the chatter bot need not continue what can be an inane conversation, but can assist the customer in resolving some problem. Like rule-based expert systems, the biggest deficit in bot technology is that bots don't know what they don't know. They can detect words and phrases they don't understand, however, which is often good enough. When a chatter bot can't recognize a question or statement, it can be used to pass customers over to a human customer representative or another bot.

In addition to generating text-based dialogues, bots can exhibit appropriate facial expressions, and can be configured to carry on a relatively decent conversation, with or without voice recognition or synthetic speech. For example, Virtual Personalities, Inc. (http://vperson.com) markets verbally interactive characters called Verbots™. These bots combine plain English understanding and real-time facial animation. *Avatars*, graphical representations of humans that are intended to interact with other human representations, can also be under bot control, especially in game situations. (See Figure 5.3.) However, even chatter bots without anthropomorphic graphics can be used as a customer-friendly alternative to excessively long lists of FAQs posted on a Web site.

Unlike lists of FAQs, bots can help a business build customer trust and loyalty. For example, Massachusetts General Hospital uses a chatter bot interface on its Anesthesia and Critical Care Web site (www.etherdome.org) to help recruit applicants to its residency program. Resident applicants can find out about life in the Boston area, program specifics, and other information in an informal, conversational setting.

In addition to customer support, bots are being used in testing and education. Simulated social encounters, whether for sales training or medical diagnoses, are all possible with bot technologies. For example, Medical Learning Company, Inc. (www.FamilyPractice.com) creates

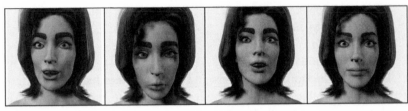

*Figure 5.3    Emotive states from a bot-based simulated patient encounter.*

bots that simulate patient encounters for testing physicians. An exchange between Mary, a simulated patient (bot), and a clinician (MD) follows:

MD: *Hello.*
Bot (smiling): *Hello.*

MD: *How's it going?*
Bot (smiling): *Oh, pretty good, doc, I'm just here for a little tune-up.*

MD: *What seems to be the problem?*
Bot (straight-faced): *Well, I'm tired and I've been losing a lot of weight lately.*

MD: *How much weight have you lost?*
Bot (concerned): *I've lost about three pounds in the past month.*

MD: *How's your vision?*
Bot (straight-faced): *My vision is fine, but I do wear reading glasses.*

MD: *Any recent changes in your vision?*
Bot (straight-faced): *No.*

MD: *Tell me about your sex life.*
Bot (sheepish): *It's okay, but it could always be better.*

MD: *How's your appetite?*
Bot (concerned): *Funny you should ask; it seems as though I'm always hungry.*

MD: *How frequently do you urinate?*
Bot (concerned): *Now that you mention it, I've had to go to the bathroom a lot lately.*

MD: *Are you drinking enough water?*
Bot (straight faced): *Well, it seems as though I'm thirsty all of the time, even though I do drink enough water.*

MD: *Have you noticed any blood in your urine?*
Bot (indifferent): *No, never.*

The interchange can be text only, or, with voice recognition and synthesis software, through bidirectional, conversational speech. In this context, an anthropomorphic interface immediately reduces the barriers between the patient and the physician, in part because the use of the interface is obvious without instruction. For example, the average adult woman is probably an expert on human–human interactions and on everyday physics. As long as an interface abides by these guidelines and her expectations, she doesn't need any instruction. It's when the interface deviates from what she would expect in an ordinary conversation that confusion results, and she many need some guidance.

***Issues with emotionally intelligent interfaces.*** Creating an Emotionally Intelligent Interface for a Web site involves much more than simply acquiring a data warehouse full of customer information, expert systems and other artificial intelligence techniques to analyze the data, and an army of bots—anthropomorphic or otherwise—to converse with customers. There are still soft issues, such as managing customer expectations and how to connect with the customer, thereby planting the seeds of an emotional bond.

The trouble with using almost lifelike, anthropomorphic figures in Emotionally Intelligent Interface designs is that customers may assume a higher level of intelligence, interactivity, and service potential than a Web site can actually provide. Although the latest generation of chatter bots can seem surprisingly intelligent, most are actually sophisticated parrot programs, echoing information back to the user, modified by predetermined content from the chatter bot developers. Some day, truly intelligent programs will be able to combine new input with databases, formulate conclusions, and offer new, creative ideas. For now, however, faced with a lifelike character, some customers may expect or even demand human-like intelligence and understanding. Bots are simply not as adaptable or as trained as customer service representatives. However, they can act much more rapidly, sifting through large amounts of data in an instant. Fortunately, in many situations, response time is everything.

Connecting with customers means paying attention to issues such as the personality of a Web site from the customer's culture and perspective. These issues are critical because the characteristics of the Web–customer interface, the ease of use, logic, and "personality," shouldn't happen by chance or receive attention as an afterthought, but intentionally reflect the mission of a company. Consider, for example, Microsoft's introduction of

Bob, an attempt at an emotional interface, in 1995. Bob bombed for a number of reasons, including its personality. Many critics found Bob condescending, patronizing, and an insult to the intelligence of the user. The unfortunate failure of Microsoft's Bob underscores the fact that anthropomorphized interfaces aren't necessarily emotionally intelligent. This is especially true when they don't cater to the customer's emotional needs or when they neglect the customer's perspective. Consider, for example, potential customers who might be blind, handicapped in some other way, or who don't read or speak English as their primary language.

## Localization and Internalization

Because the Web, like the telephone, extends a business' reach around the globe, it provides the business with an opportunity to expand its market. If the business' plans include competing in the global economy, management will have to extend considerations of customer needs and preferences past immediate experience. It will have to invest resources into *internalization*, matching its site to the language and culture of its customers, and localization, translating its site for the language and culture of a specific locale. For example, it's important for businesses to be attuned to the significance of certain colors that may offend and certain phrases that may be too confusing when translated from English in the Asian markets, and to localize parts of Web sites to suit Japanese and Korean customers. To maximize effectiveness in communicating with offshore customers, the presentation of textual information should be such that the level of sophistication suits the reader's needs, background, and familiarity with the products and services.

Since most of the world is non–English-speaking, preparing a Web site for a global market will involve selecting character sets; determining the most appropriate numeric formats, including dates; modifying English-based searching routines to work with non-English text; and dealing with currency, sales tax calculations, and a variety of potentially confusing address formats. The Web development team will have to be certain the character sets needed by the site are available. In addition, something as simple as the sorting order of addresses in a scrolling text field can cause confusion. Sorting order can be language-specific because of characters such as ô, umlaut, and ñ. For example, in English, sorting "côte" will follow "Czech," but if the locale is French, "côte" should follow "cote."

Similarly, currency can be displayed as $100.00, with cents following the decimal point in the United States, whereas a comma is interpreted as a numeric separator for the deutschmark. One hundred Italian lira are expressed as Lit. 100, without a decimal. Sales tax calculations can be complicated, with European VAT, for example. Address formats are country specific. In Italy, for example, the street number follows the name of the street, and the postal code precedes the name of the city and province. Even dates, if improperly formatted, can give an impression of a "foreign presence," and subliminally distance the customer from a site. For example, in Germany, 1/2/01 would be interpreted as February 1, 2001; in the United States, it would be interpreted as January 2, 2001.

# Profiling

To develop a relationship with customers, the management of a business needs a good idea of where customers are coming from. With this data, management can present itself in a way that customers can relate to. Although this is obvious with international customers, it's true of all customers, even if they live and work in the same town as the business. Hence the importance of generating a customer profile for all customers. Profiling (see Figure 5.4) is the process of taking a few key customer data points, such as name, occupation, age, and address, and generating best guesses about other characteristics. The probability of guesses' being true depends on the techniques used to assign traits to customers, and on the nature and amount of information available. For example, customer data are rarely accurate or complete. A single customer may be registered multiple times in a Web visitor log, and appear as several customers. These and other common errors highlight the importance of cleaning customer data before it is included in a data warehouse.

A profiler can be thought of as a probability matrix. For example, given the customer's name, there's a good chance that someone can guess the customer's sex as well, unless the names aren't familiar to whoever established the criteria for naming. For example, in English-speaking countries, "Jane" is probably female and "John" is probably male, each with a high degree of likelihood. Nicknames, unfamiliar names from non-American cultures, and otherwise ambiguous names can diminish the likelihood of a proper classification. For example, "Jae," a popular name for Korean males, may be mistaken for the name of a female in the United States.

Similarly, given a customer's occupation, it's possible to make an educated guess, within a range of certainty, about his income. If nothing else, a business can get a good qualitative estimate of a customer's potential purchasing power from his occupation. Professionals are

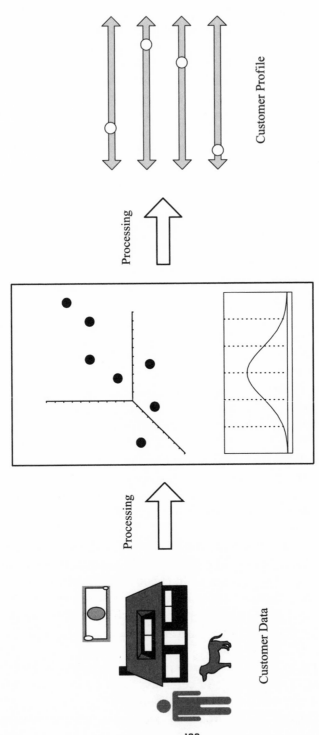

Customer Profile

Processing

Customer Profiler

Processing

Customer Data

*Figure 5.4 Customer profiling involves making best guesses from known customer data.*

more likely to have higher incomes than bus drivers, for example. Given the customer's age and occupation, it's possible further to refine the estimate of his likely worth, salary, and likelihood of purchasing a product or services. For example, a 45-year-old physician is likely to have much more money for investment purposes than would a 23-year-old recent college graduate.

Furthermore, a customer's address may provide information on everything from a customer's likely political affiliation to her religion. For example, some suburbs of Boston are known for their public school systems, and well-to-do families with school-age children tend to settle there. Other suburbs are known for affordable housing for single professionals. These and other data are available from the national census and other readily available sources.

Ultimately, a sampling of customer information can be used to determine the likely demand for a company's products and services and suggest steps the company might take to foster customer loyalty. For example, if a business has the ability to modify the personality of its Web site to suit that of potential customers, making an educated guess about the customer's profile can have huge economic consequences. If a company is in the business of selling luxury sailboats, then it probably isn't going to have much luck with fast-food servers in North Dakota.

## Looking Ahead

The days of basic Web "brochureware" are over. Customers expect not only quality graphics and catchy screens, but relevant interactivity and service. Whether companies use bots and Intelligent Agents, or human customer service representatives, their goal should be to build customer loyalty for a Web site by providing prioritized content and personalized customer interactions with minimum delay. If companies do everything reasonable to create an emotional bond between a business and its customers, such as providing a high level of responsiveness, customers will repeatedly return to a Web site for business. In the next chapter, we'll look at the likely trajectory of technologies relevant to developing Emotionally Intelligent Interfaces, and how EII techniques are being applied today.

## Executive Summary

To reap the benefits of the Web as a touch point that provides a company with an opportunity to further customer relationships, the company must go beyond a simple marketing veneer. To personalize a customer's Web experience, companies will need to endow their sites with memory and some type of intelligence.

The memory component of an ideal site, a data warehouse, provides a central repository for all business and customer-relevant data. Since a data warehouse draws upon data throughout an organization and on different hardware platforms, it can save management time in making key business decisions, as well as support real-time customer service functions.

The intelligence component of a site can be developed through a number of statistical or artificial intelligence techniques. Cluster analysis is a relatively efficient process for searching for patterns in customer data. Rule-based expert systems, neural networks, and genetic algorithm programming have various strengths and weaknesses relating to the quality of data and the processing time available. For example, rule-based systems are easy to construct and execute rapidly. Neural networks are resistant to errors in the data. Genetic algorithm programs, like neural networks, can search through vast amounts of customer data and arrive at one—but not necessarily the best—solution to patterns in customer data.

Bots and intelligent agents, akin to expert systems entrapped behind a veneer of plain English text understanding or natural language processing, can create an emotive dialogue between customers and a Web site. However, when anthropomorphic interfaces are used, the current level of graphic rendering is so high that customers may expect more than the site can deliver. Success at this stage of development entails managing customer expectations.

Internalization and localization will be key issues in the overall Web design if management plans to expand the business overseas. Profiling can give management a better idea of what customers want and need, even if the customer base is limited to the business' immediate geographical area.

## Technological Trajectory

*Our imagination is our
preview of coming attractions.*
Albert Einstein

I t's hard to imagine, but when the telephone was first introduced to American business executives, many actually signed up for classes to learn the intricacies of operating and troubleshooting the new tool. For example, when the connection became too noisy with intermittent static, they were trained to rap the receiver of those early black rotary dial phones sharply with the palms of their hands. To the executives, this process, which was intended to unpack the carbon granules in the phone's microphone element, was like magic. In contrast, today, even Web-enabled cellular phones, which are infinitely more sophisticated than the first commercial telephones, are mere appliances in the hands of technophobic executives. What's more, the communications infrastructure that supports cellular phones, which is itself orders of magnitude greater in functionality, complexity, and scope than that in the early analog phone system, is virtually invisible.

Some people believe that everyday computers are making employees easier to use by corporate America. After all, a significant portion of the productivity increase attributed to computer technology may be due to people's using technology to work longer hours. Answering work-related email at home can take an hour or more every day. Others take the stance that people are making computers easier to use, for personal and business purposes. Whether the truth is one of these extreme views or somewhere in between, it's clear that distributed, interconnected data and computational resources will continue to play an increasingly important role in the future of business and personal life. Regardless of the attitude someone takes toward the trajectory of technology, they can't help but acknowledge their reliance on computer technology. It seems that every few months there is another computer virus scare that ends up costing businesses across the globe millions of dollars in lost productivity.

The communications medium called the Web is maturing, moving from a free-for-all, minimally policed environment to something else. Although the end-point is virtually impossible to predict, it's obvious that the Web will continue to evolve, at least for the foreseeable future. It will undoubtedly continue to converge with other technologies and diverge into niche areas, just as the telephone, fax, television, and other business touch points have evolved since their inception. The initial stages of this convergence are obvious within several industries. For example, the America Online and Time Warner merger signifies the convergence of the entertainment and communications technology industries. Web phones are blurring the lines between the Web and traditional telephone carriers. Game console manufacturers, such as Sony and Microsoft, are introducing game hardware with DVD and built-in, high-speed Internet capabilities, further blurring the line between education and entertainment.

The most likely advances in the field of information technology can be categorized as either assisting in the creation and capture of data or modifying the process of data dissemination and utilization. That is, technology that either makes data, moves them around, or both. As illustrated in Figure 6.1, the data creation and capture category includes voice recognition and digital imaging. Technologies for data dissemination and utilization include the Web, cell phones, pagers, and other wireless devices.

This chapter explores the potential trajectory of these and other technologies that will likely have a direct bearing on the success of any Web presence. This book is not directly about creating a successful Web presence. It's about having a responsive, personal Web presence to

PROJECTED INFORMATION TECHNOLOGY ADVANCES

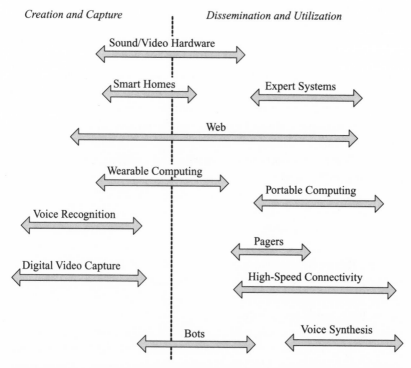

***Figure 6.1*** *Likely information technology advances can be categorized as primarily related to either data creation and capture or data dissemination and utilization. Note that the Web falls into both camps.*

increase customer retention and therefore lead to success. In particular, the focus is on technologies that will most enable a business to provide personalized customer support, including the creation of emotionally intelligent interfaces. But first, let's do a little time travel to the recent past and a few possible futures.

# It's the Law

Pick up any computer trade magazine, and it has the same information on the front cover: news on faster processors; thinner, larger displays; lighter portables; higher-resolution scanners and cameras; lower prices; new standards for peripherals, networks, and the Internet; more feature-packed software; and new peripherals. Given the dozens of computer magazines that have managed to survive over the past decade in spite of the resources available on the Web, it's clear that there is sufficient consumer appetite for new technology to keep the hardware and software advertisers happy.

It seems impossible, but the computer industry is constantly inventing more powerful solutions for the creation, capture, storage, manipulation, transport, and exchange of information. Even more remarkable is the expectation that these technology offerings will continue to develop at a nearly exponential rate, based on several laws attributed to visionaries in Silicon Valley. There's the oft-cited *Moore's law*, named after Gordon Moore, the former chairman of Intel, which states that the number of transistors that can be placed in an integrated circuit of any given size will double every twenty-four months. Then there's *Metcalfe's law* (named after Bob Metcalfe, inventor of Ethernet), the prevailing measure of the Internet's worth. Metcalfe's law, which is more difficult to quantify, states that the prevailing measure of the value of the Internet is a function of n-squared, where "n" is the number of individuals connected. More recently, *Brown's law*, after John Brown of Xerox PARC, asserts that the power of the Internet grows as a function of $2^n$, which represents the number of possible communities that can form with "n" people.

Whether these predictions and observations are ultimately regarded as laws or simply heuristics, they have an effect on the consciousness of both consumers and producers of computer technology. For example, software developers, such as those who work on voice recognition systems, games, and 3-D rendering environments, all assume that by the time the software they're working on hits the market, their customers will be using hardware at least twice as fast and probably less expensive than their development platform. When hardware is cheap and fast, developers are less constrained by code efficiency or size. What's the problem with a bloated software package when multi-gigabyte hard drives are inexpensive? Why should programmers spend weeks optimizing code to execute ten percent faster when faster processors are so affordable?

Unfortunately, there has yet to be a law advanced that predicts the bandwidth of the Internet in such a positive light. In this context, a law would be most important if it accurately predicted continually increasing Internet bandwidth, especially as it relates to the bandwidth available at the computer-to-Internet connection. There have been various predictions, some stating that the Internet will have excess bandwidth soon, owing to the investment in the fiber backbone. Others predict saturation of the Internet within a few years, even with a new national backbone and direct satellite links.

All the laws proposed for the evolution of technology over the next few years take a back seat to economic Darwinism. That is, to survive in the market, a business isn't going to be affected by Moore's law as much as it will be by changes in the federal tax laws, interest rates, and the whims of customers. There will always be outside pressures to which the business will have to adapt if it's going to survive. Despite the storm, businesses will have to focus on quality, price, or their ability to deliver, and make their customers happy in the process. The fastest CPU on the market won't do a company any good if it can't convince customers to enter into a business relationship—and recommend to their associates that they do the same.

# Great Expectations

In C. Clarke's *3001: The Final Odyssey*, the main character is a modern-day Rip Van Winkle rescued from a thousand-year sleep to discover himself in a nearly incomprehensible world of 3001 A.D. Surprisingly, the greatest departure from current reality isn't nano-technology, cortical implants, or space travel, but rather the attitudes and interactions of the Earth's future inhabitants. Virtually all the technology that Clarke describes is conceivable today. What is remarkable from a current perspective is that while humans in 3001 are immersed in technology, they are not interrupted by it. The technology that swaddles them doesn't carry with it an expected sense of awe; they don't even seem to notice it. This attitude may be in part because they don't interact with or think about mice, keyboards, or PDAs, but with what most people would consider everyday objects. In their time, acquiring information with the use of a keyboard makes about as much sense as it would for someone today to interface a keyboard with a bar of soap to take a bath.

Clarke's vision provides one possible way technology could evolve to serve us, or at least meet some of our perceived needs. Following this line of thought, information technology will become even more ubiquitous than it is today, to the extent that it will permeate virtually every aspect of life. Eventually, people won't even be able to hide from the scrutiny of the government or some corporation in their own homes. What they buy, eat, and do, and whom they meet will all be cataloged for possible review.

While some people might consider this an extreme invasion of privacy, Clarke's inhabitants of Earth in 3001 don't seem to mind. They are willing to sacrifice their individuality—if only subconsciously—in order to enjoy the benefits that technology offers. If a businessman uses a cell phone, he is in a similar situation—that of being forced to trade one freedom for another. Not only can the FBI track his exact location whenever he uses his cell phone, but several government agencies and his phone carrier may compile detailed records of whom the business-man calls, when, and how long he talks. By using his cell phone, the businessman is tacitly agreeing to trade his privacy for his freedom to communicate with whomever he wants, whenever he wants—for a price. That said, there are companies in eCommerce that will use the same technology to help the businessman locate, for example, the near-est service station or golf course.

# Let Your Imagination Soar

The typical, modern knowledge worker—an executive or professional who creates and moves thoughts and words for a living, enjoys a lifestyle derived in part from ubiquitous and, for the most part, afford-able information technologies. Cell phones, ultra-portable computers, wireless Internet access, high-capacity data storage devices, and per-sonal digital assistants are all part of his work arsenal.

Imagine the possibilities of a ubiquitous Web of personal informa-tion at a woman's fingertips. How could it completely, and yet almost imperceptibly, transform her life—and create a multitude of business opportunities? Not only would the woman's information be of personal interest to her, and perhaps to her physician and employer or board of directors, but also to hundreds of future businesses that would repur-pose her data.

Visualize the future Web-enabled smart home, outfitted with the lat-est in entertainment and information electronics. Software of every variety, from games to movies, is downloaded from the Web in seconds. Room cameras, together with instrumented floor tiles that detect weight and movement, control the lights, temperature, and appliances. The Web-enabled refrigerator tracks the shelf life of everything inside and determines what to add to a Web-based shopping list. Similarly, the other Web-enabled appliances capture and distribute data on activity, diet, and habits without any conscious effort on the woman's part, or any change in the way she currently lives or works.

Web-enabled objects, from cups, bowls, and eating utensils, to shoes, clothing, and jewelry, collect data such as heart rate, respiration, blood pressure, and diet. The woman's shoe inserts capture data on impact, mileage, and pace of her travels, and her chair records how long she's been working and warns her to sit up straight if she's slouching.

Everything and everyone the woman comes into contact with is cataloged and categorized. That means no more forgetting names or phone numbers, since she can exchange name, address, and other demographic information with a handshake. Similarly, every time she handles a piece of food, or touches an appliance, the transaction is recorded.

Consider how painless and effortless nutrition tracking could be. When the woman has a bowl of cereal for breakfast, the amount of cereal and milk that she consumes is recorded. Similarly, when she eats out, data collected from the woman's utensils and the dinnerware calculate what she's ingested. With her exact nutrient intake known from minute to minute, her local grocery distribution center can be notified of exactly what should be included in the woman's next order. By exploring her weight and caloric intake trajectory, she'll know—along with her physician and perhaps the marketing director of a diet supply company—whether her personal RDA has been satisfied, and how her diet is progressing.

Aside from the obvious efficiency and lifestyle implications of automatic nutrition tracking, including freedom from compiling shopping lists, calorie counting, or budgeting, there are medical, legal, and right-to-privacy issues as well. For example, if a man is in great shape, counting calories or the amount of saturated fat or sodium in his diet may seem inconsequential. However, if he's a diabetic, has a family history of heart disease, or suffered a heart attack in the past, these seemingly inconsequential data could be used to extend his life by several years and to avoid costly medical care. Similarly, since the man could exchange viruses and pathogens through direct physical contact, it may be necessary from a public health perspective to know every person he's been in contact with. From a legal perspective, the information might be useful in court, providing evidence of whom he was with, and where, on a specific date. The context could range from a casual meeting to casual sex or even murder. Of course, these illustrations ignore the obvious invasion-of-privacy issues involved in collecting and disseminating what most people would consider very personal data.

These ideas aren't as far-fetched as they might seem. For example, Polar, Inc. (www.polar.fi) is one of several companies that market heart rate monitors for casual and professional athletes. The monitors, which look like ordinary digital watches, capture information from an athlete's heart through a thin band that straps around his chest. He can go for a run or attend an aerobics class and then download his heart rate data into his home computer or laptop. The athlete can then analyze the data, including his recovery time and maximum heart rate, and plan the optimum duration and pace of his next exercise routine in order to reach his fitness or performance goals.

There are a variety of similar, ultra-portable, sports-specific physiological monitoring devices made for cyclists, rowers, and other sports enthusiasts that are designed to capture blood lactic acid, torque, and other data for later analysis on a desktop computer. Although most of these monitoring devices download data through a cradle or infrared beam, the data download process could be made even simpler if the monitoring device automatically put in a call through a woman's cell phone to deposit the information on the Web. The information could be delivered to a Web-based database, which could be accessed by the woman or her physician. Information the woman gathers through her own efforts could be combined with data from, for example, a medical kiosk in her local mall, to create a more complete picture of her health. It seems inevitable that, with time, the term "personal network" will come to mean the network of the woman's watch, shoes, personal digital assistant, and clothes, not the tangled mess in her cubicle or home office.

# Digital Cloning

Once a customer's personal data have been captured, the universe of possible applications is nearly infinite. Described below are only a few of the many possibilities associated with digital cloning, from both consumer and business perspectives. In reviewing the applications of digital cloning, it's important to realize that every consumer application is mirrored by one or more business opportunities.

*Consumer implications.* From the consumer's perspective, digital cloning represents a host of possibilities, from personal simulations that have medical implications to visualization tools, time capsules, resurrecting ancestors, education and training, and digital surrogates. These possibilities are described in more detail below.

*Creating personal simulations.* With his Web-based health status database, including information on his diet, exercise routine, and medical status, a man can play the ultimate game of "what if" with his life. With a digital clone—a simulation of the man's physical self, instantiated with his current medical status information—he could ask, for example: What would be the effect on his weight and blood pressure if he took up tennis for a few months? What would be the likelihood of a knee injury if he started running? If he has that bypass operation, how long will it be before he can go sailing again?

Imagine the man's personal health-state simulation, a 3-D projection of the man, modeled on his personal data, days, weeks, months, or years into the future. He can see the result of today's or next week's actions or inactions, and project the results, in the form of a 3-D rendering of himself, into the future. That extra piece of pie every week, or that extra set of sit-ups at the gym, may have greater meaning when he can visualize the results in his girth over months or even years. Similarly, if the man is a diabetic, he could see firsthand how failure to take his medicines or follow his diet could result in deterioration of his vision. The man could view an image of the Empire State Building, for example, as it might appear through his future diseased eyes. Using the same approach, the result of a surgical procedure could be illustrated with an internal view of the organs involved and the most likely outcome of the surgery.

***Providing visualization tools.***  Using a personalized 3-D model to communicate physical or medical findings and to visualize the effects of diet or clinical intervention is a very powerful technique. Unlike an incomprehensible list of laboratory values, a man can probably relate to an image of himself in various health states, even if it is somewhat stylized. It's one thing to have the man's physician tell him that he has to lose ten pounds, and quite another to see himself, fit and trim, in the future. As most athletes know, positive visualization is key to winning; if it can be visualized, it can be achieved.

The use of personal visualization on a Web site interface is illustrated by Figure 6.2, which shows the Lands' End Personal Model (www.Landsend.com) that was introduced in Chapter 1. A Web-enabled 3-D rendering program generates the personal model, which hints at the eventual power of *clone bots* in affecting customer loyalty. To create a personal model, a woman enters her personal physical parameters, including height, weight, hair color, hairstyle, and skin tone, and a 3-D representation of her description appears in her Web browser. She can then pick items from the Lands' End wardrobe and see for herself how they would look on her.

The model isn't perfect, but it's close enough to allow the woman to visualize herself. Future versions will likely provide higher resolution and more realistic models, perhaps incorporating the customer's actual features that have been extracted from a digital photograph. Someone at Lands' End apparently realizes that customers who can visualize themselves wearing Lands' End clothing end up buying Lands' End clothing. A supermodel wearing a dress has much less of an impact on woman than seeing herself as the world would see her wearing that

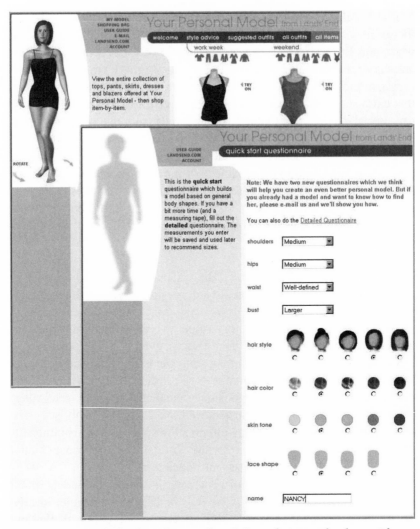

*Figure 6.2*   Lands' End combines online 3-D rendering technology with an Emotionally Intelligent Interface that allows the customer to create digital clones of themselves. Customers can visualize themselves wearing the products and sell themselves on those products. Permission granted by Lands' End, Inc.

same dress. The Personal Model represents personalized service that, by its very nature, creates an emotive bond with the customer. After all, that's a potential customer depicted on the screen.

*Creating time capsules.*   Digital cloning isn't limited to creating a 3-D representation of a woman that can be used like a modern Barbie doll, or even to creating a personalized physiological model that a man or his physician can use to explore the effect of a new exercise routine or drug on his physique or blood pressure. The real power will come from modeling, or at least simulating, a person's thoughts and personality.

Imagine that, every year on his birthday, a man answers a computer-based questionnaire of about a hundred items, for the purpose of creating a digital clone. The questions range from his religious beliefs, favorite activities, books, and movies, to his fears, thoughts about his job, what he's most proud of, and his top goals for the next year. In addition to these and other questions that might be of interest only to the man's family and perhaps historians, there could be additional questions that might find their way into his medical record, to be accessed by an emergency room clinician or perhaps a court of law. For example: if the man were found in a coma after being hit by a truck, and full recovery was virtually impossible, would he want medical intervention? The man's last will and testament and his living will may eventually be a digital clone, able to converse with attorneys and his family if he is ever incapacitated.

By answering these and other questions, the man would create a living diary of sorts, on his behalf, as well as for his children and their children. His responses to the questionnaire could be processed to create a chatter bot that reflects and represents his current personality and beliefs. With the appropriate data, the man's chatter bot could either answer questions outright, or guess what he would probably say if he were asked in person. Of course, the man wouldn't want his beliefs or other personal information in the hands of politicians, his neighbors, his employer, or his employees.

As a means of achieving immortality, it may become common practice for politicians, movie stars, famous writers, and others wanting to be remembered to commission chatter bot personalities. In the near future, sitting presidents may commission presidential chatter bots, accessible over the Web, which may be routinely interviewed in high school history classes. Candidates for public office—even at the local level—may commission chatter bots to answer questions about their positions on a variety of issues. Given enough valid information to create a personality profile, one could even conceive of resurrecting great religious figures, from Mohammed and Jesus to Buddha to God, in the form of chatter bots.

A man could enjoy interacting with his chatter bot for personal reasons. He could converse with a lifelike 3-D rendering of himself, looking back over 30 years, remembering what it was like when he was his teenage son's age, for example. Similarly, one of his children could ask the clone of the man's twentieth birthday about issues that the man may not be able to appreciate at fifty. The man's grandchildren could ask his digital clone to tell them a story before bedtime, and enjoy the man's wisdom and wit long after he's gone. The grandchildren would develop and benefit from a strong emotional bond with their grandfather to a degree that would have been impossible without chatter bot technology.

***Resurrecting ancestors.*** In addition to creating a digital sarcophagus, the same bot technology will soon be able to resurrect ancestors as well. A woman will be able to take an old black and white photograph of a deceased relative, say her grandfather, a character profile that she's created, and, if she has it, a sample of his voice, and have a conversation with her deceased grandfather the next morning—well, almost. The woman and her family could complete a detailed online questionnaire, including relevant quotes and personal correspondence, and this information would be fed into a personality profiler. The result is that her ancestor's chatter bot will produce realistic responses to any problems and questions addressed by the profile. With voice samples of her deceased relatives, and a voice recognition system on her computer, realistic conversations will be possible.

***Providing education and training.*** The digital cloning technique could be extended to include educational purposes. For example, consider the utility of an Abraham Lincoln or Henry VIII chatter bot, wearing period-correct clothing, in a history class. Students could ask Lincoln what he felt moments before his assassination. A Martin Luther King, Jr. chatter bot could recite his "I have a dream" speech, in 3-D, and then be available to students for questioning. Or consider creating chatter bots of a man's business associates at an upcoming negotiation. He could try different techniques of negotiation and explore the various what-if scenarios in a lifelike simulation. A human customer service representatives could use chatter bots of difficult customers for practice. On the other end of the spectrum of applications, a woman could throw verbal darts at a chatter bot of her employee, difficult client, or someone on her Board of Directors, and have the bot beg for mercy. Chatter bots could also be used in training employees, not just about customer service issues, but about improving their writing and speaking, and for instructing customers about products and services.

***Creating digital surrogates.*** At one time or another, most business professionals wish they could be in two places at the same time. If a woman is in the service industry, there often isn't a way to take on more

work or get more accomplished without hiring and training assistants—
or cloning herself. As the ultimate office assistant or stand-in, a digital
clone, a chatter bot with the woman's face and at least a modicum of
her knowledge, could triage email and other time consuming tasks.

Meetings on the Web or email conversations could occur between
the woman's digital clone and her colleagues, or even with another
bot. What's more, with bot-to-bot communications, her bot could
translate the other person's or bot's messages to better fit her pre-
ferred language, style, and level. As an anthropomorphosed language
assistant, the woman's bot could translate, for example, medicalese or
legalese into ordinary English that she can understand. Her physician's digital clone bot could even tell the woman's personal assistant
bot to send a message to her cell phone to remind the woman to take
her medication.

Consider how the woman's clone bot, used as a triage, could make
giving a live presentation over the Web to thousands of viewers easier
for both the woman and her audience. Imagine the woman's state as she
begins to review her address to her stockholders, and feel the inevitable
migration of butterflies toward her belly as the log-on count of participants peaks past 8,000. On the woman's view panel, she sees the demographics of her audience, by age, sex, education level, language, and
location. She's fully aware that the majority of overseas participants will
be using their clone bots as translators, replacing her obscure or technical words and phrases with localized, more readily understood terms, in
their native languages. As the woman faces the bidirectional video
panel, she's prepared to deliver her speech and to monitor the inevitable
questions as they are handled by her army of clone bots. Her clone bots,
which look and respond to questions just as she would, could handle all
but the most obtuse or ridiculous questions. With all this backup, the
woman is cool, calm, and ready to start her presentation.

As a surrogate, the woman's clone bot could have other uses as well.
It could interview potential employees or employers, for example. A
dating service could create a clone bot for her, which resides on its Web
site, ready to interact with other clone bots searching, for example, for
a tall, athletic blonde male with a fondness for Latin dancing. If she
were to interview a potential date's clone bot, the woman could ask it
questions she might not be comfortable asking the bot's owner on a first
or even second date.

***Business implications.***    So much for science fiction—which has a
sneaky way of becoming science fact overnight. What are the business
implications of the potential future of the Web and related information

technologies? In short, they're startling. Consider the amount of information that would be available from a smart home, and the value of that information to manufacturers of home appliances, online grocery delivery services, or producers of consumer goods.

Customer data are now so valuable that, in medicine, companies are giving physicians electronic medical record (EMR) systems—the programs that physicians use to keep track of their patients' medical status—worth thousands of dollars in exchange for patient and practice data. Similarly, online stores, such as Priceline.com, are offering heavy discounts on groceries in exchange for preference information.

Consider the value of knowing that a customer's supply of orange juice is running low in her refrigerator. As a service to the customer, does a business flash a banner ad for orange juice on her cell phone? If a company is in the business of restocking customer refrigerators when they're empty, how does it go about differentiating itself from the business one mouse-click away? Should the company use a chatter bot that appears on the various flat panel displays in the customer's house or at work, asking the customer to order more juice?

Similarly, what if the customer recently ran a "what-if" analysis of the combined effects of her consumption of calcium and phosphorous and her exercise program on her bone density and explored her likelihood of developing osteoporosis—a disease characterized by porous, fragile bones? Furthermore, what if the analysis suggested that she increase her calcium intake in order to reduce the risk of osteoporosis? What are the odds that a customer in this situation would be responsive to an ad for calcium-fortified orange juice? How much would that information be worth to an orange juice distribution company?

Given these expectations and predictions of vast business opportunities afforded by future Web-based technologies, how are they going to be realized? More important, how is a business going to capitalize on them? A lot of this also has to do with bandwidth, and broadband is fast approaching the consumer's homes. Broadband, wireless, and other technologies that can increase the bandwidth of the business-customer communications channel are enabling technologies, in the sense that they facilitate the possibilities discussed above. Clearly, in assessing the business opportunities that lie ahead, the first step is to follow the current trajectory of the Internet's infrastructure and recent developments in computer hardware and software, including taking a look at some of the commercial tools available today.

# Making It Happen

Reaching for the stars can be exciting, especially when there are wonders and new technologies creating new business opportunities around every bend. And yet, businesses have to keep their feet on the ground in order to provide their IS staffs with realistic visions of Web sites that can engender trust and loyalty in their customers. Looking at the present, what is the status of the tools and technologies available to make a business's dreams a reality? Although there are seemingly hundreds of new techniques and tools announced weekly, the most significant developments are in three areas: infrastructure, hardware, and software tools. These developments, and their potential to create new business opportunities, are described in more detail below.

*Infrastructure.*    A business can have the best data warehouse technology, the sharpest graphics, the smartest expert systems, and the most lifelike, responsive bots, but they're worthless if the infrastructure between the business and its customers won't reliably support the technology. The most important recent developments in Internet infrastructure are about increasing the bandwidth of the connection, especially to and from the customers' sites. Improvements in bandwidth through the use of DSL, cable modems, fiber to the home, and wireless communications are creating new business opportunities.

*Bandwidth.*    With a high-bandwidth connection, it suddenly becomes feasible for customers to download several megabytes of music or computer software from a Web site for immediate purchase. A high-bandwidth Internet connection also allows a business to offer streaming media, Web-based voice recognition, and highly interactive bot interfaces. Adequate bandwidth can make the difference between a talking head that looks as though it came from an old black and white martial arts movie, where English is poorly dubbed over Japanese or Chinese lip movements, and a lifelike, believable character. If a business plans to use video and other streaming media, it will need the appropriate player or client software, such as Apple's QuickTime, Macromedia's Flash, or RealNetwork's RealPlayer7, in addition to high-speed connectivity. In deciding which standard to choose, management will have to assess the capabilities of each environment with its own particular requirements in mind.

A high-bandwidth infrastructure also validates the Application Service Provider (ASP) model, in which customers run applications directly from a vendor's Web site. Databases, expert systems, and even graphic programs can all be run directly from a Web browser, without having the actual application on customers' computers. Because of the marginal cost of providing additional users with access to applications, vendors can offer ASP products at a fraction of the cost of traditional programs. For example, in medicine, ASP-delivered office practice systems are available at one-tenth the cost of local server-based systems offering the same functionality. Thanks to high-bandwidth connectivity to the Web, even the most complex applications can be shared with a virtually unlimited number of customers.

*Wireless.*    Wireless communications, with geographically limited intranets, are also a key component of the evolving Internet infrastructure. For example, store owners in mixed office and residential buildings are creating building-wide intranets to entice tenants to shop where they work or live. The threat of brain cancer notwithstanding, wireless communications, from cell phones to wireless Internet modems, is expanding. Wireless network connections are opening up new markets in personal computing devices. For example, in the futuristic scenarios discussed earlier, the data-aware jewelry and clothing are not tethered by massive cables, but rather the communications occurs through wireless technology.

The future of wireless communications can be seen by examining the new standards. For example, the Wireless Application Protocol, an emerging standard for the delivery of wireless information and telephony service, is being applied in mobile phones and other wireless appliances. Similarly, many companies are backing the Bluetooth communications standard (www.Bluetooth.com) for small–form-factor, low-cost, short-range radio links among mobile PCs, mobile phones and other portable devices. Imagine a woman's cell phone calling her refrigerator for a shopping list, or her cell phone contacting her PDA for a phone number. Thanks to new technologies and standards, cell phones, pagers, and other portable devices will never be the same.

*Hardware.*    As pointed out earlier, hardware capabilities seem to be increasing at breakneck speed every day. There doesn't seem to be an inherent limitation in desktop hardware, as far as access to the Web is concerned. There are, however, issues of standards, and several minor compatibility problems. For example, there are remnants of the Apple/Motorola versus Intel/Windows battle over the desktop, which Windows won. Some of the more interesting developments in the area of hardware pertain to the ergonomic component of the physical interface, especially alternatives to the standard mouse and keyboard and the desktop video display.

Hardware development relevant to emotionally intelligent interface design includes dedicated media-capture hardware for images and sound. For example, there are video cards, initially developed for the game industry, that can provide DVD-quality video on a desktop computer. In addition, the new generation of sound cards is capable of producing high-fidelity output that matches the ability of most stereo systems. Synthetic voices and pre-recorded human voices sound crisper and more natural than they do with previous sound output technologies. Since most sound cards double as sound capture devices, improvements in their DSP capabilities will translate into higher-quality speech recognition and higher-quality audio for playback through bots.

At the leading edge of interface hardware development is specialized input and output hardware than can make computer interactions much more realistic. For example, Motion Ware (www.vm3.com/motionware) uses galvanic stimulation of the vestibular system—that is, electronic stimulation that influences the user's sense of balance—to impart the sensation of motion. An electronic headband simulates the sense of motion by sending small electronic pulses to the area behind the wearer's ear that controls balance. On another front, Eye Control Technologies (www.eyecontrol.com) offers a system that bounces light off the back of a man's eye to determine where he is looking, much like the systems used in high-end consumer cameras and in targeting devices on some Army helicopters. With the eye control system, a man can interact with his computer by using his head movements to control cursor position while using intentional blinks to trigger mouse clicks. One day, patterns in electroencephalogram (EEG) signals may be harnessed to control computers as well.

Display hardware is also evolving at a rapid pace. For example, consider Sony's Glasstron (www.ita.sel.sony.com/products/av/glasstron/), a lightweight visor-type device with built-in headphones. This unit, which looks like a pair of glasses, provides a viewing experience analogous to a 52-inch monitor viewed from approximately six feet away. A "see-through function" electronically adjusts the transparency of the liquid crystal shutter to change the viewing environment, giving the wearer the impression, for example, of being in a cinema theater, or of watching a video screen hanging in mid-air. The Glasstron, or something like it, will usher in the eventual era of wearable, Web-aware computing. Another hardware development is eBooks, Palm Pilots on steroids, designed to download reading material from the Internet. The flexibility of the hardware form factor may be enough to entice customers to take a good look at the technology, much as the simple Palm Pilot virtually recreated the PDA market overnight.

*Software*   Advances in software tend to lag behind hardware, in terms of taking full advantage of the available options. This delay occurs because software developers generally have to wait for the hardware configuration to stabilize before they can fully debug, test, and deliver a final software product. Software developments in the areas of standards, data warehousing, expert-system architectures, graphics, and bots are all relevant to a company's Emotionally Intelligent Interface aspirations.

*Standards.*   Software standards are often partially defined by the underlying hardware limitations, and partially defined by whichever firm controls market share in a given technology area. When there isn't a clear market leader, standards tend to proliferate. For example, there is a potentially confusing array of standards available for sound transport over the Web, from DVD, MIDI, DLS, and streaming, to DSP filtering, Internet Voice Chat, DirectX 7, Dolby Surround, Q-sound, and CD Audio.

Some standards really have helped stabilize the Web. For example, Hypertext Markup Language (HTML) is the very fabric of the Web. However, even HTML is being pushed either to include or transform itself into other, more powerful standards. Extensible Markup Language or XML is being promoted as the best alternative to HTML. Whereas HTML is primarily a fixed formatting language, XML excels in dynamic content delivery, in part because it allows interactions across platforms that otherwise don't share common data formats. From an emotionally intelligent interface perspective, the ability to configure content dynamically is key to providing personalized Web content for customers. An interim standard, a combination of HTML with XML extensions, called Extensible Hypertext Markup Language or XHTML, may prove useful, since it allows backward compatibility with HTML-based Web sites.

*Data warehousing.*   As discussed in Chapter 5, data warehousing is in many ways a response to the "be careful of what you ask for; you might get it" saying. If a business is lucky enough to have a site that captures thousands or even millions of clicks a day, then the business may or may not have enough data on each customer to create a reasonable customer profile. What the business will have is a lot of user data. The challenge in data warehouse development is how to deal with very large, rapidly growing databases. There's so much data being captured from Web sites that there often isn't really time to figure out what to do with the data, other than stick it in a data warehouse. Because it often isn't clear, for example, at what granularity to save data or how long it should be kept, a typical data warehouse for a busy dotcom business is well past the 1 terabyte size. With so much data, the emphasis is on new architectures and software that simplify data warehouse design, as well as tools that provide increased performance; that is, an ability to work with increasingly large databases with faster searches.

Research into data warehousing architectures includes exploring alternatives to the relational DBMS model, such as the object-oriented model. In this model, complex structures are represented by composite objects, ones that contain other objects, allowing structures to be nested to any degree. For example, in an object-oriented world, the structure of a car contains an engine object, which contains cylinder objects. The major advantage of the object-oriented model is that it can be used to represent information in an easily understood or "natural" way, one that doesn't compromise flexibility.

From the performance perspective, data mining and analysis tools are being introduced that will make it feasible to search through terabyte-level databases. These tools will sift through the information to create a picture of who is using a Web site and offer a view of the way they use it. Other tools offer template data warehouse design, based on standard relational database architectures.

*Expert systems.* The trajectory in expert system development, or, more correctly, machine learning development, is toward hybrid systems. There are machine learning systems that incorporate the best aspects of rule-based expert systems, neural networks, and statistical methods in their design. The idea behind the hybrid approach is to use the strengths of each technology to nullify the inherent weaknesses of the others. For example, neural networks can't explain their reasoning, whereas the rule base of an expert system can be examined and modified if necessary. Neural networks are relatively immune to occasional errors in the data; in contrast, rule-based systems are not. By combining the two, a business can have a system that adapts to noisy data, and yet has a rule base that can be verified and more easily modified.

*Graphics.* The video entertainment and gaming industries are fueling rapid advances in the area of graphics creation software, especially applications for creating anthropomorphic characters. Action-packed video games and special effects in movies all have an almost insatiable demand for synthetic actors. Developments in these fields are typified by products like Metacreations Poser, LifeF/X, and Lipsinc's Mimic and Ventriloquist.

Metacreations Poser is a popular, entry-level anthropomorphic modeling environment that runs on ordinary desktop hardware. With Poser, a graphics artist can create full-body or facial close-up stills and animations that can be used as the visual basis of a virtual customer service representative. In addition, there are utilities, developed for the game industry, which can aid in creating more realistic characters. For example, Lipsinc, Inc. (www.lipsinc.com) offers Mimic, a utility for Poser, and Ventriloquist, a similar utility for more advanced 3-D rendering environments, that automate the process of lip-synching. These programs analyze a sound file, automatically identify the phonemes, and animate the character's mouth in synch with the spoken word. Like Poser, Mimic and Ventriloquist are intended to be used as a production tool to create canned sequences.

Whereas Poser and most other graphical development environments create fixed or canned images, LifeF/X (www.lifefx.com) creates virtual, photorealistic, animated talking head characters called Stand-Ins that speak in real time. In other words, LifeF/X can take the text output of a bot, for example, and not only synthesize the speech, but provide lip-synching, blinking, and eye movement. Lipsinc, Inc. is in the process of introducing two similar real-time environments, Talk Now and Talk Back, that can sample voice tracks coming in from the Web and generate the appropriate expressions. One of the strengths of LifeF/X technology is its ability to take a standard photograph, process it, and create a lifelike, talking, 3-D representation of the person in the photograph. LifeF/X is much more than a graphics creation program. It's a system designed to provide interactive, free-running, humanlike talking characters over the Web through relatively slow analog Internet connections by virtue of its proprietary playback technology. All of these tools have the potential to create a sense of realism. However, it's up to the development staff to employ the realism in an emotionally intelligent manner.

*Bots.*    Bots are hot. They are a growing area of software development, as anyone can tell from visiting BotSpot (www.BotSpot.com), the Internet clearinghouse for bots and intelligent agents. There are dozens of academic bot-related projects and a number of commercial products introduced weekly. Some bots, such as Zabaware's (www.Zabaware.com) Ultra Hal Representative (see Figure 6.3), are focused more on carrying on a conversation, without the data warehouse and other back-end processing required for customer support.

In commercial bot development related to customer support, activity is focused on three areas. The first is a hybrid, integrated approach

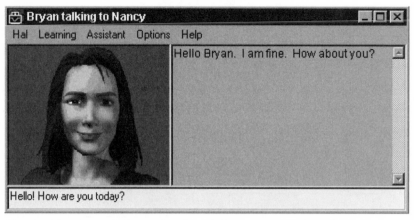

**Figure 6-3**   *A visual chatter bot from Zabaware responds with text and synthetic speech. Voice recognition is also supported. Permission granted from Zabaware, Inc.*

involving a mix of text-only chatter bots and live support. This approach to providing an Emotionally Intelligent Interface to a Web site is exemplified by Brightware, Inc. (www.Brightware.com). Brightware uses intelligent agents to converse with customers in real time over the Web and over email. If necessary, these automated services can be supplemented with live assistants. For example, Web-based customers can interact with Brightware's Web Assistance Bot. The responses created by the Web Assistance Bot are realistic and personalized, in part because the system incorporates customer data in the message. Complex inquiries or those acquiring immediate live interaction can be transferred to Brightware's Live Assistance. By providing a mix of intelligent agent triage and more expensive human backup, personalized, responsive customer service can be created without the cost of full-time support staff.

The second approach is to provide text-only chatter bots, without any emotive graphics. This approach to customer support is exemplified by NativeMinds (www.nativeminds.com), which offers vReps™, their version of virtual customer representatives to answer customer questions in real time. Like most chatter bots, vReps supports natural language customer queries (See Figure 6.4). The dialogue is text based, without the overhead—or emotive cues—of different graphical characters with each response.

The third major area of bot development activity is in creating chatter bots accompanied by images that convey appropriate emotional cues. Big Science Company, Inc. (www.BigScience.com), which markets

**Figure 6.4**    *Interface to NativeMinds virtual representative, Red. Red, like all of NativeMinds vReps™, converses with the customer in English using natural language processing (NLP) technology. Printed with permission from NativeMinds, a leading supplier of automated natural language customer service representatives for the Internet.*

Klones™, illustrates this third approach. Klones are chatter bots in the form of graphical characters that can converse with customers in plain English (see Figure 6.5). Like the service offered by Brightware, Inc., and NativeMinds vReps, Klones can be programmed to answer customers' questions about a company's products and services, and assist customers in problem solving. In addition, like Brightware's offerings, when faced with unanswerable questions or customers who demand immediate attention, Klones can transfer customers to call tracking, telephone callback, instant messaging, or email contact.

Brightware, NativeMinds, and BigScience Company are only three examples of the many commercial bot developments underway. They

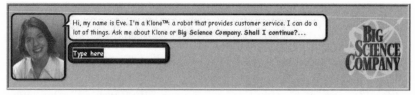

**Figure 6.5**    *Big Science Company offers virtual representatives called Klones™ that converse with customers in English. Responses are accompanied by emotionally appropriate still images of the Klone. The Eve Virtuel customer representative is used with permission from eGain Communications Corp.*

demonstrate, in varying degrees, the usefulness of applying bot technology to improve customer support, and provide a foundation for an emotional bond with customers. A business can work with products like these to populate its Web site with synthetic characters (whether text based or 3-D animations) that can converse with customers. Bots can assist customers in navigating through a site, selecting products, purchasing, and other routine tasks normally performed by human customer representatives. Unlike humans, however, these bots are available on an immediate, 24/7 basis, and, with sufficient customer data and a sufficiently rich data warehouse, can provide personal and personalized service. As some of these products demonstrate, if a bot can't handle a customer's problem, the customer can be automatically connected with a human representative, allowing a company to employ a smaller customer support staff while handling a larger volume of customers.

In evaluating the many commercial and academic bot offerings, the gold standard for bot responsiveness is, of course, a trained, courteous, motivated human customer service representative. In fact, just as telephone support service providers make 24/7 telephone support available for any product, there are Web equivalents that can provide live customer service, via the Web, to customers. One such example is LivePerson (www.LivePerson.com). In normal operation, customers click on a LivePerson link on a Web site to launch a window where a live customer service operator initiates a secure, one-on-one text chat. Because of the way LivePerson is configured, the chat window appears to reside on the company's server, giving customers the impression that the company, and not a third party, is providing the real-time customer service support. Innovative communications technology, together with trained human customer support representatives, is one approach to providing an emotionally intelligent interface to a Web site.

One level up from direct human phone support is computer-assisted email response, typified by Amazon.com, which handles customer complaints in a semi-automatic way. As the 20,000 or so emails come in every day, over 200 human operators quickly scan them, and then pull up a canned response from a library of about 1,400 pre-scripted remarks. The remarks are personalized for the recipient, using the customer's name and the appropriate book title, for example, and sent to the customer as a reply. Unlike bots, Amazon.com's human representatives can defer shipping charges, suggest alternative or replacement products, and, if appropriate, go beyond what's normally expected.

PeopleSupport, Inc. (www.peoplesupport.com) is another company that focuses more on the human touch than on bots for providing emotionally intelligent customer support. They specialize in live 24/7 online help through over 500 customer representatives called eReps™ that support one-on-one interactive chat, personalized email, telephone, and voice over the Internet. In addition to the human customer support, PeopleSupport provides searchable, interactive knowledge bases of FAQs that can be accessed without human intervention.

## Build or Buy

As the commercial bot systems illustrate, there's much more in creating an Emotionally Intelligent Interface than simply buying or building a bot. Even without addressing the complexity of the back-end processing and the data warehouse requirements, developing an integrated bot environment can be very resource intensive. To illustrate, consider the effort that typically goes into the development of the visually interactive components of a virtual customer service representative. First, the very process of picking the face of a business can be daunting. After all, this virtual customer representative embodies the entire Web site and, by extension, the entire company. Should the customer representative be male or female? Should he or she be of distinctive ethnic origin or something non-discernible? If male, should he have facial hair? How old should the virtual representative look? Are glasses appropriate? Sports jacket or pullover sweater? Long or short hair? Getting these decisions through a committee meeting can be daunting enough, and then there's the implementation issue.

Taking examples from the game developer community, virtual personality developers know that attractive people are treated better than unattractive people. Beautiful or handsome people are often thought to be more poised, independent, sociable, interesting, exciting, and even more sexual than their average looking counterparts. Unattractive super heroes and heroines are rare. Game developers know the importance of having a strong character, and of conveying its personality through body language and poses.

Then there's the need to deal with the unconscious attention to human physiology. For example, most people breathe about twelve times a minute, perhaps double that when they're excited or running up a flight of stairs. Eyes are important in an animated character. For example, when a customer talks to a customer representative in person, the customer unconsciously examines the exact gaze direction, border shape, eyelid movement, glint, and pupil size to gauge the representative's thoughts and emotions.

In order for virtual customer representative bots to convey complex human emotions through the use of animated graphics, they must have expressive, humanlike eyes. In this regard, graphical bot designers use certain heuristics based on human physiology. For example, it's normal to occasionally wink, blink, and nod, and to look around to get a sense of our surroundings when idle, with the eyes always leading any head motion. In addition, eyes always move in quick, darting movements, from one focal point to another. Even eye shape, as defined by eyelids and eyebrows, affects perceived expressions.

Consider the complexity of an appropriate blink. Blinks are important because we all blink periodically, with different events, and at various speeds. Automatic blinks occur rapidly when a woman moves her gaze from one focal point to another. Conscious blinks, such as in batting the eyelashes for flirting, take longer. Excessively long blinks confer an air of drowsiness. Exaggerated blinks suggest disbelief. Even the details of blinking have significance. For example, in normal blinks, the upper eyelid moves down to meet the lower eyelid. In contrast, in blinks of disbelief and sleepiness, both upper and lower eyelids move to meet in the center of the eye.

Pupil size also contains emotional cues. Although pupils normally respond to light, with smaller pupils in brighter light, they're also indicators of emotional status. If a woman likes what she sees, her pupils will get larger. For this reason, small pupils can look cold and menacing. Aware of this subconscious reaction, many photographers use dark rooms with flash to capture their subjects with wide, friendly pupils. Clearly, simply within the area of facial expressions, someone on the development staff will need an understanding of the subtleties involved in eye movements, as well as the nuances of lip-synching, or how and when to move the eyebrows in order to create an expressive face.

## Technology Wrap-Up

This chapter ends the section on the primary technologies for developing Emotionally Intelligent Interfaces. The discussion underlines the importance of the human-computer interface in establishing a meaningful dialogue between customers and a Web site, and the various tools and techniques that can be used to provide the "meat" behind the thin veneer of a pretty face. The next section will discuss how to integrate business and technology perspectives to create Emotionally Intelligent Interfaces and make a Web site a warm and fuzzy place for customers.

# Executive Summary

Constantly improving processor speeds and network connectivity, progress in ultra-miniaturization, the increasing popularity of the Web, and the permeation of computer technology in the very fabric of our society will continue to feed the growth of information technologies for the foreseeable future. The positive expectations surrounding the trajectory of the Web stem in part from the paths established by related technologies, such as the telephone, fax, and television. An overwhelming air of positive expectation is also established by the prevailing attitudes set by technology visionaries such as Moore, Metcalfe, and Brown.

At the current rate of computer-related technological development, it's often difficult to differentiate science fiction from economic forecasting. Current trends suggest that in the near future, our lifestyle will be even more profoundly and yet subtly affected by ubiquitous information technology. Data-aware, Web-enabled objects, appliances, and clothes will dramatically increase the amount of personal information available for practical uses that range from market analysis and diet planning to providing medical care. Digital cloning, creating lifelike, 3-D bots modeled after human physiology and personality, is only one of several application areas of this inevitable body of personal information.

All of these technological advances bring with them virtually unlimited business opportunities, from providing customers with "what-if" analyses of their personal health, to creating an automatic means of communicating customer needs to suppliers. Realizing the potential of the Web and related technologies is contingent upon developments in the areas of communications infrastructure, hardware, and software tools and standards. Assuming developments in these areas follow their current trajectories, affordable, off-the-shelf tools will soon be available, for example, for any business to create interactive virtual customer service representatives. However, whether a business decides to purchase a complete virtual customer system from an established vendor or create its own system depends on the business' goals, time constraints, and budget. In the end, it still comes down to providing excellent service and to finding some way to create an emotional bond between a business and its customers.

**3**

Part
**Putting It All Together**

## Leveraging Technology

*He that will not apply new remedies*
*must expect new evils,*
*for time is the greatest innovator.*
Francis Bacon

For many eCustomers, the Web is like an infinitely large shopping mall they have all to themselves. Although the absence of long lines at the checkout counter and the freedom from the hassles of parking are welcome, the lack of other shoppers and even salespeople can make it a lonely experience. For a social shopper—a woman who enjoys shopping with friends—looking for a product on the Web can be akin to going to a movie alone. The fun factor is missing, regardless of how great the movie is. On the other hand, if she's a mission shopper—she enters, extracts the goods, and then make her exit as soon as possible—then shopping on a highly structured Web site can be a welcome respite from the time-consuming task of searching the malls. In either case, even a potentially pesky salesperson can be a welcome sight when the woman simply can't find the product she's looking for.

A good salesperson knows how to satisfy both types of customers and keep an eye on the bottom line of her business. She also knows how to create a win–win scenario in which the customer gets the desired item, she receives her well-deserved commission, and her business makes a profit. Regardless of the product or service involved, a good salesperson knows how to use basic sales techniques—and her knowledge of human nature—to sell customers what they want. Of course, it may not be what the customer really needs, but how often do customers require a salesperson to sell them on what they need? If they need milk and bread, they go to their corner grocery store, pick up the milk and bread, and bring it to the checkout counter. They don't need to be sold on the benefits of eating. Grocery stores have been self-service establishments for years, despite a huge inventory of constantly changing offerings.

This section, Part Three, illustrates how advanced technologies in the current business environment can be used to create a sticky Web touch point to a business. Using sales as a backdrop, this chapter explores the differences between human- and computer-mediated sales and customer service representatives. It examines how technology can be used to assist representatives or replace them completely. In particular, it explores how interactive Web technology, including Emotionally Intelligent Interfaces, can leverage the Web's strengths to compensate for differences between the real and virtual worlds, thereby inspiring trust and loyalty in online customers.

## The Sales Process

Imagine that a man is shopping for a new suit at a quality establishment. He knows it's a quality store as soon as he walks in, because of how the staff treats him, and by the inviting decor. First, the greeting: The salesperson, a well-groomed, smartly dressed woman approaches the man and acknowledges his presence. The salesperson offers him a friendly, genuine smile and gives him plenty of personal space while she unobtrusively observes him. She doesn't ask, "Can I help you?" or anything else that might invite a "no" response from him. At this point, she doesn't assume anything, and, unless he's obviously been living on the street, she avoids pre-qualifying the customer based only on his appearance.

After the customer has had sufficient time to orient himself to the store and its products, the salesperson re-approaches him and politely asks him a few product-oriented and qualifying questions. She knows when to direct him elsewhere if she senses that he has no intention of buying, and to focus her attention on customers who need and can afford her company's products. She does her best to determine the customer's needs, all the while attempting to build rapport with him. She knows that for a sale to occur, it's imperative that he feel as though both of them are working together to solve a problem in a trusting relationship of equals. His problem—finding a new suit—becomes her problem.

To initiate the problem-solving exercise, she explains the various lines of suits carried by her store, including the special features and benefits of each suit. At an appropriate point in the conversation, she personalizes his shopping experience by offering her name. She also makes an effort to mirror the customer in speech and body language to enhance rapport. For example, if he's a fast talker, she talks fast, and if the man talks with his hands, she does the same.

After the two of them have selected a suit, the salesperson escorts the customer to the ward robing area, and hands the suit to him. After he's changed and looked at himself in the mirror, she offers product knowledge, speaks of the benefits and versatility of the suit, and demonstrates the resilience of the fabric by grabbing a piece of cloth in her fist. She helps the customer to visualize ownership of the suit by asking questions about where and when he plans to wear the suit. The salesperson listens with the intent of diagnosing the customer's needs and confirms his opinion of the suit he's trying on before she introduces another piece of clothing. The salesperson doesn't use or invite a "no" and doesn't use empty adjectives in her conversation. She continues to suggest shirts, shoes, and accessories until he asks her to stop. She reinforces his "buy" decision with sincerity, and doesn't abandon him for other customers, even if he's reached the point where the sale is already "in the bag."

As a professional, the salesperson is focused on building a relationship, not on simply achieving a single sale. She listens for the customer's objectives, and asks more questions, if necessary. She discusses the benefits of the suit he's contemplating purchasing, and, if appropriate, suggests alternatives. At some point in the sales process, she'll introduce the customer to the store's client book. The book formally establishes a link for future business. By gathering the customer's contact information, she can follow up on her commitment to inform him periodically of special sales.

Proceeding to the close, the salesperson is assertive and comfortable. She makes certain that the customer has finished shopping, and then, unlike many amateur salespeople, asks for the sale—and he gives it to her. Next, she establishes information for future business, such as promising to call him when a new shipment of belts arrives. She determines what his final, lasting impression of her will be by being positive, open, and genuine. As she introduces the man to the cashier, she doesn't express doubt or uncertainty, but exudes certainty that his suit is perfect for him.

Now consider an equally imaginary but unfortunately possible encounter with the Internal Revenue Service. A woman's first contact with a "customer representative" is by mail. The computer-generated notice is personal: it has her name, social security number, and address plainly printed at the top. The contents of the notice are equally personal; it lists a discrepancy in her reported income two or three years ago. Even though she can't recall anything out of the ordinary in her previous tax returns, she has been given thirty days to respond to the notice under threat of certain financial and legal penalties. She's told to write to the Internal Revenue Service with her response.

The woman knows from experience that calling the Internal Revenue Service with questions results in a variety of different answers, depending on which customer service representative she happens to talk to. In addition, if it's near April 15, her odds of winning the lottery are probably better than getting through to a customer service representative without spending hours on hold. Even if she manages to get through, the Internal Revenue Service doesn't stand behind what their customer service representatives say on the phone. She'll have to resort to snail mail for her communications while interest and penalties accrue daily.

# When Humans Aren't Enough—Or When There Aren't Enough of Them

These two experiences highlight several important elements in human customer service interactions. The most obvious is variability; what constitutes good customer service in one area doesn't necessarily apply to another. There is also variability at the trade, organization, and individual levels. For example, an individual may have different expectations of what constitutes good customer service in the airline, hotel, and restaurant industries. He probably has specific expectations about his favorite airline or hotel chain. Furthermore, he no doubt expects different levels of service at each location. For example, even McDonald's service varies somewhat from franchise to franchise.

Variability in service can result from a variety of factors. Perhaps the staff in one location has insufficient training to understand their customers' needs. Maybe they just don't care. Perhaps they're simply having a bad day. In the case of the Internal Revenue Service, the issue could simply be the enormous amount of information each customer service representative is supposed to know. It's one thing to familiarize oneself with the suits in a clothing store, and another to memorize and understand the U.S. tax code, especially if it's being amended every few months and overhauled every year. Today, many new products last only three months in the marketplace, making it virtually impossible for a salesperson to become an expert on the particular product before another replaces it. Clearly, with some products and services, it's simply absurd to expect a salesperson without extensive training to become proficient at interfacing with customers in more than a superficial way.

If someone were to ask the person who manages the customer service division of a business to name his greatest assets and liabilities, he'll say that the answer to both is people. It's a challenge to attract and keep attentive, articulate, educated people, but it's usually worth the effort. Good customer service representatives can provide personal, empathetic, quality, reassuring service, especially when they interact with the customer in person. Nothing beats an attentive, knowledgeable sales or support person in terms of bonding customers to a company. Great sales and service representatives create a loyal following that's often independent of the company they represent.

Although there are situations when only a live customer service representative will do, this isn't always possible. With today's busy lifestyles, there often simply isn't time to meet face to face. Increasingly, sales and support interactions occur with the assistance of communications and computer technology, even for big-ticket items. For example, when time is of the essence, and an unstructured conversation can resolve things in a few seconds, the telephone is a great technology, especially since it's universally available.

Despite these advantages of personal service, sales and service representatives are expensive from a practical perspective, especially in a 24/7 support model. In addition, there is the aforementioned variability in service, due to dozens of possible issues, such as a representative's disinterest in a particular product because there are dozens of other products he needs to know about. One of the major limitations of human customer service representatives is that they normally work with customers one-on-one. Scalability, the ability to work with multiple customers at once, is possible in group presentation situations, but then the personal, one-on-one interaction suffers. There are also errors, of both omission and commission, which can appear in any human-mediated transaction, regardless of the touch point. This is especially true when the transaction involves the manual entry of data.

As the effective interaction distance between customer and support staff increases from personal to phone to live Web chat to email interactions, many of the positive qualities of personal interaction normally ascribed to a good customer service representative decrease. The potential for using the touch point in an Emotionally Intelligent Interface diminishes as well. For example, it's much easier to foster an emotional bond with a customer through personal interaction than it is through email. In addition, human-mediated interactions tend to generate fewer data and less granular data than is available through computer-assisted means. Often, this is simply because someone has to take the time to record the data. Furthermore, it may be impossible for some employees to fulfill their data-logging requirements because they may lack the education needed to understand the product or service. For example, a new employee may not be able to differentiate between fabric types, suit styles, or designer labels. Another characteristic of human customer representatives is that they bring with them a variety of security and confidentiality issues, from both an employee and a technology perspective. That is, the equipment the support staff uses must be protected from viruses and break-ins, and employees must be trusted or guarded as well.

## How Technology Can Help

Interactive computer and communications technology can assist in the sales and support process in several ways. Telephone, live chat, and email can enhance the effectiveness of overworked or outnumbered customer service representatives. Computer-mediated email, chat, and animated chat can take over when a human representative is overwhelmed. They can serve as a triage barrier, answering all but the most difficult questions for the representative.

Web technology can also help offload the support issue to customers who enjoy helping each other on the Web. For example, as mentioned in Chapter 1, Lands' End (www.LandsEnd.com) adds to the fun of shopping with its *Shop With a Friend*™ option. Two shoppers can browse together and add items to the same shopping cart. For example, two friends working in different companies can go shopping during their lunch break, just as though they had met and gone shopping in the same brick-and-mortar retail outlet. There isn't any elaborate data warehousing or cluster analysis involved, just a two-way Web chat connection and a slight modification in their shopping cart model. The customers take care of navigating the Web and of helping each other with product selection.

In a similar vein, several vendors, including Cahoots, Hypernix, ICQ, MyESP.com, Third Voice, and WebSideStory, offer live-chat technology to make online shopping less sterile and more emotionally engaging. Their idea is to create a sense of community for a particular Web site by allowing prospective customers to communicate with each other at any time, even without knowing each other's name.

For example, customers shopping for widgets on a particular Web site could ask if other customers had a good or bad experience with the widgets purchased there. Anyone visiting that Web site could respond to the inquiry and discuss the merits of those widgets. The goal is to improve upon the Web's record of two-thirds cart abandonment. That is, about two-thirds of all shopping carts are abandoned at some point before final checkout. From the perspective of a Web site owner, and the one paying for the live-chat capabilities, the danger is that the discussions may become derogatory and out of control.

Figure 7.1 illustrates several characteristics of selected human- and computer-mediated touch points, and how these characteristics vary when the amount of technology is increased. For example, moving from left to right, human-mediated personal contact, phone contact, live Web chat, and email, to computer-mediated email, Web chat, and animated Web chat are representative of the range of possibilities currently available, where animated Web chat represents the greatest level of technological involvement. Note that there are many more potential points of contact than are listed in Figure 7.1, such as human-mediated faxing, as well as automated fax-back services. There are also several technologies on the horizon, such as two-way Web-based video links, but the realities of current bandwidth limitations of the Internet are holding these technologies at bay. Also, the value for each characteristic attributed to a touch point represents a typical case. As with any measurement or estimate, there is variability in the actual value shown.

***Reducing cost per contact.*** One of the effects of adding the appropriate technology to the customer support or sales mix is that there is often a reduction in the cost per contact—the money spent to connect with each customer. The cost per contact tends to be highest for personal, one-on-one interactions, simply because the representative's full attention is necessarily focused on a single customer. The customer receives the full benefit of the representative's training during the period of contact, as well as many of the resources that result in direct and indirect costs to the company.

With the addition of phone technology, the support representative is freed somewhat from dealing with one customer to the exclusion of all else. For example, he might be on the phone with one potential customer while simultaneously composing an email to another potential

| CHARACTERISTIC | HUMAN | | | | COMPUTER | | |
|---|---|---|---|---|---|---|---|
| | Personal | Phone | Live Chat | EMail | Email | Chat | Anim Chat |
| Cost per Contact | High | Medium | Low | Low | Low | Low | Low |
| Development Time | High | Medium | Low | Low | Medium | Medium | High |
| Emotional Bond | High | Medium | Medium | Low | Low | Medium | Medium |
| Emotive | High | Medium | Medium | Low | Low | Medium | Medium |
| Empathetic | High | Medium | Medium | Low | Low | Low | Medium |
| Error Prone | High | High | High | High | Low | Low | Low |
| Flexibility | High | High | High | High | Medium | Medium | Medium |
| Interactivity | High | High | Medium | Low | Low | Medium | High |
| Longevity | Low | Low | Medium | Medium | Medium | Medium | Medium |
| Personal | High | High | High | High | High | High | High |
| Personality | High | Medium | Medium | Low | Low | Medium | Medium |
| Quality | High | Medium | Medium | Medium | High | High | High |
| Reassuring | High | High | Medium | Low | Low | Medium | Medium |
| Reliability | Medium | Medium | Medium | Medium | High | High | High |
| Responsive | Medium | Medium | Medium | Low | Medium | High | High |
| ROI | Low | Medium | Medium | Medium | High | High | High |
| Scalability | Low | Low | Low | Medium | High | High | High |
| Transference | High | High | Low | Low | Low | Low | Medium |
| Variability | High | High | Medium | Medium | Low | Low | Low |

● High ● Medium ○ Low

***Figure 7.1*** *Characteristics of human- versus computer-mediated customer service representatives over a variety of touch points. For example, variability in service is greatest with personal, one-on-one contact and telephone service.*

customer or client, filing papers, cleaning up his desk, or in some way contributing to his own and the company's future success.

Similarly, live, Web-based chat and email have a relatively low cost per contact, in part because the support representative can multitask. For example, in the case of a live chat, the representative can communicate with potential customers on the Web in spurts, and, in between sessions, handle other support issues. Furthermore, since email is normally handled in batches, often with canned responses, a customer service representative has time between email runs to perform other functions.

Moving from primarily human- to computer-mediated interactions, the cost per contact is potentially even lower. Computer-mediated email, in which email is generated by a bot, can respond to hundreds of emails in the time it would take a human to answer one or two. Similarly, computer-mediated chat, where real-time chat bots help customers, can reply to hundreds of queries per second. The same rationale holds for animated chat bots that incorporate emotive, animated graphic characters. The marginal cost of handling an additional customer is an insignificant increase in the server power and Internet bandwidth requirements.

***Decreasing development time.***    Customer representatives are expensive to train, keep motivated, and retain, especially in this economy. Training a representative for a new product or service may take a few days or up to several weeks, depending on the complexity and number of products and services the representative is expected to sell or support. Development time is greatest for representatives who work face-to-face with customers. One reason that development time is so great is that it includes recruiting time. Good all-around salespeople and representatives with winning manners, speech, dress, and charisma are hard to find. A business may be lucky enough to locate a representative who has excellent live chat skills, but whose squeaky voice may not do in phone support and whose green hair might not present the image the business is looking for in person-to-person sales.

With computer-enabled tools, such as a library of canned phrases, customer service representatives can be trained to become proficient users of live chat and email even if they are slow typists. As long as the representative can recognize which phrases or responses to use in specific circumstances, even minimal keyboard skills will do. Email is one of the most forgiving touch points, since the dialogue doesn't occur in real time. A customer service representative has time to refer an unintelligible email to a supervisor who can then answer it or route it to the appropriate person to handle.

In comparison to training human customer representatives, computer-mediated email and chat have moderate development times. The likely questions and the corresponding answers have to be gathered and compiled into a knowledge base. The normal software development cycle of testing, modifying, testing, and remodifying the code and the knowledge base until everything checks out can take weeks, even with a simple support problem. Computer-mediated animated chat can require as much development time as training a human representative. However, as discussed earlier, this cost can be spread out over possibly hundreds of simultaneous customer interactions, resulting in a very favorable cost per contact. In addition, there isn't the recurring recruitment and training cost associated with upwardly mobile representatives.

*Creating emotional bonds.*    Although the gold standard for creating an emotional bond between the customer and a company is a dedicated, charismatic salesperson or representative, technology can help create an emotional bond. As illustrated in Figure 7.1, personal contact is capable of the most profound emotional bond. Live chat is also capable of supporting a meaningful dialogue that can help create an emotional bond, but it's not as powerful as the phone or direct contact. Because email lacks most of the cues we normally associate with a conversation, such as immediacy, it has the lowest likelihood of creating a meaningful emotional bond.

Computer-mediated chat and animated chat, when appropriately implemented, have the best chances of creating an emotional bond in the customer's mind. In this context, "appropriately implemented" includes providing an emotionally intelligent interface that is personal, reliable, responsive, and reassuring.

*Presenting emotive content.*    Humans are emotional creatures. We react to not only language and voice intonation and content, but to dozens of subtle cues, from body posture to pupil size. The more access we have to these multiple channels of information, the more emotive the dialogue. For this reason, personal interactions convey the most emotive content. It's always easier to tell someone something confrontational on the phone, for example, because the caller doesn't have to face him or her. Live chat can have considerable emotive content as well, but because the many subtle cues in the representative's voice aren't available, the possible emotive content is lower than that supported by phone. Email has the lowest emotive content capacity, in part because of the lag time. Bot chat and email can improve the emotive content with the use of emoticons or emotive icons, such as (:-). Of the computer-mediated options available, animated chat has the greatest potential for conveying emotive content to a customer.

*Displaying empathy.*    Great salespeople and customer representatives are empathetic; they can identify with the customer's situation—or at least give the impression that they do. It's the impression that matters to customers; they want to feel that they've been heard. This feeling can be communicated best in person, but to some degree over a phone conversation, and, to a lesser extent, over a live chat conversation. Because it lacks immediacy, email tends to be a poor communications conduit for empathetic thoughts and feelings. Think about it; when most people have an issue, they want it addressed immediately.

Computer-mediated communications such as email and live chat don't fare very well when the goal is to communicate feelings that may be difficult for a computer to convey. In this regard, animated chat communications can sometimes convey a sense of understanding when used as the touch point. In addition to text conversations, the animated character can provide emotive cues that the customer may appreciate, even at the subconscious level. For example, a look of concern instead of an inappropriate smile may go a long way in making the customer feel heard. The underlying assumption is that the bot is responsible for recognizing customers' problems. For example, the bot could key in on certain phrases, such as "I'm very frustrated" and "I'm angry."

*Reducing human error.*    Face it, humans are simply more error-prone than computers when it comes to manipulating symbols and values. Assuming there is accurate customer data to work with, computer-mediated customer communications can have a much lower error rate than human-mediated communications in tracking orders, verifying charges, and identifying repeat customers. Even when customer data are in error—and there is always error—computers tend to fare better. Although there are exceptions among trained customer service representatives, untrained representatives tend to compound or at least propagate errors, often with the assistance of computers.

*Increasing flexibility.*    While computers might excel at flawlessly following instructions, good customer service representatives excel at flexibility. Regardless of the touch point, a good representative, when properly trained, can provide remedies for mistakes, errors, or missing data that current computer-mediated systems cannot. For example, if a product evolves quickly, a customer service representative may at least be able to provide some level of support. In contrast, computer-mediated systems must be reprogrammed to support a new product or service.

*Improving interactivity.*   Interactivity, the ability of representatives to respond to a customer's queries in near-real time, is best in person and over the phone. Email interactivity suffers from an inherent lag from the time a problem statement is made to response, but the lag time tends to be smaller when the email is computer-mediated. Chat, whether live or computer-mediated, can support a moderate level of interactivity.

*Increasing longevity.*   Longevity, the expected working life of a customer representative, depends not only on the individual but also on the nature of the business, how it treats its employees, and other soft factors. However, from the customer's perspective, longevity can be extended with computer-mediated chat and email. Longevity, perhaps better thought of as continuity, is important in forming a bond with customers, especially with personal and, to a lesser extent, phone interactions. Computer-mediated communications can provide infinite longevity and continuity. For example, the names used to identify a chat bot can be held constant, and the appearance of animated figures used in animated chat communications can remain constant as well.

*Adding a personal touch.*   All the touch points listed in Figure 7.1 can provide personal communications—the use of a customer's name, for example—contingent upon the availability of customer data. Even human-mediated communications tend to rely upon computer-generated or warehoused customer data to the same extent that computer-mediated communications do. In other words, most touch points are already leveraging computer technology to provide a personal touch.

*Communicating personality.*   As noted in Part Two, computer hardware, programs and Web sites all have personalities. However, just as personal interactions tend to have greater potential to exhibit personality, animated chat, where an anthropomorphic figure can communicate with visual cues, text, and even voice, has a much greater chance of communicating personalities to customers. The challenge is to create personalities that customers can relate to in a positive way.

*Increasing quality.*   The quality of customer dialogue tends to be highest when it's controlled by a good salesperson or motivated customer service representative. Phone, live chat, email, and other touch points can also be high quality, but are usually not as high as with a good salesperson. Computer technology can help with these other touch points by minimizing variability and otherwise contributing to quality control. Computer-mediated communications can have consistent, high-quality dialogues with the customer because all possible responses can be validated before they are presented to customers.

***Providing reassurance.*** An important aspect of the sales process is reassuring customers that their purchase decisions are correct, their problems are solved, and that their products are on the way. Computer technology can be used for something as banal as helping reassure customers about the status of their order, or as sophisticated as creating a personal profile of customers and using it to explain why the products they just ordered are in their best interest.

***Increasing reliability.*** Humans vary in their reliability from person to person and from day to day. We all have good and bad days, sick days, and days we have to pick up the kids from school. On the other hand, computers are reliable machines when human-generated viruses are not attacking them. A business can rely on computer-mediated communications with customers to occur within very tightly controlled parameters. In short, computers excel where reliability is an issue.

***Improving responsiveness.*** Properly trained sales and support staff can do a good job of responding to customer needs in a timely manner. Email has the lowest responsiveness of the human mediated communications simply because of the inherent delays of email communications. By definition, email carries with it a perceptible delay that isn't noticed or at least isn't significant with live chat, for example. Because of the rapid 24/7 response made possible by computers, computer-mediated chat and animated chat are potentially much more responsive than a customer representative or salesperson could be.

***Improving return on investment (ROI).*** Generalizing the Return on Investment (ROI) for a customer representative or computer technology is complicated. There are always specific circumstances, such as the cost of money and specifics of the people or computer technology involved. However, in today's economy, it's generally understood that turnover is high. This is especially true in the customer support area, where temporary and seasonal workers fill a relatively large number of representative jobs.

Because of the variable nature of the labor supply, and the low cost per contact for computer-mediated dialogue, the ROI for computer-mediated support of all types is potentially greater than for human-mediated support. Conversely, because of turnover at point-of-sale positions, ROI tends to be lowest for human-mediated support.

*Increasing scalability.* In general, humans don't scale very well. Most interactions are on a one-on-one basis, from personal, phone, and live-chat communications. Email is scalable because it may be handled in batches, with the same generic answer applied to hundreds of questions. In contrast, computer-mediated touch points are virtually infinitely scalable, given an adequate infrastructure, including supporting server hardware.

*Controlling transference.* Transference is ascribing the characteristics of one person to another, often at a subconscious level. This may be the result of similarities in appearance, speaking style, or mannerisms, and can be a positive or negative factor in the sales and customer relations process. For example, a salesman may subconsciously remind a woman of a trusted relative, and she'll instinctively believe everything he says. Conversely, the same salesman could remind her of an unscrupulous salesperson she dealt with in the past, and she develops the same negative attitude toward this one. In human-mediated communications, transference occurs primarily with personal contact, but may also occur in phone conversations.

Transference can be an asset in computer-mediated interactions. For example, a business can provide customers with the ability to modify the animation and synthesized speech to suit their preferences. For example, a business could present customers with a menu of animated figures, including male, female, young, and old, from which they could choose. In addition, the business could allow customers to specify the speaking style of each figure, from businesslike to casual. Customers don't generally create figures to learn from or to deal with that they don't relate to positively.

*Decreasing variability.* As discussed earlier, variability is a characteristic of human-mediated communications that is virtually absent in properly designed computer-mediated dialogues. This variability may be a nuisance; for example, if the customer is inquiring about tax code information. An animated chat bot may not be as engaging as a human, but a business will know to what information *its* customers are being exposed.

# Economic Darwinism in Action

There are obvious benefits of incorporating computer-mediated support into the overall customer support strategy. A business can support multiple customers simultaneously, standardize the level of service, and potentially realize a much higher ROI. The technology, however, isn't perfect. Modifying a computer-mediated system to cover a new product can be equivalent to training a human, in terms of the time and resources required. Even with adequate time and resources devoted to developing computer-mediated support, the functionality of the final product depends on the quality of the programming staff, and of the computer scientists employed by the vendors.

The use of technology in support and sales is accelerating despite the current limitations of the Web, in areas such as bandwidth and security. It's likely that the problems associated with variability in human performance, the difficulty in recruiting quality representatives, and of retaining them once they're trained add to the increased use of technology. This increase can also be attributed to the realization that technology can make international support issues easier, compared to providing 24/7 live cultural- and language-sensitive phone support to overseas customers. It may also be that the 40 percent of households that own a computer are more likely to buy a product or service than are non-computer owners.

The economic Darwinism that is being fueled by the Web seems unstoppable. Businesses can either view the natural mutations and evolutions of technology on the Web as either threats or opportunities. If a business takes the latter stance, it might be able to steer the evolutionary pressures to its benefit—before the competition does. For example, consider voice on the Web. While still evolving past scratchy connections, poor security, and poor audio quality, this technology may help build community and will provide another touch point for customer sales and support. Voice on the Web is especially helpful for customers with only one phone line who can't simply disconnect from the Web to call customer support. With voice on the Web, customers can converse with customer service representatives while looking at their screens, much as they do now with text through instant messaging. Despite pressure from the traditional phone carriers to limit the use of this competing technology, voice will eventually find its way on the Web, in one form or another.

Similarly, two-way Web videophone technology is destined to become a force on the Web, pending sufficient bandwidth at the customer's connection to the Internet. DSL, cable modems, and other high-speed connections are not yet standard configurations for most consumers.

However, consider the enormous potential, from the perspective of assisting customers over the Web, of a high-quality video and audio link. Imagine a woman contacting her favorite customer representative online, where she can chat and, if needed, view samples of clothing or machine parts to verify that he has what she's looking for.

Music on the Web is in the same position as voice in that an optimum delivery configuration is materializing, shaped by the evolutionary pressures of the Web. For example, Napster (www.Napster.com) offers an integrated browser and communications system that enables music fans to locate bands and music on the Web. Napster is the controversial search engine for music, designed for the MP3 music culture. However, unlike most Web browsers, the content it indexes isn't published to the Web in the usual way, but sits on individuals' hard drives. It's a way for individuals to share music and CPU cycles with total strangers.

Napster is unique in that users decide what content to make available to others using the Napster browser, and what content to download. Although users are responsible for complying with all applicable federal and state laws applicable to such content, including copyright laws, Napster is being sued because it's enabling massive copyright infringement. The music industry may shut down Napster and similar noncommercial copy enabling. However, what matters is that Napster has hit upon a Web-based distribution model for music that will likely survive and become a win–win situation for customers, artists, and the recording industry.

# Where Interactive Web Technology Shines

From the above discussion, it's apparent that of the characteristics listed in Figure 7.1, the addition of computer-mediated interactive technology to Web-based customer support has the following advantages:

- Lower cost per contact
- An emotional bond with the customer
- An ability to communicate with more emotive content
- Fewer errors
- Greater customer interactivity with a Web site
- Improved reliability
- Greater responsiveness
- Greater return on investment
- Improved scalability
- Less variability in the quality and content of communications.

What really matters is how businesses apply these potential benefits of interactive technology to their Web presence. If the goal is to create an Emotionally Intelligent Interface, then a business could use these technologies toward setting the tone of interaction, involving its customers in a mutually beneficial dialog, and using interactivity to establish a meaningful relationship.

When potential customers visit a Web site, they should be made to feel comfortable with the company and confident that it can fill their needs efficiently and economically. At a brick-and-mortar store, the sales staff and the layout and decoration of the reception area of the store perform this function. The environment established by the technologies incorporated in the Web site can dictate its customers' responses to its business, and how long their visit to the Web site lasts. Creating a welcoming environment can entail something as simple as creating a panel of potential customer service representatives and allowing customers to choose which one they would like to interact with, whether the representatives are real or virtual. Let the customers decide if they want to interact with someone with blonde hair and blue eyes, or dark wavy hair and brown eyes. An advantage of using virtual customer representatives in the form of animated Chat Bots is that every company can precisely control the customer experience. The business can be assured that interactions are politically correct, for example.

## Converting Clicks to Customers

Part of the Chinese belief system is that the good or bad luck that happens to someone depends on the state of the universe when they were born. However, the person isn't powerless to change their fate, as long as they know what the luck is likely to be—good or bad—and when it is likely to occur. The belief is that someone can use techniques such as Feng Shui to determine the various enhancements and remedies required to prevent or avoid any bad luck. The underlying principle of Feng Shui is to live in harmony with the environment so that the energy surrounding a person works for him, and not against him. Whether or not adhering to these principles can help someone avoid a tax audit or simply provide a more pleasant work environment, the system may be of value in determining how to best apply technology in a Web site.

To leverage technology and thereby realize the greatest benefit from a Web presence, a business must first know what it's after, in terms of a relationship with its customers. Assuming that the goal is to provide a Web site with an Emotionally Intelligent Interface, management also has to appreciate the possibilities, within the business' resource and technology constraints. For example, Figure 7.2 shows the relative potential of selected computer- and human-mediated touch points for contributing to an Emotionally Intelligent Interface for a Web site. Note that the technologies with the greatest degree of interactivity provide the greatest potential for an EII. Finally, as in using Feng Shui, a business needs to pull everything together in a way that harmonizes with its customers; the business should use the technology at its disposal so that the odds of creating a loyal customer following are maximized.

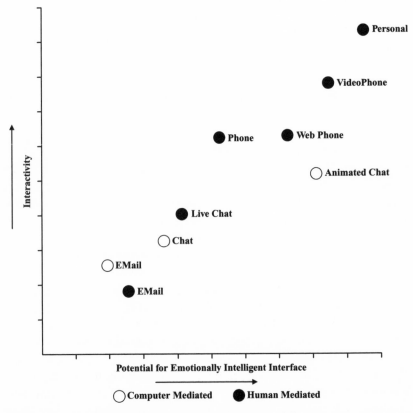

***Figure 7.2*** *Level of interactivity versus the potential for use as a component of an emotionally intelligent interface for computer- and human-medicated touch points. Note that personal interaction represents the maximum for both interactivity and Emotionally Intelligent Interface potential.*

In deciding on a business' goals for a Web presence, management has to keep customers in mind as well. For example, although the popularity of the Web for consumers was initially driven by price, those days are over. Today, the battle is over customer service, excellent product information, and ease of navigation through a Web site. Web sites stand out because they offer wide inventory, fast searches, and compelling promotions. The interface must be especially easy to navigate. Just as customers may refuse to go to department stores that make them wander through a maze of promotions to reach the escalator, Web customers won't likely appreciate delays that aren't in their immediate best interest, such as having to fill out a questionnaire before they're allowed to enter a site.

Let's assume that the goal is to use technology on a Web site to replicate the capabilities of a personal salesperson. Before making a judgment on what's feasible, consider the requirements. For example, consider, from a human customer representative's perspective, what's involved in listening to a customer's needs. A salesperson has to start with a customer-first mindset; ask questions that encourage the customer to talk; use active listening; ask additional questions to probe deeper; and repeat the customer's statements to make certain that the customer understood what she said. Active listening means involving the customer in the dialogue. A salesperson has to translate the customer's statements into his own words, and then repeat the statement to the customer to verify that his meaning was correct.

Consider also how simply establishing a relationship in only a few minutes is a hallmark of a great salesperson. These high achievers come to the table prepared. They know as much about the customer as possible before the interchange, mirroring the customer's personality type. They respect the customer's time; they introduce themselves, and then stop talking. Great service providers and salespersons also pay attention to the customer's appearance, attitudes, and actions.

In looking at the possibilities for a Web presence, consider the capabilities of the technologies available. For example, as shown in Figure 7.2, personal interaction is the gold standard in relationship building. Chat, especially animated chat, has good potential for creating a computer-enabled Emotionally Intelligent Interface.

Having the technology is one thing, and applying it correctly is still another. For example, management has to decide if it will temporarily increase Web traffic to the site through viral marketing, competing on price, or creating evangelists. Viral marketing, spreading word of a Web site through free email accounts or free online greeting cards, doesn't require much more sophistication than a "dead" Web site with an email address. Similarly, if management decides to compete on price, it won't need much in terms of technology. Management should ask itself if it's trying to buy customers, akin to using an escort service, or develop a relationship with someone who's going to bring chicken soup when they're sick. The third alternative, creating evangelists, involves creating an emotional link to the customers. For this goal, management will have to use advanced technologies such as animated chat to the their fullest potential as components of Emotionally Intelligent Interfaces.

The leaders in the emotional interface arena—Nintendo, Sega, and Sony—illustrate how to combine technology in a way that creates customer loyalty. Even as these entertainment giants broaden their market from games to networked digital entertainment, a significant portion of their market still involves putting customers in role-playing situations. Their customers form an emotional bond to the games with which they're interacting. The most emotionally engaging games on the market allow a player to put the faces of his friends on the various characters in the game. He can play basketball or hockey with his friends, with their faces attached to the virtual players. These companies have most of what they need to create a loyal following, and the connection with the Internet is making it possible further to customize and personalize the customer's experience.

The next chapter follows the premise that in order to avoid the potential pitfalls of Web-based technology, management has to know what to look for. It examines issues that can impede progress in developing an emotionally intelligent Web site and formulates a plan that management can use to avoid these pitfalls.

# Executive Summary

Interactive technology can be used to leverage the Web's strengths to compensate for differences between the real and virtual worlds, thereby creating a mechanism for inspiring trust and loyalty in online customers. Recent advances in interactive Web-based technologies, from computer-mediated email to chat and animated chat, are driving the use of technology to move the Web from a highway littered with billboards to one lined with online stores. Similarly, the problems associated with variability in human performance, the difficulty in recruiting quality representatives, and of retaining them once they're trained, create an environment that favors the increased use of interactive technology on the Web.

Interactive Web-based technologies can address many of the shortcomings associated with customer service representatives, such as poor scalability and frequent errors. Similarly, telephone, live chat, and email can enhance the effectiveness of overworked or outnumbered customer service representatives. In addition, computer-mediated email, chat, and animated chat can take over when a human representative is overwhelmed. These and other technologies can serve as a triage barrier, answering all but the most difficult questions for representatives who work online.

From the customer's perspective, the use of interactive technologies represents a move toward more emotionally intelligent interactions with a Web site. For example, live chat, which relies on attentive customer service representatives, can make online shopping less sterile and more emotionally engaging. There are numerous additional potential benefits of integrating interactive technology into a Web site as well, ranging from reduced cost per contact, increased quality of interactions, increased reliability, and increased responsiveness, to increased scalability, controlled transference, and decreased variability.

In looking at the possibilities for a Web presence, consider the capabilities of the available technologies. What really matters is how these potential benefits of interactive technology are applied to a Web presence.

## Rate-Limiting Factors

*To dare is to lose one's footing momentarily.*
*Not to dare is to lose oneself.*
                    Soren Kierkegaard

Perhaps it's simply human nature, but change is more challenging than it should be at first, even when it's obviously for the better. For example, imagine that an overworked CEO is lucky enough to find himself eligible for a coronary bypass operation. He's lucky because he has options, thanks to modern medicine. He can choose to undergo surgery and have a good chance of avoiding a heart attack and of enjoying a reasonable quality of life for the next few decades. By investing in the surgery, his most likely return is an improvement in the infrastructure of his coronary arteries.

With the continuous stream of marketing information focused on today's medical miracles, he might have an unrealistic view of the current state of medical technology. The man may expect that his bypass procedure will be quick, completely safe, painless, and affordable. It won't be. Despite the development of new, microinvasive surgical techniques, he'll still need several months to recover fully and he'll have to take drugs before, during, and after the surgery. What's more, these miracle drugs all have side effects or additional actions unrelated to their intended purpose. For obvious reasons, these actions are rarely highlighted in ads. Furthermore, there are no magic pills. Even if he takes his medicine, he'll be right back on the operating room table unless he changes his lifestyle. The man will have to invest the time to eat right and exercising regularly. Fortunately, he'll probably experience several positive side effects of exercise, such as a slimmer waistline and an overall better outlook on life.

In a similar vein, transforming the heart of a business's existing Web presence into something that's going to impart a sense of trust and loyalty in its customers is going to involve some hard decisions and overcoming significant obstacles. Management must critically evaluate the technology, economics, and processes of the business. When management initiates the transformation of its Web presence, it will have to deal with the reality that the planned improvements won't occur overnight, but may take several months or more. In addition, during this time of change, management may feel that the pace of the Web, including the competition, is accelerating, leaving the company behind, or even causing it to recede into oblivion.

This chapter explores the various rate-limiting factors that can impede a company's progress in developing a personal, loyalty-evoking, emotionally intelligent Web presence. Armed with this knowledge, management should be better prepared to formulate and act on an implementation plan while avoiding problem areas. For example, reworking the current IT infrastructure, which may involve replacing antiquated hardware and software with updated versions capable of supporting new bandwidth and throughput requirements, will likely demand a significant investment in time and money. Furthermore, as in a coronary bypass operation, the outcome won't be a certainty, but only a probability of success. Odds are, however, that if management makes the right moves and avoids or addresses problem areas, a more successful site and, by extension, a more prosperous business will result.

## Overview

Although management should consider the effect an improved Web presence will have on its customers, it will first need to modify its business processes. For example, numerous potential data acquisition bottlenecks may impede a company's ability to acquire the information it needs to create a personal Web experience for its customers. Not only is the typical data acquisition process time consuming, but it tends to be expensive and error prone as well. Furthermore, even though there may be several cookbook methods available, management will have to use its knowledge of the industry and of its customers to determine the best way of acquiring customer information, whether through questionnaires, transaction tracking, or other methods. Data acquisition bottlenecks, like many other challenges, are the result of several interrelated rate-limiting factors that the business will have to address on its path to an emotionally intelligent site. These rate-limiting factors can be categorized as technical, social, managerial, economic, or political (see Figure 8.1).

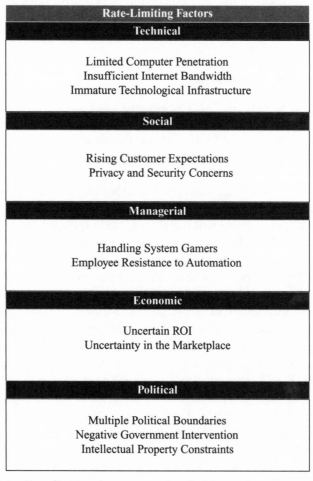

**Figure 8.1** *Rate-limiting factors associated with creating an emotionally intelligent Web presence.*

Technical factors that may limit progress include an immature technological infrastructure within a business, Internet bandwidth limitations at a customer's site, and varied penetration of computer technology in some customer markets. Social factors include rising customer expectations and customer concerns over online privacy and security. Managerial factors include making allowances for those who would game the system and employees who resist automation. Economic factors include uncertainty about the return on investment and the evolution of the marketplace. Political factors include the challenge of working across multiple political boundaries, the negative effects of governmental intervention, and overly aggressive internal and external intellectual property constraints. The most significant of these rate-limiting factors, any of which may limit the viability of the Web as a touch point to a business, are detailed below.

# Technical Factors

## Immature Technological Infrastructure

To the uninitiated, a good way to assess the success or failure of a coronary bypass or even a minor surgical procedure is to rate the appearance of the incision or scar. After all, the incision site is normally all that's plainly visible. A straight incision with clean margins and snug sutures suggests the underlying surgery was expertly executed. A jagged incision with angry margins that tug at irregularly spaced sutures suggests a poorly done job. However, below the cosmetics of a wound closure, what really matters is the fundamental improvements to the underlying organs and other structures below the incision. What this means is that a successful surgical outcome requires more than simply having the appropriate technology at the surgeon's disposal. It means having an entire process established to use the technology. Two surgeons can use the same scalpels and sutures and yet their patients may have very different outcomes. From the surgeon and nurses to the technicians, anesthesiologists, and room monitors, everyone is critical to the success of a process that has been perfected through hours of study, trial and error, and practice. Technology and process are equally critical to the successful outcome of a surgical procedure.

Similarly, both technology and process will be critical to a company's success on the Web. However, the technological infrastructure of the Web is still in its infancy, and the information infrastructure that provides integration, allowing customers to see the company as one seamless entity, is still evolving. Wireless Web connectivity, high-speed, secure direct Internet connectivity, and standard communications protocols have yet to be fully realized. The developmental history of the PC and of the Web illustrates that the technological infrastructure of the Web can evolve rapidly; in a matter of a few weeks, to months, whatever can be imagined can be achieved.

Consider the technological and process infrastructure behind *choice boards*, the Web-based, multi-user ordering system that approximates the Japanese method of just-in-time delivery. In this paradigm, suppliers deliver parts on the day that they're needed, allowing customers to avoid paying warehousing costs and management to avoid overhead associated with maintaining an inventory. A few companies, such as Dell and ChipShot.com (see Figure 8.2), use choice boards to involve their customers in an active process of creating custom products. Customers make selections from choice boards to define a product's features, and the information is automatically routed to the manufacturer and suppliers at the time the order is placed. The manufacturer usually assumes many of the usual business risks, such as customers failing to pay or returning the item for a refund. One role of the customer in the choice board model is as a custom designer. For example, ChipShot.com's choice board allows customers to design their own golf clubs, and Dell uses choice boards to enable customers to define a computer that suits their needs.

Despite the potential of choice boards to change the face of eCommerce, they account for only a small percentage of overall sales, in part because the infrastructure of most businesses in the United States doesn't support this degree of automation. Although Dell and a few other companies have been able to apply choice board technology successfully, the process infrastructure lags sorely behind the enabling Web technology. Choice boards have yet to proliferate on the Web because there isn't a significant customer base, which is in turn partly due to the novelty of the model. In addition, most potential customers aren't knowledgeable about digital matters, and even if they own home computers, general computer literacy across all age groups in the United States is low. On the supply side, distribution and manufacturing networks aren't available. Despite these limitations, the choice board model will likely become more dominant as the overall economy moves from a supply-driven to a demand-driven system, where customers' needs drive business decisions.

Choice boards are particularly well suited for use with Emotionally Intelligent Interface designs, in part because they generate so much transaction data. For example, in designing a pair of custom golf clubs,

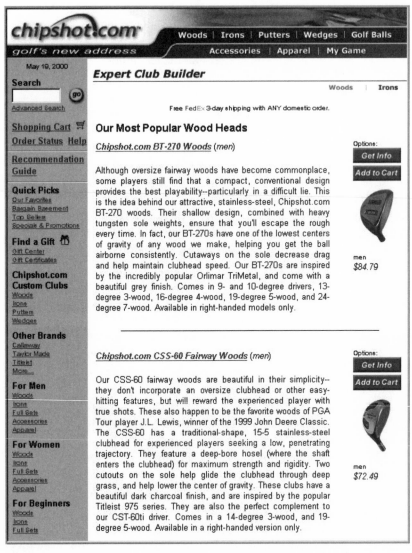

**chipshot.com**
*golf's new address*

Woods | Irons | Putters | Wedges | Golf Balls
Accessories | Apparel | My Game

May 19, 2000

**Search**

Advanced Search

Shopping Cart

Order Status  Help

Recommendation
Guide

Quick Picks
Our Favorites
Bargain Basement
Top Sellers
Specials & Promotions

Find a Gift
Gift Center
Gift Certificates

Chipshot.com
Custom Clubs
Woods
Irons
Putters
Wedges

Other Brands
Callaway
Taylor Made
Titleist
More...

For Men
Woods
Irons
Full Sets
Accessories
Apparel

For Women
Woods
Irons
Full Sets
Accessories
Apparel

For Beginners
Woods
Irons
Full Sets

## Expert Club Builder

Woods | Irons

Free FedEx 3-day shipping with ANY domestic order.

### Our Most Popular Wood Heads

*Chipshot.com BT-270 Woods (men)*

Although oversize fairway woods have become commonplace, some players still find that a compact, conventional design provides the best playability--particularly in a difficult lie. This is the idea behind our attractive, stainless-steel, Chipshot.com BT-270 woods. Their shallow design, combined with heavy tungsten sole weights, ensure that you'll escape the rough every time. In fact, our BT-270s have one of the lowest centers of gravity of any wood we make, helping you get the ball airborne consistently. Cutaways on the sole decrease drag and help maintain clubhead speed. Our BT-270s are inspired by the incredibly popular Orlimar TriMetal, and come with a beautiful grey finish. Comes in 9- and 10-degree drivers, 13-degree 3-wood, 16-degree 4-wood, 19-degree 5-wood, and 24-degree 7-wood. Available in right-handed models only.

Options:
Get Info
Add to Cart

men
$84.79

*Chipshot.com CSS-60 Fairway Woods (men)*

Our CSS-60 fairway woods are beautiful in their simplicity-- they don't incorporate an oversize clubhead or other easy-hitting features, but will reward the experienced player with true shots. These also happen to be the favorite woods of PGA Tour player J.L. Lewis, winner of the 1999 John Deere Classic. The CSS-60 has a traditional-shape, 15-5 stainless-steel clubhead for experienced players seeking a low, penetrating trajectory. They feature a deep-bore hosel (where the shaft enters the clubhead) for maximum strength and rigidity. Two cutouts on the sole help glide the clubhead through deep grass, and help lower the center of gravity. These clubs have a beautiful dark charcoal finish, and are inspired by the popular Titleist 975 series. They are also the perfect complement to our CST-60ti driver. Comes in a 14-degree 3-wood, and 19-degree 5-wood. Available in a right-handed version only.

Options:
Get Info
Add to Cart

men
$72.49

*Figure 8.2*  *A view from the head selection component of Chipshot.com's expert club builder option board. After the customer selects the handle and shaft, and answers questions about her skill level and handicap, a custom set of clubs is built to specifications. Permission granted from Chipshot.com.*

a man may willingly offer personal information on his game, shoe, and clothing sizes, build, weight, and overall fitness level so that he can receive the best clubs possible. Since customer information is a natural byproduct of service, choice boards can use customer data to better their product offerings. From a process perspective, it's also important to note that whoever owns choice boards controls customer relations. Although a customer may generate data that go directly to a choice board's suppliers, as far as the customer is concerned, the choice board is the only touch point involved.

## Internet Bandwidth Limitations

Often the bigger the crowd, the better the performance, but not so with the Web. Restricted bandwidth at the customer site, whether due to the customer's Internet Service Provider or computer hardware, can limit a business' ability to provide customers with interactive, multimedia-rich experiences through its Web site. As described in the previous chapter, the potential for a touch point to provide an Emotionally Intelligent Interface is positively correlated with the level of interactivity that the technology used can support. That is, talking face to face or through a two-way videophone is fundamentally more interactive and more likely to result in a trusting relationship than is communicating via a text-based chat connection. In addition, through viewing television and playing electronic games, customers have come to expect a certain level of interactivity from electronic portals.

Even though the majority of personal computers shipped today are capable of moving data internally at several million bits per seconds, and the Internet's backbone is capable of handling even higher data rates, most home-based customers communicate with the Internet through 28.8K analog modem connections. This huge disparity between the potential bandwidth of the Internet and customer-to-Internet connectivity at the home necessarily limits interactivity. 56K analog modem connections to the Internet are increasingly common, and high-speed DSL and cable modem connections embraced by most businesses are becoming popular among the well-heeled Internet crowd at home. Depending on a customer's demographics, the business may be forced to create the equivalent of two Web sites. While focusing its main efforts on highly interactive but bandwidth-hungry technologies, the business may have to be content with supporting the lowest common denominator: home-based customers with 28.8K connections.

Fortunately, even customers with low-speed dial-up connections aren't limited to one-way interactions with Web portals. Because of customer demand for two-way, interactive communications, there is an extensive software industry based on serving customers with limited bandwidth access to the Internet. There are numerous utilities for Web-based video, animation, and audio compression, streaming, transport, and decompression. Most of these utilities rely on run-time engines that reside on the customer's computer and provide the real-time decompression and rendering or playback. As with closet space, there never seems to be enough bandwidth, and these utilities quickly fill any bandwidth void. Therefore, a variety of compression utilities and thin-client applications will likely remain popular, even after the majority of customers switch to high-speed access. Customers will continue to rely on bandwidth-enhancing utilities to keep up with the technology made possible by even higher speed Internet access.

Unless a business' products and services appeal to the technologically elite who have high-speed connectivity, digital video cameras, and other data-dense peripherals, designing a customer support function based on two-way live video isn't practical. If a business assumes that most of its customers have a 28.8K connection to the Web, human-computer-mediated chat are viable options. However, animated chat may not be appropriate because of the bandwidth limitations. If the low bandwidth connection supports a smaller image, or fewer frames per second, then the emotional impact of the images will be lessened. That is, the emotive bandwidth is limited by the communications bandwidth. The differences in emotive bandwidth can be appreciated by viewing AnaNova (www.AnaNova.com) at high and low resolutions. The smaller, lower-resolution image, suitable for customers with 28.8K connections, simply doesn't communicate the emotional nuances of eye movement and facial expression as well as the larger, more detailed image designed to be viewed by customers with high bandwidth connections.

## Varied Penetration of Computer Technology

Although corporate America is replete with computers, the varied penetration of PCs in the home may influence a business' Web initiatives. Short of giving PCs away, there isn't much that a company can do to increase the penetration of computers and computer technology into the homes of some potential customers. Despite massive marketing campaigns by Apple, IBM, Dell, and others, fewer than half of all Americans have access to computers at home. Similarly, although K–12 schools in well-to-do neighborhoods typically have elaborate computer laboratories, four or five students in less affluent areas may have to share a PC. Clearly, a business must be aware of computer ownership demographics when formulating a marketing strategy.

If a business needs to reach a broad segment of the population, it may have to rely on telephone, television, and direct mail as well as its

Web touch point. Conversely, if the target audience is upper-middle-class America with a significant disposable income, or white-collar employees on the job, then the Web may be the best opportunity to reach these customers. Over the next few years, as computer hardware continues to drop in price, and even inexpensive game consoles support high-speed Internet access, the Web will be available in the home of virtually anyone who wants it. The convergence of technologies, where television sets, game consoles, cell phones, cars, and even appliances are Web enabled, portends a future when the Web will be as ubiquitous as television is today. Given the rate at which technology is being developed and deployed, the issue may soon become not one of computer availability in the home, but one of how to train customers to use the computer technology at their disposal.

# Social Factors

## Rising Customer Expectations

Fresh technology just doesn't have the same connotation as fresh bread; technology is considered old even before it hits the retail or virtual shelves. The engineers in Japan and marketing gurus in the United States and Europe have trained customers to expect constant improvement from any line of electronic products. For example, most customers know that if they want a faster computer, they need only wait a few months and the nominal clock speed will not only be faster, but the price may have dropped as well. Unfortunately, this continuous rise in customer expectation also thwarts sales of current products. Many customers now wait as long as possible before buying a new PC, simply because if they only wait a month or two more, they'll get more for their money. The effect of rising customer expectations can be seen in the game console market, which is currently playing a game of virtual catch-up. All the major manufacturers are extolling the virtues of their next-generation game consoles, some of which don't even exist in prototype form. Given the huge marketing blitz of what customers can expect to own in only a few months, why would anyone buy an existing game console? Why not wait for the next great game console from Microsoft or Sony? Moreover, why invest in a PC-based game when consoles are so affordable and powerful? By extension, why should customers purchase a business' technology now, instead of waiting for something better?

When customers deal with a business, they expect seamless touch points. In other words, if a business offers products through a mail-order catalog, the same products should be available through the business' Web site. A company simply can't put a subset of its offerings on a Web site and expect to satisfy all its customers. A visit to a Web site can be a major disappointment if only a small number of products from the retail portion of a business are available online. It is acceptable, however, to offer Web specials, just as some retail outlets offer "catalog only" specials. Differences between touch points may give customers the impression that the Web site is only an afterthought. If a business doesn't take its Web site seriously, neither will its customers. In other words, companies should put everything their retail store or mail-order catalog offers online or shouldn't go online.

For most business processes, the Web is an accelerant. When customers realize that real time and Internet time are interdependent and yet operate at almost incomprehensibly different rates, many experience tempo shock. That is, they can't understand why they can't have whatever they want now. Thanks to maddening progress in information technology, everything is accelerating, and the time machine called the Web only adds to the fury of the clock. For many customers, technology is synonymous with time savings. If a business can't satisfy a customer's needs immediately, the customer will go elsewhere—and elsewhere is usually only a click away.

Management has to recognize that time is the most precious resource for its customers. Customers will respect a business only if it recognizes the value of their time. This display of respect includes taking every reasonable step to ensure that a customer's time is well spent when she's interacting with the business, whether through a Web site or any of its other business touch points. Responsiveness is also essential; a Web site must respond quickly to queries, commands, and orders. In addition, customers expect the widgets they order from the business to arrive promptly, with at least an option for overnight or even same-day delivery.

Because all customers value their time, when management designs or builds a more interactive, emotionally intelligent site, it should keep in mind the time overhead that could be imposed by an "improved" interface. Animated chat bots and colorful backgrounds may be emotionally appealing, but if their use results in decreased responsiveness, then management's efforts to improve the site won't be appreciated. Customers will be off viewing another site. Paradoxically, because of the incredible tempo of technological and process innovation occurring on the Web, if a business doesn't continually work to improve its Web site, the Web image might only be recognized as an historical document. Regardless of the interface and customer support innovations planned for a Web site, it has to provide performance at least as good as what the business and its competition have now. From a practical perspective, this means that a business may have to throw more powerful hardware at the site to improve information throughput. Another option is to have programming staff craft code that can execute more efficiently.

In the design of a Web presence, it's important to consider the premium customers place on their time. BizRate.com (www.BizRate.com) is one of several companies that compiles customer survey information to rate online retailers. Of the ratings listed on BizRate.com's site, from ease of ordering and product selection, to product info, price, Web site, product representation, customer support, privacy policies, and shipping/handling, the most prominently displayed is on-time shipping. It's not rocket science, but a customer who orders a product on the Web wants it now. Furthermore, customers don't expect to wait longer than it would take a mail-order firm to deliver the product.

Given the value that customers place on their time, management may want to evaluate alternative, timesaving user interface options. Many online retailers are beginning to recognize that anything they can do to save their customers time will result in a better customer experience and, by extension, increased sales. For example, online grocery delivery services are looking at providing customers with bar-code readers for their homes. The idea is to reduce the time it takes customers to complete a grocery order. Because of the excessive time involved—typically over an hour for the first order—most online grocery shoppers walk away from their shopping carts before they make it to the checkout counter. The challenge is to create a system that can manipulate, analyze, and apply customer information to create a better Web experience in real time. An automated, near-real-time data warehousing and data mining system is needed to provide the information that an Emotionally Intelligent Interface must respond to and adapt to customers in Internet time, not weeks or months later.

## Customer Concerns Over Online Privacy and Security

To create a personal and personalized Web experience for its customers, a business needs access to customer information, from general preferences to demographic data. By creating an extensive tracking file for each of its customers, the business will eventually own a comprehensive library of client profiles. These could be used to build models of likely customer behavior during visits to the site. The profiles may also have value to insurance companies, who might use the data to assign insurance rates. Customers who routinely engage in high-risk behavior, such as hang-gliding, could receive higher rates. Potential employers may avoid hiring applicants who frequent the home pages of certain special-interest groups, such as those dedicated to certain chronic diseases or former addicts. A business may discover that selling customer information is more profitable than its main business.

The problem with this latter approach to profitability, illustrated by DoubleClick, the Internet's largest advertisement placement company (www.DoubleClick.com), is customer backlash. DoubleClick set off widespread concern about privacy on the Internet when it announced plans to merge a customer database it acquired containing names, addresses, and off-line buying habits of millions of customers with information it anonymously gathers about Internet users as they surf the Web. The company's plan triggered a probe by the U.S. Federal Trade Commission and at least one potential lawsuit at the state level. Bowing to this pressure, DoubleClick delayed the merger plan. Many online customers don't want their personal information sold or traded over the Internet to third parties without their explicit knowledge.

To add to customer concerns, what is considered private in the workplace is under legal debate. Most courts have held that if employers own the computers, they can do whatever they please with them, including tracking employees' time on the Internet. Customers may be less likely to visit a Web site from their office computers, even when they are on break, for fear of their purchases or inquiries being recorded. Since most customers are aware of these realities, personalization efforts won't go very far unless a business fully addresses customers' privacy concerns. For example, the primary obstacle to the use of electronic money is the customer's desire for privacy. While cash is anonymous, the use of electronic money, especially on the Web, is anything but anonymous. This lack of privacy is credited with keeping financial portal use low and limiting commerce on the Web in general.

Supreme Court nominees and children receive special attention when it comes to privacy. Because of political outrage after Judge Robert Bork's video rental habits were uncovered during his Supreme Court nomination hearings in the late 1980s, it's now illegal for video stores to reveal a client's rental records. More important, the Children's Online Privacy Protection Act of 1998 bars any business from collecting personal information from children under 13 years of age who visit a Web site, unless the business obtains parental consent. Because of parental concern, Congress is also considering legislation that would require parental permission before schools could allow companies that donate computer equipment to monitor students' online activities. In deciding how a business is going to address its customers' privacy concerns, the Federal Trade Commission's "Fair Information Principles" provides helpful guidelines (www.ftc.gov).

The FTC advocates a policy of notice and awareness, where a business posts its privacy policy for customers to examine. It also supports choice and consent, where customers can control how their information is used. Another factor is access and participation, which includes allowing customers to view and correct information collected about them. Finally, there is the security and integrity issue, where customers are notified about the safety of their data from theft or hacking. In short, businesses should openly disclose privacy policies, let customers see what the business is tracking, and let customers opt out of the tracking-for-personalization system. Businesses should also keep informed on the latest trends in consumer privacy by checking with the Electronic Privacy Information Center (www.epic.org) and Privacy International (www.privacy.org/pi). As far as privacy issues are concerned, it's much better to be creative than simply to respond to customer complaints. After all, most customers won't bother to notify the business. Why bother, when the competition, which may have a more reasonable privacy policy, is only a click away?

To address customer privacy concerns, a number of companies have established themselves as clearinghouses for users who want either to surf the Web anonymously or only to visit sites that abide by certain privacy rules. Zero-Knowledge Systems, Inc. (www.zeroknowledge.com) takes the former approach, allowing customers to forgo the Faustian arrangement of trading personal information for access. Their privacy system allows customers to surf the Web, send email, chat, and post to newsgroups in total privacy without having to trust third parties—other than Zero-Knowledge—with personal information. Their system works by linking all traffic to untraceable digital identities called "nyms," rather than the customer's identity. Customer messages are then encrypted and routed, somewhat randomly, through a globally distributed network of servers. It would be impossible for a business to build up a customer profile on a customer using the Freedom system because his identity would be different every time he visited the site.

Enonymous Corporation, Inc. (www.enonymous.com) takes the approach of warning customers about the privacy policy of the Web site they're entering. Armed with this knowledge, customers can opt to stay or leave. Enonymous maintains a database of privacy ratings for over 30,000 Web sites that request personal information. Their product,

Enonymous Advisor, detects requests for personal information and then queries its Enonymous database to retrieve the site's privacy policy rating, which is communicated to customers in real time. The best rating is four stars, which is awarded to sites that do not contact customers without their explicit permission and do not share personally identifiable information with third parties. Their lowest rating is given to sites without a privacy policy, or sites that were not reviewed by Enonymous. With the rating in hand, customers can decide whether to divulge personal information or not. Customers can also check for the privacy rating of a particular Web site by looking up the rating manually from their database (www.PrivacyRatings.org).

PrivaSeek, Inc. (www.PrivaSeek.com) is also working to automate privacy policy verification while adding time savings to Web site interactions. PrivaSeek allows customers to create their own Persona, an encrypted, password-protected online identity. The advantage of using Persona is that, for sites that support their standard, registration forms are automatically filled in, allowing customers to shop or ask for information faster. Along the same lines of Enonymous and PrivaSeek, but on a much grander scale, is the work behind the Platform for Privacy Preferences (P3P) Project. This standard, which is being adopted by Microsoft and others, enables a business to encode its Web site's privacy practices in a standard, machine-readable format. The encoded message can be retrieved automatically and interpreted by software agents. This automated approach to privacy notification saves customers time because they don't have to read the privacy policy of every site they visit.

Whereas privacy is concerned with intentional distribution of what customers might consider confidential information, security is concerned with the malicious or illegal destruction of, access to, or removal of information. Security is a major concern on the Web, as customers' apprehension about disclosing credit card information over a Web site remains the major detractor to buying online. When Web stores first opened, the greatest concern was over the security of the transactions. However, Web-based credit card fraud is only slightly higher than other types of credit card fraud. Whereas privacy tends to be more of a policy issue, Web security depends on selecting the right tools and knowing their limitations. Security on the Web involves three sets of challenges: protecting data inside the business; handling the transmission of data to others; and deciding how much to trust outside parties. Despite the high media profile on hackers and viruses, careless employees and disgruntled former employees threaten security more than any outside factors.

The steps a business should take to provide adequate security depend on the degree of security it needs to establish, which depends in turn on the potential economic loss involved in a breach of security. Various options are available for confirming a user's identity and permitted access level, ranging from the usual name and password scheme to more exotic—and more expensive—biometric characteristics, such as finger or voice prints. The American Express Blue Card has an embedded chip that stores data such as the customer's billing address, and an accompanying piece of hardware allows customers to swipe their cards for an online sale. In addition, secure server protocols have been developed and adopted by most online retailers. Another approach to providing Web security is to use public keys and digital certificates. These certificates rely on encryption to ensure the confidentiality and integrity of the data, and private keys are used to control access. In this scenario, documents are authenticated using digital signatures. The downside is that this level of security is expensive, complex, and difficult to maintain.

In the end, customers must trust that a business is doing everything it reasonably can to provide a secure, confidential transaction environment. From a business perspective, providing a secure online environment and maintaining customer confidentiality results in improved customer attraction and retention. The associated expenses are therefore a necessary cost of doing business.

# Managerial Factors

## Handling Gamers

A customer-focused business, where the customer is always right, seems fine in theory—until management considers the reality that some customers will try to play games with their system. Although most customers will use a Web site for legitimate acquisition of information or products, some will try to thwart the operation just as they do with real customer representatives. To protect itself, a business can establish managerial processes to handle disgruntled former employees and hackers who will try to take advantage of its good will. Management may find it necessary to train its customer representatives to bend over backwards for a customer only to a point, regardless of how the customer contacts the business. Serious customers, such as those with a history of ordering from the business in the past, may deserve special attention, from a real or virtual customer representative. Analysis of information in the business' data warehouse, especially a history of frequently returned merchandise, can be used to identify those playing games.

## Employee Resistance to Automation

Internally, employees may resist automation because it disrupts their role in the current business process, or because it highlights that there is no process infrastructure in place. There is also the perceived threat that customer loyalty to lifelike bots may replace customer loyalty to human customer service representatives. Programmers and others in the high-tech industry have unprecedented job security, to the point that many are pulled from one dotcom to another several times in the course of a year. However, for the workforce not involved in the high-tech arena, computers and computer automation can represent a threat to their livelihood.

# Economic Factors

## Uncertain ROI

Uncertainty is an inescapable part of life—and business. There's always a component of risk in any business venture, and, in that respect, conducting business on the Web is no different from retail sales. As many dotcom failures have pointed out, a company can't expect to succeed, or even survive, by pouring capital into its marketing budget in the hope that slick ads will attract loyal customers. A business can't even guarantee success by giving away products. While the practice of bribing customers with goods and even old-fashioned cash is great for customers and manufacturers of digital cameras, PDAs, and other giveaways, where is the long-term profit? Many of the fundamental brick-and-mortar principles, such as Return on Investment, apply equally to click-and-mortar companies.

Business—even non-profit business—is at least partially about profiting from a business' efforts. It doesn't matter whether a business is customer focused or primarily responsive to its stockholders or board of directors. A business has to make a decent ROI to survive. The uncertainty of ROI for Web investments may make it difficult for management to determine how much of its company's capital should be devoted to projects such as developing Emotionally Intelligent Interfaces, data warehouses, and virtual customer representatives.

The real question, in terms of ROI and the Web, is not whether to invest, but how much and where. There is a significant challenge and cost in creating an Emotionally Intelligent Interface or otherwise advancing a Web presence past a simple electronic billboard. This cost is primarily in developing the supporting infrastructure. To create even the most rudimentary personal Web site, a business needs to collect enough timely customer information in a way that is non-threatening and doesn't impinge upon the customer's right to privacy. In assessing ROI, the cost of timely customer information includes the increased complexity of a business. A business will need to store and manage transaction and preference data from all its touch points, and make the data available through all touch points as well. There is also the associated cost of data warehousing and of Web programming. On the return side of the ledger is the likelihood of developing a loyal customer following, and, by extension, mutually beneficial repeat customer business.

At some point in management's ROI assessment, it will have to decide how many quality data are enough. If management's goal is to provide personal, one-on-one marketing to its customers, for example, it will soon discover that investment requirements grow with increased granularity. That is, management has to decide, for each stage of its Web site's development, the point at which the benefit of additional customer granularity doesn't support added economic investment. For example, if, in profiling customers, a business can identify 60 percent correctly, that may be sufficient, as long as it does not alienate the other 40 percent. For example, don't advertise Viagra to elderly women or fur coats to animal rights activists.

With the Web and the new economy in flux, it may be impossible for management accurately to calculate the ROI for investing in a particular technology. All the technology and infrastructure development in the world may not be met, at least immediately, with customer demand. Potential returns on investment aren't always obvious when working with the Web. There is obvious potential for savings in replacing customer support representatives with virtual representatives. If a business relies heavily on mail-order business, then publishing on the Web instead of in print could save the business the cost of printing and mailing. If all a business' customers have Web access, it may attract new customers who did not know about the business' other touch points.

A business can have the best Emotionally Intelligent Interface, with the smoothest video, and the most lifelike computer-mediated virtual customer representatives possible, but if its core business doesn't make sense, then it will not see a return on its investment. If the business is trying to sell snow blowers in Silicon Valley, then chances are the company won't survive! The days of hollow dotcoms are over. The business needs to have a product and a business plan that makes sense in the short term. The Web won't save management from a poor business model, any more than a great telephone system or fax system will.

However, a bad telephone or fax system can kill a business. If the product is right, the customers will come. The question is when and in what numbers. Whether it is luck or the uncertainty of the marketplace, some factors will always be out of a business' control. However, if a business positions itself correctly, it will be able to take advantage of uncertainties, should they favor its business model.

# Political Factors

## The Challenge of Working Across Multiple Political Boundaries

Every time a business crosses a political boundary, it adds legal, ethical, cultural, and technical complexity to each of its business transactions. Conducting business over the Web in foreign countries or even other states can subject a business to unknown laws, taxes, cultures, and jurisdictions. For example, the United States and the European Union (EU) have been working for years on a data privacy agreement that would require U.S. companies to respect the privacy of EU citizens. U.S. companies may eventually have to provide EU citizens access to any information they have on file and give people an opportunity to change the information or delete it entirely, upon request.

Sometimes the political restrictions within one country are more formidable than obstacles in the international arena. For example, despite the ready availability of technology, information, and customers, online wine retailers in the United States attempting to connect small wineries directly to consumers have failed. The online wine retailers that have managed to survive do so by working within the entrenched three-tier system of wine suppliers, state wholesalers, and local retailers. Although the Web theoretically allows a company to bypass the system—which includes a hefty state sales tax—and sell wine directly from the vineyard to the customer, state and local regulations don't permit it.

Similarly, consider the restrictions placed on the practice of telemedicine, a theoretically superior way to bring quality medical diagnosis to rural communities using images transmitted through the Internet. If a radiologist licensed to practice in New York offers a diagnosis based on a chest x-ray from a Native American Indian in a tribe in New Mexico, then the radiologist is considered to be practicing medicine in New Mexico. If the clinician isn't licensed to practice in New Mexico, then he is breaking the law. He could easily lose his license to practice in any state. In another medical example, consider the likely fate of Web sites that allow clinicians to bid for elective surgery. Customers select the procedure they want and provide their medical history, and clinicians auction off their services. Although the concept is too new to tell how this model will affect the practice of medicine and clinical specialty areas, businesses can expect profound resistance from professional medical organizations for the wholesale auctioning off of medical expertise. The bottom line is that businesses should expect and prepare for political challenges as they use Web technology to extend their reach around the globe.

## Governmental Intervention

Thomas Edison's 18-second "Kiss" (http://memory.loc.gov/ammem/edhtml/edmvhm.html), the most popular Vitascope film ever, propelled the projected film standard above other formats. In so doing, it paved the way for the modern cinema industry. Similarly, adult videos fueled the rise of the VCR and the growth of the video rental business. The first major application of streaming video on the Web was to deliver adult content, and today the majority of video conferencing is adult related. Despite unresolved moral and ethical issues about sex on the Web, especially in regard to child pornography and the exposure of children to adult content while they are surfing the Web, sex has helped make the Web what it is today. However, blanket censorship by the government threatens freedoms that are enjoyed on TV and in print. Blanket censorship of nudity could have an impact on a business' Web presence, for example, if it were selling stock photography that might include some degree of nudity.

Similarly, an Internet tax at this stage of the Web's development would hinder exploration by businesses venturing onto the Web. The uncertainties of Web-based business are enough of a deterrent without an additional tax burden. An Internet tax might lower the attractiveness of this touch point and decrease the amount of money a business could invest in Emotionally Intelligent Interface development, given that a tax would bite into its projected ROI.

## Overly Aggressive Intellectual Property Constraints

Overly aggressive copyrights and patents, like the threat of blanket censorship or an oppressive Internet tax, may threaten a company's ability to provide innovative solutions to its customers' needs through the Web. Some intellectual property concerns regarding the Web are reasonable. For example, MP3.com was found liable to the Recording Industry Association of America for violating music industry copyrights because it allowed customers to address huge online databases of popular, copyrighted songs, from any computer. Fortunately, that suit and others like it haven't quashed legitimate distribution of free music on the Web. Thanks to Web-based labels, many unknown bands have a chance to get their music noticed. The utility of other intellectual property concerns is less clear. For example, German courts ruled that America Online is responsible when users exchange bootleg music files on their service. In this case, censorship is at odds with the rights of creative artists. The solution may be to employ technologies, such as online encryption, to protect copyrights online.

Patents on software and business practice have successfully thwarted competition—as they were designed to do. After all, Wall Street values software patents. Companies like Walker Digital, an intellectual property incubator, are quietly amassing patents to increase corporate value. At issue is how the very broad patents will affect every business. For example, Walker Digital's first spin-off, PriceLine.com, is based on their patent for buyer-driven commerce. With such broad patent grants, with time, any conceivable software idea will be patented, and every business is likely to be infringing on someone's patent. Consider that Amazon.com was awarded a patent for its "one-click" shopping, which allows customers to make purchases with a single mouse click. With the patent on its side, Amazon.com subsequently successfully sued BarnesAndNoble.com, prohibiting it from using any one-click shopping method. Whether or not these and other recent patents for software and business methods will hinder a company's ability to compete on the Web depends on how these patents stand up in court, and whether or not reasonable licensing arrangements can be established.

Despite this example of overly restrictive business practices on the Web, some would argue that patents are crucial to the survival of the Web, where it's possible for anyone to duplicate a site in a matter of days. The only real protection a company has against this outright copy-and-compete mentality is to patent its software or process so that some new startup only a click away can't take the work and run without fear of legal recourse.

In exploring the issues surrounding Web-based copyright, consider the disruptive effect of metabrowsers, such as QuickBrowse (www.QuickBrowse.com), OnePage (www.OnePage.com), and Octopus (www.Octopus.com). These and other services allow customers to see all or parts of multiple Web sites on in one composite Web page. A sports fan can take the sports information from one site and combine it with the want ads from another, in ways the original designers never imagined. Therein lies the rub. Some metabrowsers allow customers to strip banner ads, for example, depriving advertisers of exposure. In addition, many Web designers work tirelessly to create an image and feel for their Web site that involves not only content, but also the adjacent graphics. With metabrowsers, other Web sites become simple data feeds. A business might contend that its intellectual property rights are being violated if its content is similarly "borrowed," especially if the composite pages are being distributed without mention of the content's origin. Most businesses would not be content if material from their sites were juxtaposed with content from other sites. An implied agreement in perspective with a religion or political party might be a result.

The turmoil over intellectual property on the Web isn't limited to battles between competing companies. Internal turmoil, though not as widely publicized as corporate battles, can be equally destructive to a business. In the dotcom industry, non-disclosure and non-compete agreements are increasingly restrictive to the point that the employees who might ordinarily give their best effort and ideas to an employer don't. The brightest and most creative employees have an incentive to keep their best ideas to themselves, for possible use in their future companies, or to land a job with other employers. As with a progressive tax, employees with the most to offer are hurt more by an overly restrictive non-compete agreement. Why would an entrepreneurial employee offer her current employer her innovative process or technology when it could land her venture capital? Instead of being offered a reward system for new technologies that make it to the patent stage, some employees are automatically set up in an adversarial relationship with employers.

Look at the intellectual property issue from a business' perspective. As employers, businesses probably recognize that what separates them from their competition is their organic knowledge base. That is, the knowledge held in the collective, organic matrix called employees, perhaps supplemented by a few documents. Management probably also knows that if employees were free to leave without some form of non-compete agreement, the business might lose trade secrets, and could face stiff competition overnight. Management has a responsibility to stockholders and loyal employees to protect the business. Clearly, a better balance between employer and employee rights needs to be established for the dotcom industry.

# Wrap-Up

Change always incurs a cost. Integrating a more robust Web storefront into an existing model may complicate existing processes because of the complexities involved in enabling disparate touch points to communicate with each other. With the increasing prominence of Web technology in a business, the IT department may suddenly gain power through increased funding and staffing. With the resulting shift in the reporting hierarchies within the business, the political consequences may be detrimental to morale. Dependencies on third-party contractors and software vendors can develop, as more and more data and expertise are farmed out for short-term cost savings. Finally, embracing any new technology is likely to result in at least a temporary disruption of a business' current operations. The extent and duration of the disruption depends on the nature of the technology. For example, implementing an extensive data warehouse is more likely to disrupt core business than is adding a natural language interface to an existing Web site.

In the laying of the technical and process-oriented foundations for future customer relationships, problems will surface, no matter how many precautions are exercised. However, if management knows what to look for, or at least has an awareness of the general nature of potential problems, it won't be blindsided by potentially avoidable rate-limiting factors.

Now, armed with this knowledge, let's move ahead to the actual process of improving a Web presence. Our final chapter explores the various technological and process steps that can be used to create a Web presence to foster a strong and trusting relationship between a business and its customers.

# Executive Summary

There are varieties of rate-limiting factors, some avoidable and some not, that can impede management's progress in developing a personal, loyalty-evoking emotionally intelligent Web presence. Most of these factors can be categorized as technical, social, managerial, economic, or political in nature.

Technical factors that may limit progress include immature technological infrastructure, Internet bandwidth limitations at the customer's site, and varied penetration of computer technology in some customer markets. The technological infrastructure of the Web is still in its infancy, as wireless Web connectivity, high-speed, secure direct Internet connectivity, and standard communications protocols have yet to be fully realized. A business will have to contend with the reality that not all of its potential customers have Web access, and many of those who do may only have slow-speed 28.8K connections.

Social factors include rising customer expectations and customer concerns over online privacy and security. eCustomers have come to expect immediate service, better products, and lower prices. In addition, many customers refuse to purchase goods or services over the Web without solid guarantees of privacy and security. Managerial factors include making allowances for those who would toy with the system and for employees who resist automation. It's clear that a business can't always let customers have their way, because there are unscrupulous customers who will take advantage of the system to their cost. In addition, the threat of being replaced by a computer program is a source of angst for many employees.

The top economic factors include uncertainty about return on investment and the evolution of the marketplace. Not only is the Web an uncertain environment, fraught with problems and an evolving customer base, but the fate of the dotcom industry as a whole is still uncertain. Major political factors include the challenge of working across multiple political boundaries, the negative effects of governmental intervention, and overly aggressive internal and external intellectual property constraints. To expand a business' Web presence around the globe, management must be knowledgeable about local, state, national, and international laws. Even here at home, blanket censorship, Internet taxes, overly broad patent awards, and internal battles over non-disclosure and non-compete agreements may stifle innovation and development of the Web.

By developing an awareness of the general nature of these potential problem areas, management should be better prepared for implementation and maintenance of a new Web presence.

*Long-term planning does not
deal with future decisions,
but with the future consequences
of current decisions.*

Gary Blair

Change happens. It's the one constant that can be counted on in
life as well as in business. The real question, from a business
perspective, is the role management takes in that change. Is management a change agent or does it simply let change happen? Assuming
that the management of a particular company is the former, it is probably well versed in the principles of effecting change through a discipline of setting and achieving goals. That is, management first determines where the company is, and then decides where the company is
going. World-class management sets a solid deadline and works backward, breaking down its goals into manageable and measurable sub-
goals and periods of time. Creative management is accustomed to setting milestones along the way to its goal so that it can keep track of
progress. Forward-thinking management is also skilled at identifying

the resources and skills it will need to overcome potential roadblocks and achieve its goal. Finally, successful management identifies a measurable end-point. It knows that if it isn't certain of where the business is going, it won't recognize when the business gets there.

Achievers know that it's one thing to plan their work and quite another to work a plan. Achieving goals takes massive focused action. Sustaining that action requires motivation: not only self-motivation, but also the ability to motivate others. The objective factors of success (identifying the obstacles likely to be encountered; securing the money, people, training, and other resources that will be needed; and analyzing the business' performance with hard, quantifiable measures) can be learned by virtually anyone. However, achievers know that it is the emotive aspect of goal attainment that separates the leaders in business from the laggards. Top-level achievers know that unless they have a burning desire to reach a goal and can instill that desire in others, they probably won't reach the goal. These same principles of goal setting and achievement apply equally to lowering a golf handicap, improving a Web site, or increasing the profitability of a business.

# The SOAP Method

At the outset, it may be difficult for anyone to consider developing an emotional attachment to an inanimate Web site. Consider again the issue of cardiac bypass surgery introduced in the previous chapter. Assume that the CEO has successfully completed surgery and it's time for his one-month post-op check up. When he visits his clinician, she goes through a process that involves acquiring data from a variety of sources, assessing the data, planning the most appropriate course of action, initiating the necessary action steps, and then scheduling regular follow-up visits to verify that the plan is working. This cycle is repeated until the CEO's goal—freedom from illness—is achieved.

In the practice of medicine, the standard process of assessing and assisting a patient's progress toward a goal, such as good health, is referred to as the SOAP method: Subjective, Objective, Assessment, and Plan. Following this method, a clinician first gathers subjective and objective data to establish the patient's current physical and mental status. Subjective data includes symptoms such as chest pain, itchy skin over an incision scar, or lower back pain, that are generally difficult for a clinician to quantify or verify. In contrast, objective data includes signs that a clinician can see or otherwise measure, but that the patient may not even be aware of. The patient's blood pressure, weight, cholesterol level, and EKG are all examples of objective measures that a clinician can use, together with subjective data, to diagnose and otherwise assess the patient's medical condition.

If the CEO had been coughing for the past week and presents with a fever, for example, his clinician might conclude in her assessment that he probably has a cold. A reasonable plan, given his surgical history, might be to treat the CEO for a presumed bacterial infection and to verify that the infection isn't viral. Her actions might include wiping the back of his throat with a cotton swab and submitting the sample to a lab to see what types of bacteria, if any, can be detected. She might then start him on broad-spectrum oral antibiotics and schedule him for a return visit in one week for follow-up. On subsequent visits, she would repeat the SOAP process, changing her plans according to the patient's progress and additional data from the laboratory.

Using the same SOAP approach, this chapter explores the various technological and process techniques that businesses can use to assess the current status of their Web presence, develop a plan, and take the actions necessary to realize its goal. Continuing with the medical metaphor, management is going to dramatically improve the heart of its Web presence. The quantifiable goal—the equivalent of good health—is the achievement of a strong, loyal, trusting relationship between a business and its customers, as reflected in the business' bottom line.

## Subjective

The first stage in the SOAP process—the "S"—is to take inventory of the business' current status, from a customer perspective. Even though many of the data may be subjective and difficult to quantify, it's important to gather the largest quantity feasible at this stage. Even highly subjective data can help management formulate an effective action plan. As illustrated in the checklist shown in Figure 9.1, these subjective data focus on the emotive content of the current Web presence. How do customers feel after visiting the site? Are they frustrated or fulfilled? Are they merely satisfied or delighted with service? What are their impressions of the core business? Does the business come across as a heartless virtual retail outlet or does the Web site impart a sense of compassion/trust? As management asks these questions, it has to formulate a plan of how it might remedy a negative finding, given the particular business scenario.

The best source of this type of subjective data is usually one-on-one interviews with a business' primary customers. Because direct data gathering may be difficult with more than a few customers due to time

---

**Does Management Know...**

- What customers want and need from the business?
- If there's a good match between what customers want and what the business offers?
- A customer's overall experience when he/she interacts with the Web site?
- The personality of the Web site, from the customer's perspective?
- The personality of the business, from the customer's perspective?
- If customers feel an emotional bond with the Web site?
- How customers think the Web site compares to that of the competition?
- How customers think the Web site compares to those of industry leaders?

---

**Figure 9.1**  *Examples of subjective data related to a Web presence. Although answers to these questions may be difficult to quantify, they provide important information for later decision making.*

and resource constraints, informal customer questionnaires, reports from television, news, and industry journals, and opinions of support staff may also provide valuable insight into customers' minds. For the most part, however, these subjective measures are best when they come directly from customers.

A customer's subjective impression of a Web presence may result from a variety of interrelated factors: everything from the color scheme, font size and type, and background graphics to the response time and availability of support contribute to the Web site's personality and "feel." Outside factors, such as the reputation of the retail operation or of the company's CEO can positively or negatively affect a customer's subjective impression of a Web site.

## Objective

To define the best path in realizing an emotionally intelligent Web presence, management has to supplement the soft, subjective data with hard, quantifiable, objective data—the "O". Examples of objective measures that quantify the customer experience are shown in Figure 9.2. For example, who are the major competitors and how do they impinge upon the business? Who are the best customers, and what does management know about them? Are they young or old? Are they male or female? What's their mean income level? Do they have children? Do they have anything in common, such as where they live?

---

### Does Management Know...

- The competition's strengths and weaknesses?
- The business' primary (best) customers?
- What differentiates the business' products and services?
- What a typical customers need help with?
- The Web site's conversion rate?
- The Web site's Loyalty Effect?
- The degree to which the Web site is emotionally intelligent?
- The personality profile of the company?
- The personality profile of the current Web site?
- The personality profile of the planned Web site?
- The personality profiles of the primary customers?
- The site's policy on security and privacy?
- The degree to which the business' touch points are integrated?
- The company's financial status?
- The budget for Web development?
- The percentage of the total budget targeted for Web R&D?
- If the business is serving customers within the business' magic window?
- What percent of future income will be Web based?
- The Web site's typical response time?
- The average time a customer spends on the site?
- The number of customer requests for assistance?
- The average time staff takes to a service request?
- The staffing needed to handle service requests?

---

*Figure 9.2*  *Objective data that should be collected in the inventory process. These data can usually be observed or measured.*

Focusing on the current Web presence, management should have data such as conversion rate, average customer visit time, average transaction value per visit, and the number of repeat customers who visit the site—the pulse of the eBusiness—at their fingertips. Furthermore, does management know if the business projects the same image or personality through all its touch points? Is management creating customer confusion by projecting a dual personality by running a hip Web site and a conservative retail outlet? Does the Web site provide transparent data flow and sharing so that if customers interact with the business through one touch point, they're also known by the business at every other touch point?

When management performs an objective comparison of its site with those of the competition, it should focus on key customer issues, such as privacy (see Figure 9.3). It's important to know not only how a Web site compares to established guidelines for privacy and security, but

---

**Does the Privacy Policy...**

- Warn customers of the site's ability to track them before they interact with the site?
- Allow customers to control how their information will be used?
- Allow customers to view and correct their information?
- Allow customers to see what is being tracked?
- Allow customers to opt out of the tracking program at any time and for any reason?

---

***Figure 9.3*** *Examples of information that should be known about a Web site's privacy policy.*

also how it compares to other sites within the same industry. For example, if a business is a defense contractor and deals with military customers, then the general guidelines for security and privacy described in the previous chapter may be insufficient.

To establish a starting point for its emotionally intelligent Web development efforts, management should know how its current Web interface compares to an ideal Emotionally Intelligent Interface (see Figure 9.4). Most important at this stage is determining if the current architecture is based on a solid, logical design that recognizes the human–computer interface hierarchy described in Chapter 4. Emotionally Intelligent Interfaces, which represent the highest evolutionary stage of interface development, are dependent for functionality upon the proper implementation of lower interface forms. Management can't simply add Emotionally Intelligent Interface elements to a Web site built around a poorly designed architecture and expect any reasonable return on investment. It may be necessary to rebuild the Web site on a solid foundation of physical, graphical, logical, and emotional interface elements that are capable of supporting the emotionally intelligent Web presence customers need.

Most of the factors found in Emotionally Intelligent Interfaces that are listed in Figure 9.4 are objective measures. For example, a static marketing site isn't interactive. However, many of the indices don't elicit simple, binary yes-no answers. Take responsiveness, for example. Most customers would probably agree that a one-second response time from a spreadsheet—the time between a mouse click and an answer— is responsive, and that ten seconds is abysmally unresponsive. However, if someone is playing a computer game where tenths of seconds in timing can mean the difference between death and the salvation

---

### Emotionally Intelligent Interfaces...

- Ask, don't demand.
- Suggest, don't tell.
- Are personal, not simply personalized.
- Are empathetic.
- Are emotive.
- Are interactive.
- Present a single, unified personality.
- Are responsive.
- Are based on a solid interface foundation.
- Make underlying rules obvious.
- Mimic customers.
- Are respectful of customers' time.
- Are helpful.
- Are socially adept.
- Are truthful.
- Are unambiguous.
- Are anticipatory.
- Are persuasive.
- Provide localized content.
- Provide internationalized content.

---

**Figure 9.4**    *Qualities of Emotionally Intelligent Interface designs.*

of the universe, a one-second response time is practically an eternity. The point is that responsiveness depends on what customers are doing on a Web site. In general, however, a second or two for most search or order submission operations on the Web is reasonable.

In the evaluation of a Web site, it's important to distinguish between a merely personalized site and one that is personal. A personalized site might simply have a customer's name plastered on the welcome page. It isn't a bad idea, but it's a long way from being emotionally intelligent. A personal site, in contrast, is on the other end of the continuum that approaches true one-on-one communications. For example, Amazon.com's welcome page, with suggested books, CDs, and videos, based on the customer's purchase history, is on the personal end of the spectrum. Similarly, the Lands' End Personal Model, a 3-D replica of the customer's appearance, as illustrated in Chapter 6, is highly personal. These two sites illustrate how it's possible to provide elements of an Emotionally Intelligent Interface by using innovative, elegant, and not overly complex technologies.

---

### Is the Personality of the Website…

- Dominant or submissive?
- Unconscientious or conscientious?
- Emotionally stable or unstable?
- Emotionally open or closed?
- The same as that of the company?
- The same as that of the customers?

---

***Figure 9.5*** *Personality features of a Web site can enhance or limit interactions with certain users.*

Determining and, if necessary, modifying a Web site's current personality is crucial to establishing the emotional tone of the Web presence (see Figure 9.5). Of particular concern is how the personality profile of a business' primary customers compares to the target personality of the planned Web site. Ideally, management will want to minimize the differences between what the new Web site will project and what future customers will relate to. A hip, dominant customer may have reservations about interacting with a conservative, submissive Web site. In other words, bold colors; short, to-the-point text; and a youthful chat bot interface would likely be a better means of reaching this customer than would windy text over a subdued gray background and a "suit" chat bot. Even though this relationship may not hold true for all customers, management needs to identify the existing Web site's personality for a reference point later on.

An important component of the objective measures of the current Web presence is the Loyalty Effect. Use the Loyalty Effect Equation, introduced in Chapter 3 and reproduced in Figure 9.6, to determine if the Web presence is associated with a significant Loyalty Effect. If management knows the answers to the previous subjective and objective questions, then it can easily compute the Loyalty Effect that can be ascribed to the current Web presence.

Management's analysis may suggest what it can do to improve the Loyalty Effect for the site. For example, has management done everything reasonable to minimize the customer's level of frustration (FL) with the business in general and the Web site in particular? Is response time short enough? Is the site logically arranged? Is the Web site providing enough value to customers? If not, how can management provide additional value? Is there room for improving the emotional bond by incorporating Emotionally Intelligent Interface components in the Web site design?

---

### The Loyalty Equation

Loyalty Effect = $(\text{Value}_{(0-10)} + \text{Investment}_{(0-10)}) \times \text{EB}_{(1-5)} -$
$(\text{Affordable Alternatives}_{(0-10)} \times \text{FL}_{(1-5)}) +$
Difficulty Locating Alternatives$_{(0-10)}$

*Loyalty Effect*—A relative value, expressed as a number between 0 and 110, that is used for comparative analysis.

*Value*$_{(0-10)}$—The perceived value that a consumer places on the product and services the business offers, expressed as an integer between 0 and 10.

*Investment*$_{(0-10)}$—A customer's total investment, in time and energy, in the relationship with the business, expressed as an integer between 0 and 10.

*EB*$_{(1-5)}$—An integer between 1 and 5, that reflects trust, and, to a lesser extent, accountability, respect, and other emotional issues. The emotional bond has a multiplicative effect on *Value* and *Investment*.

*Affordable Alternatives*$_{(0-10)}$—Expressed as an integer between 0 and 10, this refers to the number of alternative businesses that offer a comparable service or product in the same price range.

*FL*$_{(1-5)}$—Expressed as an integer between 1 and 5, this represents the customers' level of frustration with their relationship with the business.

*Difficulty Locating Alternatives*$_{(0-10)}$—Expressed as an integer between 0 and 10, this refers to the number of alternative businesses that offer a comparable service or product in the same price range.

---

***Figure 9.6*** *The Loyalty Effect Equation. See Chapter 3 for a more detailed explanation.*

It's important to note that it may take management weeks or even months to gather data on the business and customers in the detail outlined above. In fact, management may never know some of the answers, because of lack of time, lack of access to customers, or because customers and the market are rapidly moving targets. At some point, however, management must determine when the data are sufficient—and that's where management's instinct as a change agent come into play. Leaders routinely make decisions while working under varying degrees of uncertainty.

## Assessment

At this stage of the analysis (the "A"), given the subjective and objective data available, management should be able to realistically assess where the business is and how far it will have to go to implement an Emotionally Intelligent Interface. If management is somewhere in the process of converting to an emotionally intelligent Web presence, then it should have a good idea of whether or not it's on track, how far it has to go, and which milestones it has met. Management should also be aware of unresolved issues and unmet milestones, and understand whether these failures were technological, process, economic, or social. Has something in the environment changed, such as a new law or regulation, requiring management to rethink its approach? Has the customer base shifted to the point that there will no longer be a good match between customers and the planned site? Is the business model sound?

Given the subjective and objective findings, the realities of the budget, the economy, and the state of the competition, what actions seem most appropriate from a business perspective? If management expects that, like the national average, five percent of its sales will be through the Internet, how much should the business invest in a new Web presence in order to realize that five percent? Conversely, if the business is projected to earn 50 percent of its sales through the Internet, and the competition is working feverishly on upgrading its Web presence, then management may have to push forward with developing the components of an emotionally intelligent site as quickly as possible. Assuming the business is on course and management has the skills, funding, and discipline necessary to move the site to the next level of customer interaction, the next step is to review and, if necessary, reformulate a plan that will propel the business forward.

## Plan

Now that management knows where the business is and where the Web site development is going, the next step is to formulate a workable plan— the "P." Whether management is primarily concerned at this stage with moving from a personalized site to one that provides a personal touch or from a simple banner site to a personalized experience, it should think customer and act business. That is, management should keep the customer's wants and needs in focus, but remember that it is running a business. As long as it's feasible, management should make it convenient for customers to do business with the company. Since speed and convenience are critical to customers' acceptance, customers shouldn't be required to fill out forms before they've even decided to enter into a transaction. The business shouldn't replicate the atrocity committed by many mail-order catalog companies that require a charge card number and shipping address up front, before customers place an order. It leaves a bitter and long-lasting impression when a customer discovers that the item she desired is out of stock or otherwise unavailable, and that she wasted five minutes giving an operator her personal information.

A reasonable plan for adding Emotionally Intelligent Interface components to a Web site would be first to develop a solid information infrastructure. This could include a customer tracking system and a data warehouse to store customer data. Management could then develop or acquire tools for accessing and analyzing the data in near-real time. Finally, management could develop a means of modifying the Web site so that it can take advantage of these customer data. This last stage may entail a computer-mediated chat facility, a hybrid system of bots and human operators over the phone, email, and chat, or even a fully functional bot with speech synthesis and recognition facilities. Depending on the business' requirements and available resources, it may be able to develop everything simultaneously or in sequence in house, or buy a total solution from a vendor.

The most efficient way for management to move forward with its emotionally intelligent Web plans may be to scoop up one of the dotcom companies or their staff. An increasingly popular way for a brick-and-mortar company to acquire a Web presence is to team up with a dotcom, resulting in a win–win situation for both companies. For example, Random House, Inc., a traditional publisher, teamed up with Audible, Inc. (www.Audible.com), a Web-based publisher of audio books online. The new company, Random House Audible, continues Audible's business of making audio books available for customers to download over the Internet on their computers or portable digital audio players.

# A Plan

To provide a concrete example of the planning stage of the SOAP method, assume that, as leader of a business' Web development initiative, the CEO's goal is to increase customer loyalty by developing an Emotionally Intelligent Interface to the company's Web site. After assessing the business and the competition, she determines that her first step toward an emotionally intelligent Web presence is to develop or acquire a data warehouse facility.

One of her most difficult decisions may be to *decide whether she will develop the requisite technologies in house or use a vendor*. The cost of outsourcing and the competency of her IT department will obviously weigh heavily in her decision. If she develops a data warehouse in house, she'll have the advantage of security and secrecy. In addition, if her data warehouse system is successful, her company may be able to market it to other businesses. However, she'll also have to concern herself with management, resource requirements, maintenance issues, and ongoing support.

As part of her decision between in-house and outside development, the CEO will have to *identify the technologies and, by extension, the technical expertise that she will need*. At the data warehouse development stage, the list of technologies will probably include databases, network connectivity, data warehousing, data mining, and knowledge bases. At some later stage of development, she may need to explore natural language processing, intelligent agents, and bot technologies as well. Her expertise requirements will depend on internal development bandwidth capabilities, in-house knowledge, and other ongoing or planned projects that will be competing for resources. She may find it necessary to use outside vendors for most or all of her development efforts.

The planning stage is the most important phase of data warehouse development, because at this stage the CEO has to decide exactly what to include in the data warehouse. Because of practical cost, resource, and performance limitations, it won't be practical to store every data element from every application in the data warehouse. It's far more efficient to identify in the planning stage data she'll need for creating personal Web interactions, rather than to blindly include every data element possible in the data warehouse.

*The next step at this stage of planning is to define the process for moving forward, from managerial, economic, legal, strategic, and tactical perspectives*. This step incorporates milestones typical of virtually every software development project (see Figure 9.7). For example, the CEO needs to meet with data warehouse development experts. Together with her IT staff, she identifies critical success factors and defines, at a high level, the project's scope, goals, and objectives.

The creation of a formal requirements specification document with a ranked wish-list of features provides a vehicle for communications and discussion that she can use with her development and managerial staff. Included in this discussion are issues such as feasibility, cost estimates, and development time estimates.

At this stage of planning, it's important to identify critical success factors. This may include holding regular meetings with her current

---

**Do Development Plans Include...**

- A meeting with the experts?
- A requirements specification?
- A ranked wish-list of features?
- Clearly defined project scope, goals, and objectives?
- A list of critical success factors?
- Copyright and trademark registration?
- A detailed timeline?
- Acquiring funding?
- Market analysis?
- Clearly defined roles and responsibilities?

---

*Figure 9.7*   *Milestones for a typical Web site development initiative.*

support staff. They may need to be reassured of their continuing value and trained to work with the new system. The CEO may need to develop a plan for training her staff to work with the data warehouse, for example, in their phone conversations with customers. Later, support staff may need to be trained in how to use virtual representatives in a triage system, with the staff acting as fallback support. This stage of planning also involves market analysis to decide how to best prepare customers—especially existing customers—to interact with the new Web presence.

As part of the CEO's data warehouse development plan, *she has to decide which data to capture.* What data will she need to capture to develop a profile of customers? Will customer preferences, buying patterns, and frequently asked questions be enough?

The CEO also has to *decide how she will capture customer data.* Will she use the direct approach, where the Web site simply asks customers their preferences? As illustrated by Reflect.com's site (www.Reflect.com) shown in Figure 9.8, customers can be enticed to answer online questionnaires when it's clear why they're being asked for personal information and when it's obviously in their best interest to provide the information. For example, Reflect.com uses customer-supplied information to configure a Web site that best suits the customer's sense of fashion, makeup needs, and lifestyle. Customers provide personal information in exchange for a personalized Web site that suits their tastes. The downside of this approach is that some customers may be turned off by the need to supply personal information before they can see what the site offers.

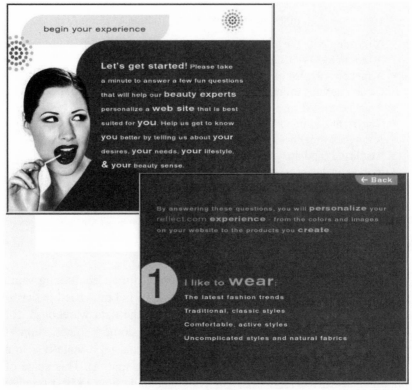

***Figure 9.8*** *Reflect.com's approach to gathering customer information is direct. Customers fill in online questionnaires in exchange for a Website that's personalized, from the makeup and other lifestyle products offered, down to the color scheme and font size used. Permission granted from Reflect.com.*

## Overriding Principles

During the planning process, if the Web site development project were a patient, the appropriate maxim would be "do no harm." In the world of the Web, the parallel might be best stated as "use common sense." In other words, management shouldn't get lost in the technology or process details, but keep its focus on providing a great customer experience. For example, it should respect customers' time, make allowances for customers who represent the lowest common denominator, and focus on developing an Emotionally Intelligent Interface that is as simple as possible, and only as complex as necessary.

In other words, the Web site must load quickly, even with heavy traffic. When features are added, they shouldn't negatively affect performance. If they do, hardware should be added to compensate for the performance hit. A text-only site should be offered to customers with old browsers or slow connections. In this way, customers decide for themselves when and if they need to upgrade their system hardware and software. Management may also want to consider parallel development for customers who may be interacting with the Web site through Web phones and wireless PDAs.

# Action Items

Even if the plan is to hand over design and development to an outside vendor, management will ultimately be responsible for the status of the site and related developments. If management elects to build everything in house, then it will have to work its plan. The IS group will be charged with the task of using sound engineering principles and good management practice, selecting and appropriately applying the right tools, within the constraints of the budget, to create a high-quality Web presence.

There is no shortage of vendors who would be delighted to sell whole or partial solutions to a business' data warehouse needs. Assume, for the purpose of illustration, that management decides to follow the plan outlined above, and the next action item is to develop a data warehouse in house. Regardless of the size of the eBusiness, creating a data warehouse system usually entails five action items: data consolidation; data transformation; selective archiving; data distribution; and ongoing maintenance.

In the consolidation phase of data warehouse development, the goal is to provide an efficient framework that supports any queries likely to be posed to the data warehouse, as determined in the planning stage. The data transformation stage of data warehouse development involves transforming or pre-digesting the consolidated data into a more useful form through summarization.

Selective archiving involves moving older or infrequently accessed data from hard disk to less expensive tape, optical, or other long-term storage media. Archiving saves money by sparing expensive, magnetic, high-speed storage, and minimizes the performance hit imposed by locally storing data no longer necessary for daily operation of the eBusiness. These data should be archived.

The distribution phase of data warehouse development is simply making data contained in the data warehouse available for viewing. Maintenance is the final, ongoing stage of data warehouse development, to support the inevitable changes in the Web site and rising expectations from eConsumers. The data warehouse must be robust enough to meet these rising demands.

One of the major challenges in creating a data warehouse system, or any other component of an emotionally intelligent interface, is *development myopia*. It's easy to be so wrapped up in creating a data warehouse that its value as a tool that supports data analysis and the structure of the eBusiness process often suffers. Another issue in data warehouse or other software component development is *complexity*. Every transaction database and application destined to feed data into the data warehouse represents a unique set of challenges. There are also practical overhead issues, such as keeping this information confidential. Security procedures, such as multi-level password controls, are necessary. In the end, the success of a data warehouse project is a function of the people and the processes in place to work with the system. Management's ability to direct the organization's dynamics are as much a key to successful implementation of the data warehouse as are the technical capabilities of the technology.

## Follow Up

If establishing a Web site is like having a child, then creating an emotionally intelligent Web presence is like raising a child prodigy. The foray into the realm of Emotionally Intelligent Interfaces can be compared to preparing a child prodigy for kindergarten. Although it's a big step and a critical milestone, there's much more to come. There will be continuous care and feeding, significant educational expenses, and surprises and disappointments along the way. If preparation is made now for college, the expenses won't be a shock later.

A business' emotionally intelligent Web site will be a growing, constantly evolving organism that will need constant care and feeding as well. In addition, just as a parent doesn't want to spoil a child—even a precocious one—management shouldn't overdo it on a Web site. The data warehouse should be used to make certain that management is not over-messaging customers. In other words, customers shouldn't be bombarded with email to the point where they ask or demand to unsubscribe from a company's emailing list. A component of care also entails regular follow-ups, such as a quarterly review of the Web site. After one or two of these reviews, management will probably learn from its IT staff or the competition that a new technology is available, and that it will need to be incorporated into the existing Web design to stay competitive.

# Resources

Managing an ongoing business may be taxing enough without taking on a potentially resource-intensive development project. Unless a company is in the Web design business, it's going to need additional resources that management can assign to the development and ongoing maintenance tasks. In addition to general technical support for software and hardware maintenance, the company will need the services of specialists as well. Management is also going to need some good advice.

Because the development and use of Emotionally Intelligent Interfaces is a relatively new phenomenon, the list of companies and available tools is growing daily. Because any list of products and services will be outdated in a matter of months—it's impossible accurately to predict which dotcom companies will merge with other companies from one week to the next—a Web site of resources is available at www.EternalEBiz.com. This Web site is updated frequently with links to sites that exemplify Emotionally Intelligent Interface design principles, as well as with contact information for relevant conferences and expositions, software, hardware, and consulting resources that management can use.

In addition to the companies mentioned in previous chapters that provide Emotionally Intelligent Interface components, including Brightware (www.brightware.com), Big Science Company, Inc.(www.bigscience.com), and LifeF/X (www.lifefx.com), there are many others focused on developing and supporting customer relationships. For example, Microsoft (www.microsoft.com/industry/crm) and its partners, including Baan (www.baan.com), Clarify (www.clarify.com), MarketSoft (www.marketsoft.com), PeopleSoft (www.peoplesoft.com), Onyx (www.onyx.com), Thinque (www.thinque.com), and Webridge (www.webridge.com), offer customer-relations management solutions. Oracle (www.Oracle.com), the database giant, and NCR Technologies (www.NCR.com) provide data warehouse tools and solutions as well. SPSS (www.spss.com), the statistical analysis company, is entering the field as a data mining specialist. A print publication that contains information on relevant products and services is *CRM Magazine* (www.CRMMag.com).

# The Long View

Achieving any goal requires commitment and an emotional connection to the end result. In other words, expect great things! After all, when it comes to technology, the greatest risk is usually not taking one. If management takes the long view, and aims for stepwise improvement in the interactivity, personality, and emotional intelligence of a Web site, it will realize its goals over several months. It will help if, along the way, management identifies the small, seemingly trivial elements of the Web site that make it memorable, and then emphasizes them. Just as painting a jumbo jet in bright colors to make it more visually appealing to potential customers can cost thousands in extra fuel consumption over the cost of a year, management has to determine whether the ROI of providing Emotionally Intelligent Interfaces for a Web site is worth the investment. More likely, the question is when, not if, to make the investment. On the Web, the virtual bar is constantly being raised. Bots and streaming media represent the leading edge of Web technology today, perhaps replaced by or at least supplemented with tactile feedback, tomorrow. At a time when even junk mail is personalized, a business can't stand by and offer a mediocre Web site incapable of providing a semblance of emotional intelligence.

In the near future, there will be more touch point transmodal translation services, moving information from one touch point such as print, filtering it, and delivering it through another touch point, in a different modality. For example, Business Briefings from Audio-Tech Book Summaries (www.BusinessBriefings.com) takes copy from professional journals, magazines, and special periodicals, and records it for distribution on audio tape. The service goes beyond the typical text-to-text shuffling that fills the current Web. Eventually, customers will be able to define the characteristics of the Emotionally Intelligent Interface to a Web site interactively. Erotic magazines won't appear in print, but as virtual information programs that can map that latest playmate image onto a customer's significant other. These and other new opportunities for expression will likely enrich, not detract from, traditional media. For example, fleeing editorial control, several artists, such as the Joe Cartoon Co. (www.JoeCartoon.com), are looking to the Web, hoping to draw fame and fortune in Web comics.

The primary beneficiaries of the Web and related communications technologies will be companies who will use the Web to meet customer needs more efficiently. Although the dotcom valuation on Wall Street may have peaked, the Web and its relevance to business will continue to evolve and expand.  For example, the telephone, another hi-tech touch point, has been around for decades, and there's still money being made by major and local carriers, telephone directory publishers, and specialized services and devices, from cordless to cell phones to answering services to wireless burglar alarm systems. The winners in the game will be those click-and-mortar businesses who pay attention to customer wants and needs, provide quality service, and do everything in their power to develop a loyal customer following.

As customers embrace the enabling information technology of the Web, it's obvious that the bottom line and society's collective concept of work, privacy, and personal responsibility will be irrevocably transformed. Whether the Web becomes specialized for certain types of multimedia communications, as did the telephone, or mutates into yet another type of communications portal, it will certainly reflect our collective visions and spirit. As we become more intensely wedded to the Web and related information technologies, information technology becomes as inconspicuous as electricity, the automobile, and jet travel. Information technology will be so immutably and subtly woven into the fabric of everyday life that technology will be as invisible to us as water is to a fish. Within the next decade, information technology will be just as critical to our everyday existence and, almost paradoxically, just as invisible.

The task ahead can be likened to building a personality or creating a living space. There's an art and at least of modicum of science involved in either activity. Like the practice of Feng Shui, there's a concept of proper proportion. Cooking a great meal is more than dumping all the ingredients, in the correct quantities, into a pot and turning up the heat. There's a process and an art involved. There's room for management to show its flair with its art, to leave its imprint on this thing we call a Web site. As in a living painting, management's brush strokes will show through to the practiced eye.

Eventually, the current infrastructure, including warehouses of customer data, will be dispensed with to allow customers to use secure information, delivered on memory sticks or smart phones. When customers enter a Web site, their personal data will be used to create a filter that admits only those items that could potentially fit or appeal to the customer. The customer will be saved the hassle of clicking around the Web to discover what suits them, and of entering billing information. After all, if a CEO visits her custom tailor, she doesn't discuss size, but focuses on fabric, color, style, and cost.

As the World Wide Web evolves into the World Wide Touch Point (WWTP), customers won't be clicking through links to find information; they'll be interacting through natural language interfaces, perhaps through cellular video phones equipped with voice recognition and synthesis. Text interfaces will be limited to research and educational information, such as newspapers. Point-and-click operations will have the cachet attributed to voice mail. Instead customers' hearing "...for sales, press 1; for marketing, press 2..." on the phone, an Emotionally Intelligent Interface will bring customers directly to their destination. The Web is likely to change other touch points as well. For example, a customer will probably bring a memory stick into a retail store, run it through a reader at a kiosk, and receive a printout of all on-sale items that fit.

In moving ahead, management can opt to increase the current Web site in stages, adding emotionally intelligent components piecemeal, or move directly to an emotionally intelligent Web presence. The former approach has the advantage of continuity and of being able to support existing customers with minimal hardware and Internet connectivity. The latter approach frees the business from legacy constraints, just as cellular phones have changed some third-world countries that never had phone cables installed. Management can similarly bypass the typical path, if the customer base will support it.

In making the move toward Emotionally Intelligent Interfaces—adding a heart, and maybe even a sense of soul to a Web presence—it may help to remember that the "e" in eBusiness, eCommerce, and eternal eCustomer stands for emotion.

## Executive Summary

Clinicians use the SOAP (Subjective, Objective, Assessment, and Plan) method to help patients realize their goals. A business can use the same approach to assess the current status of its Web presence, develop a plan, and take the actions necessary to create an emotionally intelligent Web presence and, by extension, the means of creating a strong, loyal, trusting relationship between a business and its customers. The SOAP approach is outlined below:

*Subjective*—The first step in moving toward an emotionally intelligent Web presence is to take inventory of current status, from the customer's perspective. Customer feelings and satisfaction levels are collected at this stage, preferably through one-on-one interviews with primary customers.

*Objective*—Business decisions require some hard data. To define the best path to realizing an emotionally intelligent Web presence, management must supplement soft, subjective data with hard, quantifiable, objective data, such as conversion rate, average customer visit time, average transaction value per visit, and the number of repeat customers who visit the site.

*Assessment*—Given sufficient subjective and objective data, management should be able to assess where it is and how far it must go to implement an emotionally intelligent interface.

*Plan*—Now that management knows where it is and where it's going with its Web site development, the next step is to formulate a workable plan. The maxim here is "use common sense."

Following the SOAP method, management will implement the plan in order to realize the business' objectives. Follow-up and periodic review are equally critical to the success of an Emotionally Intelligent Interface project.

In the long view, management has to consider that despite the relative enormity of the task before it, moving to an emotionally intelligent Web presence can be broken down into achievable components. The only limiting factor is enthusiasm.

## References

1. Johnson, S., *Who Moved My Cheese?* 2000, Newark, NJ: Penguin Putnam, Inc.
2. Fisher, R. and W. Ury, eds. *Getting to Yes.*, ed. B. Patton. 1987, New York: Simon & Schuster.
3. Downes, L. and Mui C., *Unleashing the Killer App: Digital Strategies for Market Dominance.* 1998, Harvard Business School Press: Boston.

**Animated chat bot**—A bot that can carry on a human-like conversation with a customer through the instantaneous exchange of text messages and one-way (from bot to customer) transfer of images that correspond to the tone or content of the text messages. The images are typically that of a person's face, but could be other characters as well.

**Anthropomorphizing**—Ascribing human characteristics to a computer-generated character, such as a human-looking bot.

**Artificial intelligence (AI)**—The branch of computer science concerned with enabling computers to simulate human intelligence. Machine learning, natural language processing, neural networks, and expert systems are all examples of applied artificial intelligence.

**Application Program Interface (API)**—A set of functions used to construct programs.

**Application Service Provider (ASP)**—ASPs provide software that is available through an ordinary Web browser, negating the need to purchase and run software locally.

**Avatar**—A graphical representation of a human meant to interact with similar graphical representations in a virtual environment, either through human or programmatic control.

**B2B**—Business to business transactions. Also known as wholesale trading.

**B2C**—Business to customer transactions. Also known as traditional retail selling.

**Bandwidth**—A measure of the information-carrying capacity of a medium. On the Internet, bandwidth is commonly measured in bits/second.

**BATNA**—In negotiations, the best alternative to a negotiated agreement. It's important for a party to know its BATNA before starting negotiations so that it knows when to walk away from the negotiations.

**Bitmapped screen**—A display screen where every pixel is represented by a memory location. The Macintosh popularized bitmapped screens.

**Bluetooth**—A hardware/software standard for handling communications among wireless devices.

**Bot**—Short for software robot. In the context of an Emotionally Intelligent Interface, a displayed representation of a person whose actions are based on programming.

**Brick-and-mortar**—A traditional business with a physical presence.

**Brown's law**—The power of the Internet grows as a function of $2^n$, which represents the number of possible communities that can form with "n" people; named after John Brown of Xerox PARC.

**Browser**—A program that allows customers to interact on the Web; a software program that interprets documents on the Web. Netscape Navigator and Microsoft Explorer are the two most popular browsers used today.

**Cable modem**—A high-speed (large-bandwidth) device for accessing the Internet. Cable modems, together with DSL, represent the most popular, affordable means for customers to gain high-speed Internet access.

**CD audio**—One of several standards for the distribution of sound and music files over the Internet.

**Certificate of authority**—An independent licensing agency that vouches for a customer's identity in encrypted electronic communications. It verifies and stores a customer's public and private encryption keys and issues a digital certificate to the business.

**Chat**—The instantaneous exchange of text messages between two or more participants. Chat is like email without the delay.

**Chat room**—A site for live, online conversations between multiple participants.

**Chatter bot**—A bot that can carry on a human-like conversation with a customer through the instantaneous exchange of text messages.

**Choice board**—A Web-based, multi-user ordering system in which a customer's order is sent to suppliers along the entire supply chain. Choice boards represent a major shift from traditional manufacturing processes in the U.S.

**Click-and-mortar**—A traditional business (represented by the mortar) with a significant Web presence (the click). A hybrid between the pure dotcom and brick-and-mortar companies.

**Client/server**—A computer architecture in which the workload is split between desktop PCs (clients) and one or more larger computers (servers) that are connected via a network such as the Internet.

**Cluster analysis**—One of several computationally efficient techniques that can be used to identify patterns and relationships in large amounts of customer data.

**Cognitive ergonomics**—The applied science of equipment design, as for the workplace, intended to maximize productivity by reducing operator fatigue and discomfort.

**Computer-mediated email**—Email that is computer generated but intended to appear as though it were composed and sent by a human.

**Convergence**—The merging of all data and all media into a single digital form.

**Conversion rate**—A measure of the number of visitors who initiate a transaction on a Web site within a particular period of time relative to the total number of visitors who visit a Web site. A high conversion rate is better than a low conversion rate.

**Cookies**—Data deposited on a customer's computer that a Web server uses to identify the customer. They can also be used to instruct the server to send a customized version of the requested Web page.

**Correction**—In the context of the stock market, a decline in stock-market activity or prices following a period of increases.

**CRT-based monitors**—An "old-fashioned" cathode ray tube monitor, still the most popular monitor type. CRTs are slowly being replaced with slimmer and less bulky LCD monitors.

**Customer Relations Management (CRM)**—The process of managing the relationship between a business and its customers.

**Data mining**—The process of extracting meaningful relationships from usually very large quantities of seemingly unrelated data. Data mining the records of charge card transactions can discover, for example, the relationship between age or sex and the purchase of suntan lotion.

**Data warehouse**—A central database, frequently very large, that can provide authorized users with access to all a company's information. A data warehouse is usually provided with data from a variety of non-compatible sources. A data warehouse can be based on a hierarchical, relational, object-oriented, or network database management system.

**Decision support system**—Software tools that allow managers to make decisions by reviewing and manipulating data in a data warehouse.

**Digital certificate**—An official electronic identity document based on public and private key encryption and obtained through a certification authority. Also called a digital ID.

**Digital cloning**—Creating lifelike, 3-D Bots modeled after a specific human's physiology and personality.

**Digital signature**—An encrypted digital tag added to an electronic communication to verify the identity of a customer. Also called an electronic signature.

**DirectX**—A system developed by Microsoft that translates generic hardware commands into specific commands for particular pieces of hardware. DirectX makes it possible for multimedia applications to take advantage of hardware acceleration features.

**Disruptive technology**—A technology, such as the Web, that causes a major shift in the normal way of doing things.

**Dolby surround sound**—A patented digital sound distribution standard.

**DSL (Digital Subscriber Line)**—A type of high-speed Internet connection based on the same copper wiring used for standard telephone service.

**DSP (Digital Signal Processing)**—The manipulation of digital information, often with the aid of specialized hardware. DSP technology is used extensively in audio and video processing.

**DSP filtering**—The use of computer-simulated filters for processing digital information. The original information is usually an analog audio or video signal that has been digitized for DSP operations.

**DVD (Digital Video Disc)**—A high-density version of the standard CD-ROM capable of storing between 4.7 GB and 17 GB of data.

**Early adopter**—In marketing circles, a customer who wants the latest and greatest gadget, regardless of cost or inconvenience.

**Ease of learning**—Regarding a user interface, the ease with which a particular interface can be learned. Contrast with *ease of use*.

**Ease of use**—Regarding a user interface, the ease or efficiency with which the interface can be used. An easy to use interface may be difficult to learn and vice versa.

**eBooks**—Electronic tablets optimized for downloading and displaying text.

**eBusiness**—Business over the Internet.

**Economic Darwinism**—Survival of the fittest—the most economically successful companies in the marketplace.

**eConsumer**—A consumer who uses the Web as a means of experiencing instant gratification. Also called eCustomer.

**Edutainment**—Multimedia designed for teaching.

**EEG**—An electroencephalogram, a brain-wave tracing. A person's EEG changes with alertness and sleep, and may eventually be used to communicate with computers.

**Emotional interface**—A computer or Web interface that creates an emotional bond with the user. Most successful video games have what is considered an emotional interface.

**Emotionally Intelligent Interface (EII)**—A computer or Web interface that not only establishes an emotional bond with the user, but does so in a way that respects the user's intelligence, time, and needs. Humans are also capable of providing Emotionally Intelligent Interfaces when they want to.

**Empathy**—The ability to identify with and understanding another's situation, feelings, and motives.

**eNovella**—A literary work, shorter than a novel and longer than a short story, published in electronic form.

**ePublishing**—Publishing over the Web.

**Evangelists**—In the context of computer hardware and software, those who back a particular product or service with unbridled enthusiasm.

**Expert system**—A type of computer application program that makes decisions or solves problems in a particular field, by using knowledge and analytical rules defined by experts in the field.

**FAQ (Frequently Asked Question)**—Lists of frequently asked questions and the appropriate answers are often posted on a Web site for users with questions of their own.

**FCC (Federal Communications Commission)**—The governmental office responsible for radio emissions, including wireless signals, and for assigning different parts of the radio spectrum for a variety of reasons.

**Fuzzy logic**—An AI technique designed to handle partial truths. Fuzzy logic is especially useful in working with uncertainty, as when only a probability of an event or an association is known.

**Game bots**—Software robots that can play against human opponents or assist humans in defeating other humans or other fun bots.

**Genetic algorithms**—Algorithms designed to mutate, breed, and spawn new, more-fit algorithms, based on their success in solving a particular problem.

**Graphical User Interface (GUI)**—The point-and-click interfaces first popularized by the Apple Macintosh and now used by Microsoft Windows.

**Haptic controls**—Also called force-feedback controls; joysticks, mice, and other controls that provide tactile feedback when used with games and certain applications.

**Heads-up display**—A graphical display in which a virtual image is projected in front of the user's visual field.

**Heuristics**—Rules of thumb. Expert-system knowledge bases commonly contain a great many heuristics.

**Hit**—The retrieval of any item, such as a page of text or a graphic, from a Web server. The number of hits is used to describe how many visits a

Web site gets, regardless of how brief. This latter definition is inaccurate, however, since a visit to a single Web page may result in multiple hits.

**HTML (HyperText Markup Language)**—The programming language used to create documents on the Web.

**Human–computer interface**—The combination of hardware and software elements that provides the communications channel between a computer and the computer operator.

**Infrastructure**—In the context of the Internet, the system of servers, cables, and other hardware, together with the software that ties it together, for the purpose of supporting the operation of the Internet.

**Instant messaging**—On the Internet, a type of communications service that allows someone to establish a private chat with another individual. AOL's Instant Messaging service is a popular means of supporting real-time communications between AOL members who are logged on to the service.

**Integration**—The process of bringing together related data from different sources to arrange them by customer.

**Intelligent agent**—In the context of the Internet, programs that perform tasks such as retrieving and delivering information and automating repetitive tasks. Also called an *Internet agent*.

**Internalization**—The process of matching the content in a Web site to suit the language and culture of specific customers.

**Internet voice chat**—A process of using the Internet as a telephone party line.

**IPO (Initial Public Offering)**—A corporation's first offering of stock to the public.

**ISP (Internet Service Provider)**—A company, such as AOL, that provides access to the Web.

**IT**—Information Technology.

**Killer app**—Short for killer application. A program that everyone obviously has to purchase and use. The spreadsheet was a killer app that transformed the accounting industry and spurred the introduction of computers into the workplace.

**LCD (Liquid Crystal Display)**—The flat display technology used on laptops, some electronic watches, and most PDAs.

**Legacy system**—An existing system in which a company has already invested considerable time and money. Legacy systems usually present major integration problems when new, potentially incompatible systems are introduced into the company.

**Live chat**—The instantaneous exchange of text messages between two or more humans.

**Localization**—The process of adapting a Web site to a particular country or region.

**Logical interface**—The component of the interface that embodies the syntax and other rules of the user interface. A user interface that doesn't follow underlying logic can be very difficult to learn.

**Loyalty**—A positive inner feeling or emotional bond between a customer and a business. Loyalty can't be assessed directly, but can be inferred from a customer's actions.

**Loyalty Effect**—The quantifiable behavior normally associated with loyalty, such as repeatedly transacting business with a particular retailer or Web site.

**Loyalty Effect Equation**—The equation that characterizes the Loyalty Effect. Solving the equation results in a Loyalty Effect expressed as a number between 0 and 110, used for comparative analysis.

**Machine learning**—Software systems that operate through some degree of self programming. Machine learning is an area of study in the field of artificial intelligence.

**Magic window**—The range of possible products and services that a business is willing to provide. Working outside the magic window to please or attract customers can result in inefficiencies, poor employee morale, and economic failure.

**Mail bots**—Bots that automatically filter email or perform other email functions, such as automatic answering.

**Mass customization**—Providing products per customer specifications using traditional manufacturing techniques. Mass customization is difficult to implement in practice.

**Metaphor**—In the realm of human-computer interfaces, metaphor is the underlying model upon which the user interface is based. For example, the desktop metaphor popularized by the Apple Macintosh is modeled on a typical office, with a trash can, files, and folders.

**Metcalfe's law**—The prevailing measure of the Internet's worth; a function of n-squared, where "n" is the number of individuals connected. Named after Bob Metcalfe, inventor of Ethernet.

**MIDI (Musical Instrument Digital Interface)**—A standard for controlling devices, such as synthesizers and sound cards, that emit music.

**Moore's law**—The prediction advanced by Gordon Moore, co-founder of Intel, that the number of transistors per square inch on integrated circuits will double every year. Moore predicted that this trend would continue for the foreseeable future. The law has been amended to predict a doubling approximately every 18 months.

**MP3**—A standard for compressing and transporting audio over the Web. MP3 provides about a 12-to-1 compression of CD-quality audio, making distribution of music over the Web tenable. Originally called MPEG-1 Layer 3.

**Multimedia interface**—An interactive computer interface that supports text, sound, and images, including static graphics or video.

**Multimodal interface**—An interface that supports multiple modes of communications, from text to voice, haptic, and graphical interaction. Multimodal interfaces are a superset of multimedia interfaces.

**Natural Language Processing (NLP)**—A system of parsing text for machine recognition purposes.

**Neural network**—A type of artificial intelligence program that can learn to recognize patterns in data through self-organization of its internal structure, which is loosely based on the architecture of the human brain.

**News bot**—A software robot that can be instructed to create a custom newspaper from online newspapers around the globe.

**OS (Operating System)**—The master software that controls a computer's fundamental operations.

**Parse**—To divide language into small components that can be analyzed into the various parts of speech. Parsing is a fundamental step in natural language processing and voice recognition.

**Personal**—In the context of a Web site, a personal Web site has several characteristics specific to the customer, from a custom color scheme to a 3-D representation of the user.

**Personal Digital Assistant (PDA)**—A personal, handheld organizer. The Palm Pilot is the quintessential PDA.

**Personalized**—In the context of a Web site, a personalized Web site has something about the customer, such as his name, listed on the site.

**Portal**—A Web site that offers a broad array of resources and services, from email to on-line shopping. Most of the popular search engines have transformed themselves into Web portals to attract a larger audience.

**Predictive engine**—An algorithm or software program that can predict customer behavior, with quantifiable accuracy, based on customer data.

**Process management**—An evaluation and restructuring of system functions to make certain processes are carried out in the most efficient and economical way.

**Profiling**—The process of taking a few key customer data points, such as name, occupation, age, and address, and generating best guesses about other characteristics. For example, teenagers are more likely to respond to an add for skate boards than are retired postal workers.

**Q-sound**—A sound distribution standard used to transfer audio files on the Web. Q-sound can be used to simulate a 3-D environment. See www.qsound.ca for details.

**RDA (Recommended Daily Allowances)**—The federal government establishes an RDA for several macro and micronutrients.

**Relational database**—A database that stores information in tables made of rows and columns. Searches are conducted by using data in specified columns of one table to find additional data in another table.

**Return on Investment (ROI)**—Profit resulting from investing in a company, process, or activity. The profit could be money, time savings, or other positive result.

**Rule-based system**—A type of expert system that uses a knowledge base composed of IF–THEN clauses as the basis for its reasoning.

**Search bot**—A bot that searches the Web for information. Search Bots are an integral part of search engines such as AltaVista, Yahoo!, and WebCrawler.

**Situational awareness**—In the context of navigating through a program or the Web, situational awareness is the user's knowing where he's been, where he is, and where he can go next.

**SOAP**—A mnemonic for the Subjective, Objective, Assessment, and Plan approach used in medicine in following and treating patients. The SOAP approach can also be applied to business challenges.

**Spider**—An agent that travels from one hyperlink to the next, retrieving HTML documents along the way, and indexing the information it finds in them.

**Stickiness**—A measure of the popularity of a Web site, normally measured in how long a customer stays on the site.

**Stock bots**—Bots that monitor stock prices and trading activity. They can send email to their owners regarding any change in prices or trends, or press releases.

**Streaming**—A technique for transferring data over the Internet, especially audio and video, in a way that it can be processed as a steady and continuous stream. With streaming video, the start of the video can be viewed before the entire file has been transmitted. An alternative to streaming is to download the entire file before playing it—an alternative that is usually too time consuming to be worthwhile.

**Test-to-Speech (TTS)**—Voice synthesis, using email or other text source to drive the voice synthesis process. Providing an animated character with speech via TTS is more bandwidth efficient than sending voice over the Internet.

**Touch point**—The point of contact between a customer and a company. Touch points include telephone, fax, email, and person-to-person conversations.

**Uniform Resource Locator (URL)**—The address for a particular page on the Web or other Internet resource.

**User interface**—The junction between the user and the computer. Microsoft DOS provides a command-line interface, whereas the Macintosh OS and Microsoft Windows support graphical user interfaces.

**Viral marketing**—In the context of the Web, spreading word of a Web site through a free service, such as email, or a product with a built-in advertisement, such as an online greeting card.

**Virtual personalities**—Computer-generated characters, which range from text-based to graphical representations with voice synthesis and voice recognition capabilities.

**Virtual representative**—A virtual personality designed specifically to support customers on the Internet.

**Voice recognition**—The automatic conversion of the spoken word into machine-readable text or computer commands.

**XHTML (Extensible Hypertext Markup Language)**—XHTML is a hybrid between HTML and XML, designed specifically for creating documents on the Web.

**XML (Extensible Markup Language)**—A markup language for the Web that supports the definition, transmission, validation, and interpretation of data between applications and between organizations.

# Index

*Note: Boldface numbers indicate illustrations; italic t indicates a table.*

# Q

Q-Sound, 156
QUAKE, 98, 100
quality of customer service, 178–179
QuickBrowse, 208
QuickTime, 153

# R

Random House Audible, 223
rate-limiting factors, 189–211, **191**
  bandwidth limitations, 195–196
  categories, 191, **191**
  censorship, 207
  crossing political boundaries, 206
  data gathering bottlenecks,
    190–191
  economic factors, 191, 204–206
  employee resistance to automation,
    204
  "game-playing"/vindictive
    customers, 203–204
  governmental intervention, 207
  infrastructure immaturity, 192–195
  intellectual
    property/patent/copyright
    constraints, 207–209
  licensing laws, 206–207
  managerial factors, 191, 203–204
  non-disclosure/non-compete
    agreements, 209
  penetration of computer technology
    into market, 196–197
  political factors, 191, 206–209
  privacy issues, 199–203
  return on investment (ROI),
    204–206
  rising customer expectations,
    197–199
  security issues, 199–203
  social factors, 191, 197–203
  tax laws, 206–207
  technical factors, 191, 192–197
RealNetwork, 153
RealPlayer, 153
reassurance, in computer-mediated vs.
  human customer representatives,
  179
Recording Industry Association of
  America (*See also* music
  industry and MP3), 208
Reflect.com, 225, **226**
relational databases, 123–124, 157
reliability, in computer-mediated vs.
  human customer representatives,
  179
resource management, 229
responsiveness, in computer-mediated
  vs. human customer
  representatives, 179
retinal imagers, 89
return on investment (ROI), 179–180,
  204–206
revenue (*See* profit vs. revenue; return
  on investment)
rewards and behavior, 59–61
*Riding the Bullet*, online novella,
  26–27
Road Runner Sports, Inc., 106
robots (*See also* bots), 44
rule-based expert systems, 42, 127,
  138, 157

# S

sales process/salesperson
  characteristics, 167–170
satisfaction–loyalty connection,
  58–61
  rewards and behavior, 59–61
  services vs. products, customer
    satisfaction, 58–61
scalability, in computer-mediated vs.
  human customer representatives,
  180
search bots, 130
search engines, 45, 130
Sears, 38
security issues (*See also* credit card
  security; privacy issues), 46,
  199–203, 217–218
  American Express Blue Card, 203
  credit cards, 76, 202, 203
  digital certificates, 203
  key systems, security, 203
  public keys, 203
Sega, 43, 98, 186
sensory stimulation in interfaces, 86,
  90, 93–94, 98–99
services vs. products, customer
  satisfaction, 58–61
session length, 39
Sharper Image, The, 9

Shneiderman, Ben, xxi
*Shop With a Friend*, customer-
customer support, 172–173
situational awareness in interface
design, 97
SOAP method, 214–223
social factors in limiting technological
growth rate, 191, 197–203
privacy issues, 199–203
rising customer expectations,
197–199
security issues, 199–203
software development, 156
software robots (*See* bots)
Sony, 43, 93, 98, 140, 155, 186
sound (*See* audio)
SoundBlaster, 91
speech recognition, 99, 100, 155
gisting techniques, 101
machine translation, 101
speech synthesis, 90, 91–93, 155
spiders, 130
SPSS, 229
standardization, 43
standards, software, 156
Staples, 29
statistical tools, 30–31, 30
stickiness (*See* loyalty; Loyalty Effect
and Equation)
stock bots, 130
streaming data, 156, 230
stylus input, 89
subjective data in SOAP method,
215–216
support staff, customer service, 171
Sybase, 123
Systran, 101

**T**

*2001, A Space Odyssey*, 42
*3001, The Final Odyssey*, 143–144
3-D graphics, 9, 43, 89
tax laws, 206–207
technical factors in limiting
technological growth rate, 191,
192–197
bandwidth limitations, 195–196
infrastructure immaturity,
192–195
penetration of computer technology
into market, 196–197

technology in business and lifestyle,
xiv–xv, 13–14, 40–46, 47,
139–164
animation, 157–158
anthropomorphic characters,
157–158
Application Service Provider
(ASP), 153–154
assessing needs, 185
bandwidth limitations, 142,
153–154, 195–196
bots, 158–162, **159, 160**
Brown's law, 142
build vs. buy, 162–163
chatter bots, 158–162, **159, 160**
data warehouses, 156–157
digital cloning, 146–152, **148**
early adopters, 64
economic Darwinism, 143,
181–182
expert systems, 157
hardware development, 154–155
implementing new technology,
153–163
infrastructure requirements, 153,
192
leveraging technology, 167–187
lifestyle tracking, 145–146
Metcalfe's law, 142
Moore's law, 142
neural networks, 157
penetration of computer technology
into market, 196–197
projected advances, 140–143, **141**
rising customer expectations,
197–199
rule-based expert systems, 157
software development, 156
standards, software, 156
video, 157–158
Web-enabled appliances, 144–145
wireless communications, 154
telecommunications technologies, 41,
47, 76, 139, 154, 230
television, 42, 47
text editors, 156
Text-to-Speech (TTS), 91
Text-to-Speech Engine, 91
Thinque, 229
Third Voice, 172
time capsule creation, digital clones,
148–150

**Bryan Bergeron** has over 15 years of experience writing and speaking about leading-edge technology and envisioning the future. He teaches at Harvard Medical School and MIT, and is editor-in-chief of e.MD and technical editor of Postgraduate Medicine. A software industry pioneer himself, Dr. Bergeron created the first medical multimedia program for the Mac and several other "first" personal health management and family planning programs. He is currently president of Archetype Technologies, Inc., a technology consulting firm, and chief scientist at Kurzweil Technologies, Inc., where he designs emotionally intelligent interfaces.